University of Plymouth Library

Subject to status this item may be renewed
via your Voyager account

http://voyager.plymouth.ac.uk

Tel: (01752) 232323

ACHIEVING SUSTAINABLE MOBILITY

Transport and Mobility Series

Series Editors: Professor Brian Graham, Professor of Human Geography, University of Ulster, UK and Richard Knowles, Professor of Transport Geography, University of Salford, UK, on behalf of the Royal Geographical Society (with the Institute of British Geographers) Transport Geography Research Group (TGRG).

The inception of this series marks a major resurgence of geographical research into transport and mobility. Reflecting the dynamic relationships between socio-spatial behaviour and change, it acts as a forum for cutting-edge research into transport and mobility, and for innovative and decisive debates on the formulation and repercussions of transport policy making.

Achieving Sustainable Mobility
Everyday and Leisure-time Travel in the EU

ERLING HOLDEN
Western Norway Research Institute, Norway

ASHGATE

Published by
Ashgate Publishing Limited
Gower House
Croft Road
Aldershot
Hampshire GU11 3HR
England

Ashgate Publishing Company
Suite 420
101 Cherry Street
Burlington, VT 05401-4405
USA

Ashgate website: http://www.ashgate.com

British Library Cataloguing in Publication Data
Holden, Erling
    Achieving sustainable mobility : everyday and leisure-time
    travel in the EU. - (Transport and mobility series)
    1. Transportation - Environmental aspects - European Union
    countries 2. Transportation engineering - European Union
    countries 3. Sustainable development - European Union
    countries 4. Tourism - Environmental aspects - European
    Union countries
    I. Title
    388'.042'094

Library of Congress Cataloging-in-Publication Data
Achieving sustainable mobility : everyday and leisure-time travel in the EU / by
    Erling Holden
        p. cm. -- (Transport and mobility)
    Includes bibliographic references and index.
    ISBN-13: 978-0-7546-4941-0
    1. Transportation engineering--European Union countries. 2. Sustainable
development--European Union countries. 3. Transportation--Environmental aspects--
European Union countries. 4. Tourism--Environmental aspects--European Union
countries. I. Holden, Erling.

    TA1055.A285 2007
    388'.042094--dc22

2007001516

ISBN-13: 978-0-7546-4941-0

Printed and bound in Great Britain by Antony Rowe Ltd, Chippenham, Wiltshire.

Contents

I dedicate this book to my father, Jakob Holden (1931–1978)

List of Figures

List of Tables

Foreword

It is now widely acknowledged that mobility patterns in developed countries have become unsustainable and moreover, that it is highly necessary to change these patterns into sustainable ones. Making mobility patterns sustainable, however, probably represents – after the elimination of poverty – the most troubling theme of sustainable development. Yet for decades attempts have been made to achieve sustainable mobility, for example, the development of more efficient conventional transport technology, the use of alternative fuels, the promotion of an efficient and affordable public transport system, the encouragement of environmentally friendly attitudes and greater environmental awareness and the use of sustainable land-use planning.

These attempts are so often presented as prerequisites for sustainability that they are taken for granted. But how successful are they really? To what extent do they contribute (or fail to contribute) to sustainable mobility? Why do some attempts succeed and others fail? Or more basically: How is sustainable mobility to be achieved? This book answers these questions. I focus on passenger mobility, partly because of the need to limit the book's scope and partly because of my professional background; the equally important challenge of achieving sustainable mobility of goods should not, however, be forgotten.

The approach taken follows four rationales: First, each attempt's appropriateness to the goal of sustainable mobility should be treated as a hypothesis rather than as a fact. Second, the research design employed is an interdisciplinary one, which is appropriate given the previous dominance of an engineering- and economic-based paradigm in research on sustainable mobility. Third, attempts at achieving sustainable mobility should include leisure-time travel (including tourism), which now accounts for 50 per cent of the yearly travel distance in developed countries. Fourth, the book's main research issue relates to the challenge of achieving sustainable mobility in the EU. However, as far as the substantive implications of the studies I draw on are concerned, they could be applied anywhere in the Western world.

The book has an introduction (chapter 1) and three main parts: Part I (chapters 2–3) presents the foundations, including the basic concepts, hypotheses and theoretical perspectives. Part II (chapters 4–7) presents the case studies which assess the respective roles of new conventional and alternative technologies, public transport, green attitudes and land-use planning in achieving sustainable mobility. Part III (chapters 8–9) presents fourteen theses of sustainable mobility and moreover discusses their EU policy implications.

I use 'I' throughout the book. However, in studies which were conducted in cooperation with colleagues, I use 'we'. The overall responsibility is, however, solely mine.

Erling Holden

Acknowledgments

This book could not have been written without the high-quality scientific work that for almost two decades has been carried out by researchers at the Western Norway Research Institute's Environmental Group (WNRI-EG). Most of the empirical investigations that form the book's core have been carried out by colleagues at WNRI-EG. In particular, the demanding, though always patient, guidance of Karl Georg Høyer, former head of research at WNRI, has been invaluable.

Moreover, this book would never have seen daylight without the post doctoral scholarship kindly offered to me by Tore Sager at the Department of Civil and Transport Engineering, Norwegian University of Science and Technology. I would also like to thank William Lafferty at the Programme for Research and Documentation for a Sustainable Society (ProSus), University of Oslo, for giving me the opportunity to dive into the mysterious world of 'green' attitudes for two years. Thanks also to the staff at the Oxford Institute for Sustainable Development, Oxford Brookes University, for accepting me as a visiting scholar, which ultimately gave me the opportunity to finish the book. Finally, thanks to Otto Andersen, Kristin Linnerud, Ingrid T. Norland and Hans-Einar Lundli who have co-authored articles which parts of the book are based upon, to Carlo Aall for valuable comments on early drafts, and to Frank Azevedo for copyediting.

Acknowledgements

Chapter 1

A New Imperative for the EU Transport Policy

...a new imperative – sustainable development – offers an opportunity, not to say lever, for adopting the common transport policy. (CEC 2001)

The relation between transport's positive effects and its negative social and environmental impacts could be compared to that of Siamese twins. Not only is it *difficult* to separate the twins, but doing so is a highly *risky* business. Separation could lead to the death of both parts. Similarly, eliminating most or all of transport's negative impacts could represent a threat to transport as we know it. Therefore, it is difficult to create a comfortable match between transport and sustainable development.

Even so, it is widely acknowledged that the increasingly devastating impacts of transport must be addressed because the overall negative impacts are beginning to exceed the overall positive ones. Therefore, business as usual is unacceptable. Making transport sustainable, however, probably represents, after the elimination of poverty, the most troubling theme of sustainable development. Sustainable transport will likely require major lifestyle changes in most developed countries – something that nobody finds easy.

Yet for decades attempts have been made to make transport sustainable by eliminating its negative impacts without too adversely affecting its positive ones. Since the beginning of the 1990s, most attempts have been of the sustainable mobility variety: the development of more efficient conventional transport technology (for example low-sulphur diesel and hybrid vehicles); the use of alternative fuels (for example bio fuels and hydrogen); the promotion of an efficient and affordable public transport system (for example buses and high-speed trains); the encouragement of environmental attitudes and awareness (for example information campaigns and environmental NGOs); and the use of sustainable land-use planning (for example densification and mixed-use development).

These attempts are so often presented as prerequisites for sustainability that they are taken for granted. But how successful are they really? To what extent do they contribute (or fail to contribute) to sustainable mobility? Why do some attempts succeed and others fail? Or more basically: How is sustainable mobility to be achieved? This book answers these questions.

The approach taken follows four rationales: First, each attempt's appropriateness to the goal of sustainable mobility should be treated as a *hypothesis* rather than as a fact. Thus, each hypothesis should be subjected to thorough empirical investigations in order to determine its appropriateness. I develop six hypotheses based on a review of the sustainable mobility literature. These hypotheses are studied in a number of empirical investigations carried out between 2001 and 2004. The results from the empirical investigations are synthesised into fourteen theses on the roles of technology, public transport, green attitudes and land-use planning, which form the basis for a theory of sustainable mobility.

Second, the research design employed is an *interdisciplinary* one, which is appropriate given the previous dominance of an engineering- and economic-based paradigm in research on sustainable mobility (Banister et al. 2000; Black and Nijkamp 2002a; Geenhuizen et al. 2002; Rietveld and Stough 2005). Thus, I draw on evidence from empirical studies using a rich variety of qualitative and quantitative social science methodologies as well as more traditional engineering- and economic-based methodologies. The empirical data is analysed by means of relevant theoretical positions within technologically-orientated environmental studies, sociology, social psychology and planning research (that is life cycle theory, attitude theory and planning theory). I focus on *passenger* mobility, partly because of the need to limit the book's scope and partly because of my professional background; the equally important challenge of achieving sustainable mobility of goods should not, however, be forgotten. Moreover, I focus on *motorized* passenger mobility because reducing its negative social and environmental impacts represents the main challenge in achieving sustainable mobility.

Third, attempts at achieving sustainable mobility should include *leisure-time travel* (including tourism), which now accounts for 50 per cent of the yearly travel distance in developed countries. Thus, I give special attention to leisure-time travel and the challenges it represents to the goal of sustainable mobility.

Fourth, the book's main research issue relates to the challenge of achieving sustainable mobility in the EU. Thus, I draw from studies carried out in EU countries. However, I also draw from studies carried out in Norway because I regard them as highly relevant to the challenge of achieving sustainable mobility in the EU. Therefore, my findings and recommendations for policy must be considered in light of the EU's and Norway's geographical, cultural and socio-economic conditions. Indeed, the impact of, say, environmentally responsible attitudes and land-use characteristics on travel behaviour varies from county to country. Most of the referenced studies are carried out in the EU-15 and Norway. However, according to the European Environment Agency, passenger travel behaviour in the EU-10 is likely to eventually parallel that in the EU-15 (EEA 2006). Thus, my conclusions are relevant for the EU-25.[1] In fact, as far as the substantive implications of the studies I draw on are concerned, they could be applied anywhere in the Western world. Indeed, the attempts at sustainable mobility, and the theories and perspectives they rest upon, are common to most developed countries. Furthermore, the conditions under which these attempts are applied are broadly

---

1   EU-25 = EU-15 + EU-10. EU-15: Belgium, West Germany, Luxembourg, France, Italy and the Netherlands (1967); Denmark, Ireland and the United Kingdom (1973); Greece (1981); Spain and Portugal (1986) and Austria, Finland and Sweden (1995). EU-10: Cyprus, the Czech Republic, Estonia, Hungary, Latvia, Lithuania, Malta, Poland, Slovakia and Slovenia (2004).

similar in many Western countries, implying that the conclusions from the EU studies must be considered to be globally applicable to developed countries. Yet, sustainable mobility is a global challenge and therefore throughout the book the challenge of achieving sustainable mobility in both developed countries and developing countries is frequently addressed. Thus, my conclusions may turn out to be relevant for a number of developing countries as well.

From 9 to 47 km a Day in Four Decades

Travel has been part of the human experience since the migrations out of Africa millions of years ago. Peoples' motivations for travelling have varied: to escape poverty or flee from aggressive intruders; to seek adventure; to trade. For the most part, people travelled to improve their lives. Whatever the motivation, travel in early times was uncomfortable, dangerous, and enormously time-consuming. Today, some would argue, not much has changed; travel is still uncomfortable, dangerous and enormously time-consuming. There are, however, two indisputable differences between travel then and now: in modern times there has been an extraordinary growth in mobility and a great increase in its environmental and social consequences.

During the twentieth century the growth rates of both population and mobility were remarkable. However, whereas population growth shows signs of becoming sustainable, the growth in mobility does not (OECD 2000). While the world's population during the previous century grew by a factor of about four, motorized passenger kilometres and tonne-kilometres by all modes each grew on average by a factor of about 100 (ibid.). In particular, the growth in mobility has been extensive during the last four decades. In 1960, Norwegians travelled an average of 9.2 km per capita daily by motorized means. By 2000 that figure had increased to 47.3 km daily (figure 1.1). A similar pattern can be found in the EU and all other OECD countries (EEA 2006; EC 2004; OECD 2000).

If the growth had resulted from increased travel by bus and train, things might not have been so alarming. Alas, more than 90 per cent of the growth in passenger travel during the last decades in Norway (and in the OECD countries) resulted from increased travel by private car and plane. This was due to the emergence of two powerful mobility phenomena during the twentieth century: the private car (and its freight counterpart, the truck) and some decades later the airplane (Black 2003). Thus, what was new during the twentieth century was not mechanized mobility but *mechanized mobility by road and air* (ibid.). Indeed, mobility by road and air as a modern paradigm is woven into the fabric of contemporary society (Beckmann 2002). According to the OECD this trend, that is increased travel by road and air, is likely to continue for many decades (OECD 2000).

The growth in transport indicated in figure 1.1 has been, according to the OECD, mostly positive:

> It has facilitated and even stimulated just about everything regarded as progress. It has helped expand intellectual horizons and deter starvation. It has allowed efficient production and the ready distribution for widespread consumption. Comfort in travels is now commonplace, as is access to the products of distant places (OECD 2000, 13).

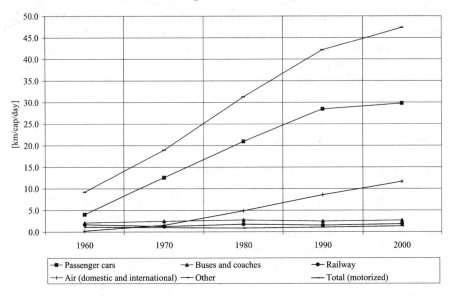

Figure 1.1   Motorized passenger transport in Norway, 1960–2000

Source: Høyer 2003.

Also the European Commission and the World Business Council for Sustainable Development cite increased mobility as a key factor in modern economies. However, during the last decades the costs – in terms of negative social and environmental impacts – associated with increased motorized mobility by road and air have been acknowledged. The intensity and scale of these negative impacts have escalated, and the negative impacts are now all too apparent as travel by car and airplane has increased.

The Troublesome Mobility

In fact, the idea that there are limits to the human occupation of this planet, setting aside the early prognostications of Thomas Malthus and others, has been recognized for perhaps five decades (Black and Nijkamp 2002a). Amongst the first to address environmental problems in modern times was the American biologist Rachel Carson. In her path-breaking book *Silent Spring* (Carson 1962) she described the ongoing disruption of wildlife and ecosystems due to man's contamination of air, soil, and water with dangerous and even lethal materials. Furthermore, she showed that chemicals sprayed on croplands, forests, and gardens remain in the soil and eventually enter into the food chain resulting in poisoning and death. Her book became serious food for thought for politicians, bureaucrats, scientists and lay people. The problems she revealed still exist; however, their causes have changed since the early 1960s. Today, environmental problems are mostly caused by high levels of private consumption in developed countries in general and growth in motorized mobility in particular (Høyer 2000; EEA 2002: OECD 2002a). In fact, it is doubtful that any other activity impacts the environment, both locally and globally, as negatively as transport does. In addition to negative environmental impacts, transport has a number of negative social impacts that should not be taken lightly:

First, transport is a major user of energy and material resources. Roughly 20 per cent of global primary energy demand is used for transport (IEA 2004). In OECD countries 30 per cent of primary energy demand is used for transport; the corresponding figure for the EU-15 is 33 per cent. At present, transport uses mostly non-renewable energy resources, which is likely to continue for decades. Globally, consumption of energy for transport is forecast to grow at 2.1 per cent yearly, which is a higher growth rate than in any other sector (ibid.). This forecast must be considered in light of the expected growth in global car ownership. The worst case scenario (or best case for car manufacturers) suggests that over the next 20 years more cars will be made than in the entire 110-year history of the industry.[2] Furthermore, production of vehicles and transport infrastructure require large amounts of materials. Such material use accounts for 20–40 per cent of the consumption of major materials: aggregates, cement, steel, and aluminium (OECD 2000).

Second, transport is a major contributor to the local, regional, and global pollution of air, soil and water. Chief among transport's global impacts is its contribution to climate change; transport activity contributes about 20 per cent of anthropogenic CO_2 worldwide and close to 30 per cent of these emissions in OECD countries (ibid.).[3] Air pollution is the main local and regional impact, with major effects on human and ecosystem health. Transport is today a main source of these air pollutants (ibid.). Air pollution is expected to decline in OECD countries, although not by enough to improve air quality to WHO standards. Worldwide however, air pollution is expected to increase.

Third, transport infrastructure, mainly roads, consumes about 25–40 per cent of land in OECD urban areas and almost 10 per cent in rural areas (ibid.). Roads and railways are cutting natural and agricultural areas in ever-smaller pieces, threatening the existence of wild plants and animals.

Fourth, 1.2 million people are killed on roads yearly and up to 50 million more are injured (Peden et al. 2004). About 30 per cent of the population of the EU was exposed to urban traffic noise levels that represent a significant cause of annoyance and ill-health (OECD 2000). Some 10 per cent of the population of the EU is estimated to be seriously annoyed by aircraft noise; however, little change in the exposure to high noise levels can be expected during the next decade (ibid.).

Fifth, transport infrastructure might lead to the disruption of communities. The increasing orientation of the urban transport system toward private vehicles can have negative effects on the quality of community life. Urban motorways are sometimes built through established communities (most frequently through communities with insufficient political power to oppose such building), resulting in physical barriers within these communities.

---

2   *Economist*, 10 September 2005, p. 71.
3   More than 90 per cent of transport's contribution to climate change comes from CO_2 produced during fossil-fuel combustion.

Sixth, mobility has not been increased for everyone. On average passenger mobility has increased, but groups of people – in this book I refer to these groups as low-mobility groups – still lack access to transport. Their low access to transport reduces their access to basic public and private services and might lead to social exclusion. This is particularly the case for poor people, disabled people, elderly, women and the growing number of low-income immigrant groups in developed countries (Root et al. 2002; Tillberg 2002; Rudinger 2002; Uteng 2006).

The rather depressing situation described above characterizes an unsustainable transport system as the term is generally understood (for example, Banister 2005; Høyer 2000; Black 2003; Black and Nijkamp 2002a; Banister et al. 2000; Tengström 1999; Wegener and Greene 2002; OECD 2000; CEC 2001; WBCSD 2004).[4] Without major changes in policies and practices, future transport activity could well continue the unsustainable trends of the twentieth century. According to the 2001 EU White Paper on European Transport Policy 2010 (CEC 2001), the principles of sustainable mobility should operate as guidelines for the necessary changes in policies and practices: 'a new imperative – sustainable development – offers an opportunity, not to say lever, for adopting the common transport policy' (ibid., 14).

The Troublesome Leisure-time Mobility

A number of complex societal conditions, or driving forces, have contributed to this unsustainable state of affairs. Amongst these forces are: globalisation, transformed lifestyles and individual travel preferences, modified demographic trends, changed household structures, increased economic growth and household incomes, increased urban sprawl, and increased specialization in education and labour. The importance of these driving forces on transport patterns and levels has been extensively investigated (Banister et al. 2000; Tengström 1999; Black 2003; Geenhuizen et al. 2002; Salomon and Mokhtarian 2002).

Closely intertwined with many of these driving forces, increased leisure-time travel represents an enormous challenge to achieving sustainable mobility. Transport research has focused on work trips and everyday travel (Banister 2005; Black 2003; Holden and Norland 2005; Geenhuizen et al. 2002; Tillberg 2002; Anable 2002; OECD 2002a; Titheridge et al. 2000); whereas leisure-time travel has been virtually unstudied. However, the relation between leisure-time travel and sustainable mobility should be given far greater emphasis. This book focuses on this relation by asking question like: Are there differences between the leisure travel of people living in the countryside and city dwellers lacking ready access to green areas? Are there different mechanisms involved when people perform their everyday travel and leisure travel, respectively? Do green individuals, characterized by a sustainable everyday travel pattern, cast aside their green attitudes when travelling for leisure?

There are five reasons for increasing the focus on leisure-time travel in transport research: First, in most developed countries average leisure travel now accounts for

---

4   Not everyone seems to agree, however. According to Camille Blum, of the European Automobile Manufacturers Association, 'Transport trends are *not* unsustainable' (OECD 2002b, 40).

about 50 per cent of the yearly travel distance by motorized transport (Vilhelmson 1990, 1992; Høyer 2000). This percentage might even be higher for people living in large cities.[5]

Second, over the next 20 years, more people will be spending more time on leisure activities because of an ageing population (Banister et al. 2000). Much of this increased leisure time may involve long-distance air travel as people have the means, time and desire to see the world.

Third, as indicated by a Norwegian travel survey (Holden and Norland 2004), although most of the year people may follow sustainable transport practices, travelling locally by low-energy modes, they may once (or even twice) yearly travel long distance for leisure, thus negating the positive effects of their sustainable transport practices. If people cast aside their environmental concerns when travelling for leisure, policy measures like information and awareness campaigns must be rethought.

Fourth, and related to the previous point, a deeper understanding of the factors that influence leisure-time travel is generally lacking. Indeed, leisure has become more than time remaining after work. Instead, leisure has become a crucial component of our lives (Anable 2002). Thus, the pull and push factors in leisure-time travel decisions tend to be different from those in, say, everyday commuting. Therefore, achieving sustainable mobility requires understanding how leisure-time travel differs from other travel.

Fifth, as the understanding deepens policy making must change. For example, traditional sustainable mobility policy measures – improved public transport, compact urban form, and green awareness campaigns – are less relevant to leisure-time travel. Policy must reflect an understanding of the psychological issues related to leisure-time travel; for example, leisure-time travel is linked to peoples' expression of identity. Moreover, leisure-time travel is politically sensitive because leisure time involves notions of freedom, choice, and self-improvement. Sustainable mobility policy measures must reflect an understanding of this.

Sustainable Mobility

Applying the imperative of sustainable development to the transport sector has led to several concepts denoted by terms such as: sustainable mobility, sustainable transport, sustainable transportation and sustainable transport systems. In the literature on transport and sustainable development these terms are essentially synonymous. 'Sustainable transport' seems to be the preferred term in North America, whereas 'sustainable mobility' is preferred in Europe (Black 2003). According to Tengström, however, a sharp distinction should be made between a sustainable transport system and sustainable mobility because striving for sustainable mobility is quite different from striving for a sustainable transport system. However, I feel that it is more fruitful to focus on concepts' contents rather than on the terms used to denote them.

---

5 A recent travel survey among households in Greater Oslo showed that as much as 75 per cent of yearly travel distance involved leisure-time trips, mainly due to a large number of long-distance trips by air (Holden and Norland 2004).

A transport system is in fact composed of three sub-systems. The first is the motorized means of transport. Sustainable mobility includes assessments of the technological development of the means of transport *and* the total distance travelled by each mode. Thus, claims of what is sustainable in transport are not limited to certain artefacts (such as vehicles) but also to the level of mobility in society. The second sub-system is the transport infrastructure. Sustainable mobility includes an assessment of all sorts of impacts due to the construction, use and maintenance of infrastructure for different modes. The third sub-system is the energy system, what fuels the means of transport. Sustainable mobility includes assessments of both the impacts of improving the existing, conventional energy system and the impacts of promoting alternative energy systems. Consequently, sustainable mobility includes assessments of the provision of transport and energy facilities (infrastructure) and the use of these facilities.

When addressing the sustainability of a transport system, I use the term 'mobility' rather than the more everyday term 'transport.' This is not an attempt to be sophisticated but to grasp the somewhat subtle division between revealed and potential mobility. On the one hand, a revealed measure of mobility is the aggregate of all journeys that have, in fact, been carried out during a period of time – that is, corporeal travel by people (Sager 2005). Mobility is identical to the sum of single transports. Sustainable mobility would therefore be a matter of minimizing the negative impacts from travel, without questioning the level of travel. Potential mobility, on the other hand, does not imply actual travelling, but rather indicates that something is mobile when it can move or be moved easily and quickly from place to place. Mobility is the quality of being mobile and indicates the capacity to overcome distance in physical space (ibid.). Sustainable mobility would therefore have to include some sort of assessment of the *level* of travel. My understanding of sustainable mobility, as set forth in this book, considers mobility as both revealed and potential mobility. Therefore, I use the term 'sustainable mobility' rather than 'sustainable transport.'

From Sustainable Development to the Sustainable Mobility Area

The four concepts 'sustainable development,' 'the sustainable development area' (SDA), 'sustainable mobility' and 'the sustainable mobility area' (SMA) are presented fully in chapters 2 and 3. A short presentation of them and their implications seems, however, to be necessary at this point.

A discussion of sustainable mobility inevitably takes us back to its mother concept, 'sustainable development.' Although this concept dates from 1980, the 1987 report from the World Commission of Environment and Development, *Our Common Future,* commonly referred to as the Brundtland Report, has set the standard and become the reference point for every debate on sustainable development. Since 1987 the concept has been widely used and today sustainable development is a major political aim of various national and international organisations and governments.

However, some scholars argue that the Brundtland Report's definition of sustainable development is hopelessly vague and thus cannot be made operational. Moreover, its vagueness has allowed people to claim almost anything as a part of

Global sustainable development			Sustainable Passenger Mobility in the EU		
SD extra prima characteristics	Indicator	2030 Goal	SM extra prima characteristics	Indicator	2030 Goal
1. Safeguarding long-term ecological sustainability	Yearly per capita Ecological Footprint	Developed countries:-50% of 1990 per capita level=3.0 global hectare per capita (Developing countries: +30% of 1990 per capita level)	1. Impacts of transport activities must not threaten long-term ecological sustainability	Daily per capita energy consumption for passenger transport	-50% of 1990 per capita level= maximum 8 kWh per capita
2. Satisfying basic human needs	Yearly per capita GDP PPP	All countries: Minimum US$ 5,000 per capita (compares to UNDP's 'medium human development')	2. Satisfying basic mobility needs	Daily per capita travel distance by motorised transport	Minimum 11 km per day *available* for all (compares to UNDP's 'medium human development')
3. Promoting inter- and intra-generational equity	the SDA	All individuals should be within the SDA	3. Promoting inter- and intra-generational mobility equity	the SMA	All individuals should be within the SMA, and the minimum daily travel distance should be met by public transport

Figure 1.2   From global sustainable development to sustainable passenger mobility in the EU

sustainable development; thus it has become a concept that entails all that is good and desirable in society. The concept, presented in such broad terms, is probably useless in guiding policy making.

Yet the concept's persistence is remarkable. Despite the problems in defining it, sustainable development as an ideal is as persistent a political concept as are democracy, justice and liberty. Rather than defining it and attempting to make it operational, however, one should ask what primarily *characterizes* sustainable development. Three characteristics can be derived from the Brundtland Report: safeguarding long-term ecological sustainability, satisfying basic needs and promoting inter- and intra-generational equity. I call these the three extra prima characteristics of sustainable development, which means that they have precedence over all other characteristics derived from sustainable development. For example, nature's intrinsic value must give way whenever basic human needs are threatened. However, aspirations for a better life should be subordinated to long-term ecological requirements.

Furthermore, I have developed an indicator and a corresponding goal for each extra prima characteristic of sustainable development (figure 1.2): Per capita ecological footprint (EF) is chosen as an indicator for safeguarding long-term ecological sustainability. The corresponding goal for developed countries, which is derived from the Brundtland Report's low-energy scenario, demands per capita EF be halved compared to the 1990 EF.[6] Furthermore, gross domestic product per purchasing power parity (GDP PPP) is chosen as an indicator for satisfying basic needs. The corresponding goal is based on United Nations Development Programme's human development index (HDI) which demands per capita GDP be above US$ 5,000 PPP.[7] Finally, the SDA (see figure 2.2 in chapter 2) is chosen as an indicator for promoting inter- and intra-generational equity. The corresponding goal is that all individuals should be within the SDA.

The three extra prima characteristics of sustainable development should logically be adapted to transport to achieve sustainable mobility. Consequently, the three extra prima characteristics of sustainable mobility (SM) are:

- Extra prima SM characteristic 1: Sustainable mobility demands that impacts of transport activities must not threaten long-term ecological sustainability.
- Extra prima SM characteristic 2: Sustainable mobility demands that basic mobility needs be satisfied. Basic mobility needs entail accessibility to appropriate means of transport in order to meet basic human needs, like travel

---

6   The Brundtland Report's low-energy scenario for 2030 is based on 1980 data. However, the Report's recommendations regarding halving per capita energy consumption were made in the late 80s and aim at 'the 21st century.' Thus, I use 1990 as a base year and 2030 as the year in which sustainability is to be achieved. Based on WWF's Living Planet Report 2004 (WWF 2004), which estimates the 1990 per capita EF in high-income countries to 5.9 global hectares, long-term ecological sustainability requires that the 2030 per capita EF be less than 3.0 global hectares.

7   Minimum per capita GDP PPP level says something about the possibility for a country to satisfy the basic needs of its inhabitants. The sum of US$ 5,000 PPP corresponds to 'medium human development' (UNDP 2005).

to work and other vital private and public services. Thus, basic mobility needs are not goals in themselves, but rather necessary means to accomplish the goal of meeting basic human needs.

- Extra prima SM characteristic 3: Sustainable mobility demands that inter- and intra-generational mobility equity be promoted. Mobility equity does not necessarily mean equity in mobility outcome (actual kilometres travelled); rather, mobility equity means that everyone should have access to a specified minimum level of mobility.

The notion of extra prima requires that these characteristics have precedence over all other characteristics of sustainable mobility. Furthermore, the SMA uses the notion of strong sustainability requirements, implying that natural capital cannot simply be substituted by, for example, human capital or cultural capital.

Also, I have developed an indicator for each extra prima characteristic of sustainable mobility and moreover suggest a corresponding EU goal to be achieved by 2030 (figure 1.2): I have chosen per capita energy consumption as an indicator of ecological sustainability. The corresponding EU goal I suggest – which is based on the Brundtland Report's low-energy scenario demanding that per capita energy consumption in developed countries be halved compared to the 1990 level – is a maximum of 8 kWh per capita daily. Furthermore, I choose daily per capita travel distance by motorised transport as an indicator for basic transport needs. The corresponding EU goal, which compares to UNDP's 'medium human development,' is that a minimum of 11 km daily must be available for all. Finally, I choose the SMA (see figure 3.2 in chapter 3) as an indicator for inter- and intra-generational mobility equity. The SMA visually represents the achievement of minimum/maximum levels for the first two extra prima characteristics. In other words: Achieving sustainable mobility means to enter the SMA. The corresponding goal chosen for the EU is that by 2030 all EU residents should be within the SMA and moreover that the minimum travel distance by motorized transport should be met by public transport.

How Developed Countries Can Enter the SMA

There are three approaches for developed countries to enter the SMA: the efficiency approach, the alteration approach and the reduction approach. The efficiency approach suggests that both environmental problems caused by transport and the lack of access to transport for low-mobility groups can be solved by developing more efficient technology. The alteration approach, on the other hand, suggests that there is a need to change to modes of transport that lead to reduced per capita energy consumption and emissions. Finally, the reduction approach suggests that neither more efficient technology nor alteration of transport patterns offers the reductions in energy consumption and emissions necessary to achieve sustainable mobility. It suggests that continuing growth in transport activity offsets the gains achieved through technology and mode shifts. Thus, it suggests that we must urgently decrease the transport volume of everyone except those whose basic transport needs are not met.

Furthermore, policy measures necessary to support these three approaches fall into three main policy orientations: Information policy based on encouraging individuals to voluntarily transform their lifestyles by both increasing their awareness and making their environmental attitudes more positive. Regulatory policy acknowledging that individuals cannot be trusted to comply with the requirements of sustainable mobility and therefore that they need to be pushed in the right direction by regulation. Technology policy relying on developing and implementing improved transport technology.

Together, the approaches and policy orientations form a *typology of sustainable mobility* which can be used as a starting point for constructing a large number of hypotheses of sustainable mobility.

In this book, six hypotheses are investigated:

- *The new, conventional energy chain hypothesis*: Sustainable mobility requires that new, conventional energy chains (energy source, fuel and vehicle drive train) be developed to reduce energy consumption for passenger transport.
- *The alternative energy chain hypothesis*: Sustainable mobility requires that alternative energy chains (energy source, fuel and vehicle drive train) be developed to reduce energy consumption for passenger transport.
- *The improved public transport hypothesis*: Sustainable mobility requires that public transport systems be improved to increase accessibility for low-mobility groups and moreover, to encourage mode switches.
- *The increased use of public transport hypothesis*: Sustainable mobility requires that the use of public transport be increased to reduce energy consumption for passenger transport.
- *The green attitude hypothesis*: Sustainable mobility requires that more environmentally responsible (or simply 'green') attitudes be encouraged to reduce energy consumption for passenger transport.
- *The land-use planning hypothesis*: Sustainable mobility requires that land-use planning be changed to increase accessibility for low-mobility groups and moreover, to reduce energy consumption for passenger transport.

Each hypothesis reflects major strategies that often are presented as necessary conditions for sustainable mobility. Their appropriateness, however, should not be taken for granted, but should instead be subjected to critical empirical investigations.

An Interdisciplinary Research Design

A research design describes the 'logical model of proof that allows the researcher to draw inferences concerning causal relations among the variables under investigation' (Nachmias and Nachmias 1992). Every research design needs a main research strategy. The two main research questions in this book are: How can sustainable mobility be achieved? and, Why do some approaches work whereas others do not? Furthermore, this study focuses on contemporary behavioural events but has little

Main research questions (a)	Hypothesis (proposition) (b)	Unit (c)	Linking data to propositions (d)			Criteria (e)
			Discipline (d1)	Theory (d2)	Method (d3)	
How is sustainable mobility to be achieved? That is, How can we enter the Sustainable Mobility Area?	The new, conventional energy chain hypothesis	New, conventional transport technology (c1)	Technologically-orientated environmental studies	Life Cycle Theory	LCA [i], EF [ii] and scenario building	As 2030 goals described in figure 1.2
	The alternative energy chain hypothesis	Alternative transport technology (c2)	Technologically-orientated environmental studies	Life Cycle Theory	LCA [i], EF [ii] and scenario building	
	The public transport hypotheses	Public transport system (c3)	Technologically-orientated environmental studies	Life Cycle Theory	LCA [i], EIA [iii] and scenario building	
	The green attitude hypothesis	Environmental ('green') attitudes (c4)	Sociology / Social Psychology	Attitude theory	Household surveys and in-depth interviews	
	The land-use planning hypothesis	Land-use planning (c5)	Planning research	Planning theory	Household surveys, in-depth interviews, documents, maps	
Chapters 1–3			Chapters 4–7			Chapters 8–9

The letters (a) through (e) refer to the main components in doing case study design (Yin 1994)

(i) LCA=Life Cycle Assessment. (ii) EF=Ecological Footprint. (iii) EIA=Environmental Impact Assessment.

Figure 1.3   The research design

or no control over them. Therefore, the preferred research strategy given these conditions is a *case study* (Yin 1994).

In case studies, five components of a research design are especially important (ibid.): (a) a study's research question, (b) its propositions (or hypotheses), (c) its unit(s) of analysis, (d) the logic linking the data to the propositions, and (e) the criteria for interpreting the findings (ibid.). This book's research design is described according to these five components (shown in figure 1.3).

The first component – the book's research questions – has already been presented. The second component – the six hypotheses – has also been introduced. The hypotheses result from a thorough review of the literature on sustainable mobility, representing the *first-level of theorizing* on sustainable mobility (chapter 3). The third component – the unit(s) of analysis – is related to the fundamental problem of defining the case. Simply, this book's case is sustainable mobility. However, the first-level theorizing revealed that there are many rival theories (hypotheses) of which six are included in this book. Each hypothesis brings one new unit into the main case, thus the case study involves subunits of analysis. These subunits are called embedded units. Thus, the research design is *an embedded, single-case study*. The subunits are: (c1) new, conventional technology, (c2) alternative technology, (c3) public transport system, (c4) environmental ('green') attitudes and (c5) land-use planning. These five[8] subunits need theorizing too, which brings us to the *second-level of theorizing*. The theorizing of the subunits is done in the introduction to chapters 4–7.

The fourth and the fifth components – linking data to propositions and criteria for interpreting the findings – represent the data analysis step. These components consist of four steps, all of which must reflect the possibility of linking the initial propositions to the final interpretation. First, a scientific discipline (d1) must be chosen for each subunit (d1). The three first subunits are based upon technologically-orientated environmental studies, whereas the fourth and the fifth are based on sociology/social psychology and planning research, respectively. Second, a suitable theory (d2) relevant to each subunit's discipline must be found (d2). Life-cycle theory is used in the three technologically-orientated studies, attitude theory in the sociology/social psychology study, and planning theory in the planning study. Third, appropriate methods (d3) must be applied to each study (d3). Life cycle assessment (LCA), ecological footprint (EF) analysis and scenario building are methods used to investigate the two technology hypotheses. Whereas the LCA and the EF put the data together and present them in easily accessible inventories, scenario building illustrates the long-term effects of the various technological solutions. The public transport hypotheses use a combination of environmental impact assessments and scenario building. To shed light on the last two hypotheses – green attitude hypothesis and land-use hypothesis – data has been collected by quantitative household surveys and qualitative in-depth interviews. In the land-use study additional data has been collected from documents of national and local authorities and relevant map sources. Finally, the criteria by which the hypotheses must be interpreted are the goals presented in figure 1.3. Consequently, if the EU were fulfilling these criteria it would meet the sustainable mobility requirements and thus would enter the SMA.

---

8   Hypotheses 3 and 4 are based on the same subunit.

The Ambiguous Role of Information and Communication Technology

None of the hypotheses includes the use of information and communication technology (ICT) as a tool for promoting sustainable mobility, even though its potential to do so has been given quite some attention. Wachs argues that: 'the social trend that is coming to have the greatest influence on transportation is the growing role of information processing and telecommunications in modern society' (Wachs 2002, 17). Giuliano and Gillespie identify ICT-related changes as the most promising research issue related to societal change and transport because 'of the fundamental nature of these changes and their expected long-term effects on travel, spatial form, and lifestyle' (Giuliano and Gillespie 2002, 27). Koski argues that 'information and communications technology plays a prominent role in transport' (Koski 2002, 44).

Indeed, various forms of ICT could increase peoples' access to services, increase transport efficiency, alter transport patterns and potentially transport information instead of people. However, empirical studies have provided very controversial conclusions about whether ICT will substitute or supplement transport (ibid.). Thus, there seems to be no hard evidence that various forms of ICT (for example telecommunications) actually change travel patterns or reduce travel volume (Banister 2002; Koski 2002). In fact, Giuliano and Gillespie (2002) conclude that very little is known about how ICT affects travel patterns.

Gillespie suggests that the increased use of telecommunication could *increase* transport: 'the partial substitution potential of teleworking should not be allowed to obscure the fact that for most human activities, telecommunications is not a substitute for the physical movement of people or goods or services, but rather a facilitator or even a *generator* of such movements' (Gillespie 1992, 76). Moreover, Gillespie concludes that various forms of telecommunication could either reduce or increase a society's mobility level, depending on the context in which they are used: 'As always, it will not be the technology itself which will determine which of these outcomes prevails, but rather the economic, social, political, and regulatory context in which the technologies are developed and used' (ibid., 76). The nature and outcome of the use of ICT will thus be mediated by local contexts (Giuliano and Gillespie 2002). Thus, whether ICT enhances sustainable mobility depends on whether ICT and transport are substitutes for or complements of each other, or whether ICT use decreases or increases industrial transport, commercial transport and residential transport (Koski 2002).

The use of different sorts of ICT in transport will not be treated to a great extent in this book. It will, however, briefly be touched upon in the review of sustainable mobility literature in chapter 3 and also discussed in chapter 9. Undoubtedly, ICT already has an important role in sustainable mobility, and it will have an increasingly important role. The exact nature of its future role, however, remains to be seen.

The Structure of the Book

The book has three main parts: Part I presents the foundations, including a presentation of the basic concepts, theoretical perspectives and hypotheses. Part II presents the studies of the five subunits – referred to as (embedded) case studies –, and part III presents fourteen theses of sustainable mobility and moreover discusses their EU policy implications.

Part I: The Foundations

Chapter 2 introduces the concept 'sustainable development' and asks what primarily characterizes it. The answer leads to a ranking of the concept's major characteristics: extra prima, prima and secunda characteristics (Høyer 2000). Based on three extra prima characteristics, a notion of strong sustainability and quantitative data (WWF 2004; IEA 2005; UNDP 2005), the SDA is constructed. The SDA shows that the main challenge to achieving sustainable development differs according to the country (or group of people). For example, developed countries must reduce their per capita ecological footprints. In an increasing number of developed counties, however, inequalities between social groups are increasing. Intra-generational equity requires that differences in income (and human development) should be reduced. Thus, sustainable development within a country would require that the least affluent citizens be allowed to increase their ecological footprints. Most likely this increase would come at the expense of their more privileged countrymen. Chapter 2 is based on an article published in *Sustainable Development* (Holden and Linnerud 2006).

Chapter 3, which introduces the concept 'sustainable mobility,' has four sections. The first section shows, in a literature review, how the typical understanding and interpretation of the concept of sustainable mobility have changed since its first appearance in the 1992 EU *Green Paper on Transport and Environment.* The sustainable mobility concept has evolved from one characterised by a single-disciplinary approach with a focus on environmental issues, everyday-travel and transport-volume issues in the early 1990s, to the present one characterised by a multi-disciplinary approach with an additional focus on social issues, leisure-time travel and transport-intensity issues. Moreover, mainstream sustainable mobility research has gradually evolved from asking Is transport sustainable? in the early 1990s, to When is transport sustainable? in the late 1990s, and finally How can transport be made sustainable? and Why are we not succeeding in making transport sustainable? today.

The second section defines the extra prima characteristics of sustainable mobility by adapting the extra prima characteristics of sustainable development to the transport sector. Based on these extra prima characteristics of sustainable mobility the SMA is constructed; it is defined by yearly maximum per capita energy consumption and yearly minimum per capita travel distance. The SMA shows that achieving sustainable mobility represents different challenges country-by-country: The main challenge for developed countries is to reduce per capita energy consumption for transport, which can be done by an efficiency approach, an alteration approach or a reduction approach. Moreover, developed countries should increase accessibility to transport for their own low-mobility groups. The main challenge for developing countries is to increase access to motorized transport even though this results in larger per capita energy consumption.

The third section presents the three main policy types for promoting sustainable mobility: information-orientated policy, regulation-orientated policy and technology-orientated policy.

Finally, based on the approaches and policy orientations, the fourth section constructs a typology for sustainable mobility, from which six hypotheses for achieving it are formulated with reference to the roles of technology, public transport, green attitudes and land-use planning. These hypotheses embrace very different ways of achieving sustainable mobility; the main point is that these different ways of achieving sustainable mobility should be treated as hypotheses rather than facts.

Part II: The Case Studies

Each chapter in part II contains three similar sections. The first presents the second-level of theorizing regarding the respective roles of technology, public transport, green attitudes and land-use planning in achieving sustainable mobility. The second section presents the results from new empirical studies in Norway which bring several fresh perspectives into the literature on sustainable mobility, particularly regarding leisure-time travel. The third section discusses the empirical studies' implications for EU policy on sustainable mobility. (This discussion continues in chapters 8 and 9.)

Chapter 4 presents the results from the first two cases: the roles of new, conventional technology and alternative technology. Due to the many similarities in the theoretical and methodological foundations, these two cases – with their respective hypotheses – are presented and analysed together. The case related to the new, conventional technology hypothesis is a study of the use of hybrid vehicles for passenger transport. Hybrid vehicles probably represent the most promising attempt to increase eco-efficiency within the existing technological paradigm. Even though they to a certain extent use alternative technology (hybrids use a combination of the internal combustion engine and the electric motor), the hybrids still use existing transport and energy infrastructure. Thus, hybrids could easily penetrate the market without significantly altering the large fossil-based transport structures. The case related to the alternative technology hypothesis is a study of the use of hydrogen as a fuel for passenger transport. The use of hydrogen has been chosen as a case for two reasons: First hydrogen has, under certain circumstances, the potential for cutting greenhouse gas emissions as well as reducing rural, urban, and regional air pollution. Second, there is presently considerable interest worldwide in promoting hydrogen as a fuel for transport.[9] The chapter is based on two articles published in Transportation Research Part D: Transport and Environment (Holden and Høyer

---

9 Probably the most notable initiative is the International Partnership for the Hydrogen Economy established in 2003. Amongst its members are the European Commission, US, Japan and the Russian Federation. In addition, a large number of 'Hydrogen Roadmaps' are now being developed worldwide: for example, HyNet – Towards a European Hydrogen Energy Roadmap, HyWays – an integrated project to develop the European Hydrogen Energy Roadmap, US Department for Energy – H2 Roadmap, UK Dept for Transport – Carbon to Hydrogen Roadmaps for passenger cars.

2005) and International Journal of Alternative Propulsion (Høyer and Holden forthcoming).

The case study related to the alteration hypothesis is presented in chapter 5. The case is based on the environmental strategy of Oslo's Public Transportation Company Ltd. ('Oslo Sporveier'). The case includes scenarios for the development of passenger transport in Oslo. Three scenarios are described as background for the company's environmental reporting: (i) a private car scenario, where the increase in passenger transport is to be met by a large increase in the use of private cars; (ii) a public transport scenario, where the increase in passenger transport is to be met by a large increase in the use of public transport; and (iii) a sustainability scenario, which calls for a reduction in total passenger transport. Emissions from, and energy and land use for passenger transport in the three scenarios were calculated. The chapter is based on an article published in *Business Strategy and the Environment* (Andersen et al. 2004).

Chapter 6 presents the green attitudes case which is based on a quantitative study of the travel patterns of members of the Norwegian Environmental Home Guard (NEHG) and moreover, qualitative in-depth interviews with households in Greater Oslo and Førde, which is a small and rural town.[10] Since its launch in October 1991, the NEHG has developed into the major green consumer's network in Norway. Over 100,000 people have joined the movement and committed themselves to changing their everyday behaviour and consumption patterns, including their travel patterns. Thus, members of the NEHG are assumed to have highly positive attitudes towards environmental issues, both in general and related to transport practices. Quantitative investigations (questionnaires) have been used to survey the members' travel patterns, whereas qualitative investigations (interviews) have been used to impart knowledge of the members' motives for travel. The travel patterns of the NEHG's members are compared to those of non-members under comparable physical and socio-economic conditions. Attitude theory forms the theoretical foundation for the study of the relationship between the attitudes of the NEHG members and their travel patterns. The chapter is based on two articles published by *Equinox Publishing* (Holden forthcoming) and *Norwegian Journal of Sociology* (Holden 2005).

The case related to the land-use planning hypothesis is presented in chapter 7, including two studies of land-use planning and residents' travel patterns in Greater Oslo and Førde. Within planning theory it is commonly assumed that the design and location of residential areas have important consequences for households' consumption of energy for transport. Thus, it is believed that physical planning and design make it possible to achieve a more sustainable mobility pattern. The selection of residential areas is based on a set of criteria representing key land-use characteristics, including housing density, location relative to the city centre, access to public transport, distance to local sub-centre and local mix of housing, business and services. Quantitative investigations have been applied to survey the residents' travel patterns under various land-use characteristics. The chapter is based on two

---

10   The NEHG changed its name to 'Grønn Hverdag' (Green Everyday) in 2001. However, NEHG was still mainly used at the time when the empirical study was performed; thus, I refer to NEHG throuhout the book.

articles published in *Urban Studies* (Holden and Norland 2005) and *Journal of Housing and the Built Environment* (Holden 2004).

Part III: The Theses and EU Policy Implications

Based on the empirical and theoretical knowledge presented in part II, chapter 8 presents fourteen theses regarding the roles of technology, public transport, green attitudes and land-use planning in achieving sustainable mobility in the EU. Some of the theses are well known within the sustainable mobility literature but nevertheless can and should be backed by fresh empirical evidence, which this book does. Others are not so well known, and some are even new, bringing new perspectives to the discussion of sustainable mobility, particularly the theses that pertain to leisure-time travel. Some of the theses are supplemented by sub-theses to give them further strength. Taken together, the fourteen theses constitute the basis for a theory of sustainable mobility.

Three theses show the challenges regarding the role of new, conventional technology in achieving sustainable mobility. Thesis 1 states that growth in passenger transport mileage constantly counteracts reductions in fuel consumption from increased engine efficiency. Thesis 2 states that heavier, more powerful vehicles with energy-demanding auxiliaries also counteract reductions in energy consumption from increased engine efficiency. Thesis 3 states that there is a significant gap between fuel consumption measured by official certification tests and actual on-road fuel consumption.

Two theses show the challenges regarding the role of alternative technology in achieving sustainable mobility. Thesis 4 states that the use of alternative fuels merely transfers energy consumption geographically (i.e. from the vehicle to the production site and the distribution process); it does not reduce total energy consumption. Thesis 5 states that there are always trade-offs involved in the use of alterative fuels because their use merely changes environmental impacts thematically, rather than reducing the total overall environmental impacts.

Two theses show the challenges regarding the role of public transport in achieving sustainable mobility. Thesis 6 states that without strategies for reducing the overall mileage for passenger transport by car and plane, the role of public transport in reducing energy consumption will be modest. Thesis 7 states that an affordable and well-functioning public transport system must ensure accessibility for low-mobility groups of people to their basic needs so as to prevent their social exclusion.

Three theses show the challenges regarding the role of green attitudes in achieving sustainable mobility. Thesis 8 states that the correlation between specific green attitudes towards everyday travel and everyday travel behaviour is significant, whereas the correlation between general environmental attitudes and everyday travel behaviour is insignificant. Thesis 9 states that people with green attitudes cast aside those attitudes in their leisure-time travel behaviour. Thesis 10 states that membership in an environmental organisation does not ensure sustainable travel behaviour by members.

Four theses show the challenges regarding the role of land-use planning in achieving sustainable mobility. Thesis 11 states that people living in high-density residential areas consume less energy for everyday travel than people living in low-density residential areas, but they consume more energy for leisure-time travel by plane than those people. Thesis 12 states that people having regular access to a private garden consume less energy for long-distance leisure-time travel by car and plane than people without such access. Thesis 13 states that people living in medium-density residential areas consume less energy for transport than people living in high- or low-density residential areas. Thesis 14 states that decentralized concentration is a more sustainable urban form than the compact city, the dispersed city or other alternatives.

Finally, in a four-step process, chapter 9 answers the questions: What combinations of approaches will make transport sustainable in the EU? and, What rolls will technology, public transport, green attitudes and land-use planning play in achieving sustainable mobility? Step 1 constructs seven scenarios each of which reflects different assumptions in terms of the transport situation in 2030. Each scenario is based upon different levels of technological improvement in vehicle efficiency, different degrees of change in transport patterns and different growth rates in total passenger transport volumes. Step 2 uses the SMART model to calculate each scenario's outcome related to the goals of sustainable mobility: yearly per capita energy consumption for passenger transport and yearly travel distance by public transport. Step 3 compares each scenario's outcome to the goals of sustainable mobility. Thus, the results from the SMART model calculations indicate whether a particular scenario will lead the EU into the SMA. Finally, Step 4 discusses the roles of technology, public transport, green attitudes and land-use planning in those scenarios that achieve these two sustainable mobility goals. The discussion draws heavily on the fourteen theses presented in chapter 8.

PART I
The Foundations

Chapter 2

If Sustainable Development is Everything…

Anything on which John Major, George Bush and Fidel Castro all agree can't really mean anything, can it? (Whitelegg 1997, 101)

Like it or not, "sustainable development" is with us for all time. (O'Riordan 1993, 37)

Some thirty years ago a paper entitled 'If planning is everything, maybe it's nothing' appeared in the journal *Policy Sciences*. The paper, by Aaron Wildavsky (Wildavsky 1973), was provocative readings for planners of that period. Wildavsky argued that the planner had become the victim of planning; his own creation had overwhelmed him because planning had become so large and complex that planners couldn't any longer control its dimensions. Moreover, planning extended in so many directions that the planner couldn't any longer shape it: 'He [the planner] may be economist, political scientist, sociologist, architect or scientist. Yet the essence of his calling – planning – escapes him. He finds it everywhere in general and nowhere in particular. Why is planning so elusive?' (ibid., 127).

About a decade later, Wildavsky got a reply from Ernest Alexander in *Town Planning Review* (Alexander 1981): 'If planning isn't everything, maybe it's something.' He took up the cudgels for planners and others associated with planning. Alexander felt that for too long he and his colleagues had failed to articulate a reasoned response to Wildavsky, because the paper's provocative title and deliberately polemic style made its unpleasant conclusions easy to dismiss: 'This last audience, of planners and people involved in planning, is the most important one for Wildavsky's argument. Unfortunately, in dismissing it, either through ignorance or through apathy, we may have thrown the baby out with the bathwater.' (ibid., 131).

Whatever the reason for Wildavsky's attack on planners and planning three decades ago, and whatever the reason for Alexander's being offended by it, they both had every right to state their case. Indeed, whether planning is everything, nothing or something, is a highly relevant and important issue. We have, however, no intention to follow up this debate here. Rather we are concerned about another concept that during the last decade apparently has come to mean everything, and thereby risks ending up meaning nothing – 'sustainable development.'

Although there is a distinction between planning (a policy process) and sustainable development (a policy goal), the link between the contemporary debate about the content and policy implications of sustainable development on the one hand and the planning controversy three decades ago on the other, is relevant: There is every reason to believe that sustainable development is about to become, like planning did, *everything*. Sustainable development is increasingly presented as a pathway to all that is good and desirable in society. However, the concept, presented in such extreme terms, is probably of little help in guiding policy making. Some of the proposed national indicators of sustainable development from the US, the UK and Finland illustrate our point: crime rate, participation of 14-year olds in social organisational work, teacher capabilities, workforce skill level, 19 year-olds with Level 2 qualifications (UK), classes taught in a minority language, children in public care, how children get to school, internet users, published domestic literature, obesity, daily smokers, research and development expenditure, and residential area satisfaction.[1]

Thus, the parallel to Wildavsky's concern three decades ago is all too relevant: The concept of sustainable development has become so large and complex that decision makers can no longer control its dimensions. Moreover, the concept extends in so many directions that the decision maker can no longer shape it.

Not surprisingly therefore, a number of scholars argue that the concept of sustainable development is about to become, if it has not already become, a useless concept. However, like Alexander stressed in his heroic defence of his profession, it is unquestionable that sustainable development is *something*. This chapter clarifies what this something is. Our point of departure is the 1987 report from the World Commission of Environment and Development, *Our Common Future,* commonly referred to as the Brundtland Report (WCED 1987). It has set the standard and become the point of reference for every debate on sustainable development (Lafferty and Langhelle 1999). Since 1987 the concept has been widely used and today sustainable development is a major political aim of various national and international organisations as well as of local, regional and national governments.

However, what is sustainable development, really? What mainly characterises the concept? Which characteristics are most important? We strongly acknowledge that the main responsibility for promoting sustainable development lies with developed countries. This raises another question: What challenges does sustainable development represent for developed countries?

The chapter consists of three sections. The first section presents what primarily characterises the concept of sustainable development and, moreover, presents three clarifications regarding our understanding of the concept. The second section constructs the 'sustainable development area' and illustrates how it can be defined by using data from 118 counties. We demonstrate that sustainable development represents different challenges for different countries and groups of people. The third section presents three approaches for achieving sustainable development in developed countries.

---

1   These are suggested as sustainable development indicators by the Sustainable Development Indicators Group with participants from twelve US Federal departments and agencies; UK Government Sustainable Development Strategy; and Finnish Indicators for Sustainable Development.

Maybe Sustainable Development is Something

The term 'sustainability' was coined already in 1980 in the *World Conservation Strategy* by three entities: the United Nations Environmental Programme, the International Union for Conservation of Nature and Natural Resources, and the World Wide Fund for Nature.[2] However, only with the publication of *Our Common Future* (WCED 1987) did sustainability, coupled to the notion of development, become a rhetorical talisman for our times: 'Pity the politician, the party programme, the long-term plan or the international agreement which does not pay respect to the idea. The prospect of a "nonsustainable society" is on a par with that of a nondemocratic society. It's simply not on' (Lafferty and Langhelle 1999, 1).

However, there is not yet political or scientific agreement on a definition of sustainable development. Rather there is a tremendous diversity of definitions and interpretations (Hopwood et al. 2005; Giddings et al. 2002), which should not come as a surprise; even in the Brundtland Report several definitions can be found (Lafferty and Langhelle 1999). The large number of definitions and interpretations of sustainable development has made some scientists avoid using the term because it is too vague, and even to dismiss the concept altogether. Whitelegg (1997, 101) puts it this way: 'One could argue that it is precisely the lack of clear meaning that allows politicians and businessmen to feel comfortable with the concept – everyone agrees that it's a good thing but no one really knows what it means.' Moreover, Luke (2005) suggests that the concept is increasingly used as a label to place over modes of existence that are neither sustainable nor developmental.

Yet the persistence of the concept itself is remarkable. Despite all the problems in agreeing a definition of it, sustainable development as an ideal is as persistent a political concept as are democracy, justice and liberty (O'Riordan 1993). According to Lafferty (2004, 26), sustainable development 'is now like "democracy": it is universally desired, diversely understood, extremely difficult to achieve, and won't go away.' Thus, O'Riordan (1993, 37) might indeed have been right in his prophesies a decade ago: 'Like it or not, "sustainable development" is with us for all time.'

Attempts at arriving at a uniform definition of sustainable development have been unsuccessful for two decades. Thus, rather than defining the concept, perhaps one should ask what primarily characterizes sustainable development. According to Høyer (2000), its characteristics can be found on three levels, which he names using terms from thermodynamics: 'extra prima,' 'prima,' and 'secunda' (figure 2.1). The extra prima characteristics express the most important features of sustainable development. The prima characteristics are more detailed features of sustainable development given in the Brundtland Report that add force to the extra prima characteristics. Secunda, on the other hand, has been used by Høyer to denote characteristics prevailing at the debate of making sustainable development

---

2   Three objectives for resource conservation were outlined by these three organisations: the maintenance of essential ecological processes and life-supporting systems, the preservation of species diversity and the sustainable utilisation of species and ecosystems (International Union for Conservation of Nature and Natural Resources 1980).

operational. For a secunda characteristic to be part of a sustainable development strategy, however, it must relate to one or more of the extra prima characteristics.

Extra prima and prima characteristics are not equal; the extra prima characteristics have precedence over the prima characteristics. Hence, nature's intrinsic value must give way whenever basic human needs are threatened. Correspondingly, aspirations for a better life should be subordinated to long-term ecological requirements.

Level	Characteristics
Extra prima*	• Safeguarding long-term ecological sustainability • Satisfying basic needs • Promoting inter- and intra-generational equity
Prima	• Preserving nature's intrinsic value • Promoting causal-oriented protection of the environment • Promoting public participation • Satisfying aspirations for an improved standard of living (or quality of life)
Secunda (examples: related to the first extra prima characteristics)	• Reducing total energy consumption in the rich countries • Reducing emissions of greenhouse gases, especially carbon dioxide • Reducing consumption of non-renewable energy and material resources • Polluting no more than ecosystems can tolerate • Developing technological for efficient exploitation of natural resources

Figure 2.1   The extra prima, prima, and secunda characteristics of sustainable development

*Ecological sustainability is often referred to as 'the environmental part of sustainable development,' whereas the latter two extra prima characteristics are often referred to as 'the development (or social) part of sustainable development.'

Source: Adapted from Høyer (2000).

Extra Prima Characteristic No. 1: Safeguarding Long-term Ecological Sustainability

The term 'sustainability' has its origin in ecological science. It was developed to express the conditions that must be present for the ecosystem to sustain itself over the long term. In the Brundtland Report (WCED 1987) there are several references to the necessity of ecological sustainability, such as: 'At a minimum, sustainable development must not endanger the natural systems that support life on Earth: the atmosphere, the waters, the soils, and the living beings' (ibid., 44); and 'There is still time to save species and their ecosystems. It is an indispensable prerequisite for sustainable development. Our failure to do so will not be forgiven by future generations' (ibid., 166).

The Brundtland Report gives two reasons for setting minimum requirements for ecological sustainability. First, if basic human needs are to be met on a sustainable basis the Earth's natural base must be conserved. Human development tends to damage ecosystems, which reduces the number of species. The loss of plant and animal species can greatly limit the options of future generations. Therefore the Brundtland report argued that 'sustainable development requires the conservation of plant and animal species' (ibid., 46). Second, the report argued that 'the case for the conservation of nature should not rest only with the development goals. It is part of our moral obligation to other living beings and future generations' (ibid., 57).

Extra Prima Characteristic No. 2: Satisfying Basic Human Needs

Satisfying basic human needs is at the core of the development part of sustainable development. Indeed, the concept of needs is embedded in the definition of sustainable development: 'It [sustainable development] contains [...] the concept of "needs," in particular the essential needs of the world's poor, to which overriding priority should be given' (ibid., 43). Thus, satisfying basic human needs and assuring long-term ecological sustainability constitute necessary preconditions for sustainable development. The other characteristics have no meaning unless these two preconditions are fulfilled.

What are basic human needs? The Brundtland Report mentions employment, food, energy, housing, water supply, sanitation and health care as basic human needs. The Brundtland Report does not, however, refer to only basic needs. People are, according to the report, entitled to have aspirations for more than just covering their basic needs: 'Sustainable development requires meeting the basic needs of all and extending to all the opportunity to satisfy their aspirations for a better life' (ibid., 44).

The Brundtland Report argues that living standards which provide for more than basic needs can be sustainable, but *only* if such living standards assure long-term ecological sustainability. Thus, not every aspiration for a better life is compatible with the goal of sustainable development. Accordingly, the aspiration for a better life is defined as a prima characteristic, whereas satisfying basic human needs is defined as an extra prima characteristic.

Extra Prima Characteristic No. 3: Promoting Inter- and Intra-generational Equity

The minimum requirement to conserve the Earth's ecosystems has led several authors to conclude that the concept of sustainable development should be understood as pertaining exclusively to physical sustainability (Wetlesen 1999). Lafferty and Langhelle (1999), however, claim that the Brundtland Report dismisses such a conclusion. They base their claim on a passage in the report that states that even physical sustainability 'cannot be secured unless development policies pay attention to such considerations as changes in access to resources and in the distribution of costs and burdens' (WCED 1987, 43).

Hence, in the opinion of Lafferty and Langhelle, even the narrowest definition of physical sustainability – as the minimum requirement for a sustainable development – must take into account social equity, which implies that the present generation must meet its needs without compromising the ability of future generations to meet theirs. Furthermore, the Brundtland Report claims that social equity *between* generations 'must logically be extended to equity *within* each generation' (ibid., 43, our italics). Thus, social equity as an integral part of sustainable development has two dimensions, time and space (Lafferty and Langhelle 1999). From this perspective, sustainable development has consequences for equity within and between generations both globally and nationally.

Clarification No. 1: Broad and Narrow Sustainability

To what extent is there a hierarchy of the extra prima characteristics and what are we to do if conflicts arise between them? Like several authors, the well-known Norwegian philosopher Arne Næss, interprets the concept of sustainable development in the following way: "development is not sustainable if it is not ecologically sustainable (Næss 1991, 37). Ecological sustainability should be understood as being synonymous with 'ecological maintainability in the long-term' (ibid., 38). This approach towards sustainable development, which also was dominant in the *World Conservation Strategy*, places great emphasis on long-term ecological sustainability, and is often referred to as 'narrow sustainability.' On the other hand, the Brundtland Report identifies a much broader spectrum of issues to be covered by sustainable development; including political, social, economic and cultural issues (Lafferty and Langhelle 1999). Thus, sustainability includes more than environmental sustainability, and this approach is therefore often called 'broad sustainability.'

As Lafferty and Langhelle point out, none of the above definitions says anything, however, about how possible conflicts between the goals should be resolved. Consequently, there is no hierarchy among the extra prima characteristics. In fact, they argue that this is exactly the intention of the Brundtland Report: 'Development is only sustainable when it takes into consideration *both* human needs and long-term ecological sustainability. The point then becomes specifically one of *not* establishing a hierarchy of values between the two dimensions, but one of excluding development paths which do not take both into consideration' (ibid., 13). This is in line with our understanding.

Clarification No. 2: Economic Growth, Economics and Sustainable Development

Contrary to the popular tripartite model[3] of sustainable development, this book has not so far given much attention to the importance of economics and economic growth. This is not a coincidence. True, the importance of economic growth for the

---

3   The tripartite model refers to sustainable development as constituted of three main issues: environmental issues, social issues, and economic issues. The tripartite model has, however, also been used to describe a model where three partners (for example, government,

future development of society should not be underestimated. However, rather than being a goal in itself, economic growth is nothing but a *potential means* to facilitate the fulfilment of the three extra prima characteristics (OECD 2002b).

Treating economic growth as a means rather than as an aim is also advocated in the Brundtland Report. The report claims that: 'Sustainable development clearly requires economic growth in places where such [human] needs are not being met. Elsewhere, it can be consistent with economic growth, provided the content of growth reflects the broad principles of sustainability and non-exploitation of others. But growth by itself is not enough' (WCED 1987, 44). Consequently, economic growth must be considered as having a *contingent* relationship to sustainable development.

To understand why an increasing number of studies on sustainability have portrayed economic growth itself as a goal, we probably need to go back a decade to John Elkington's 'triple bottom line' (TBL). Elkington coined the TBL in 1994 as he was looking for a new language to express what he saw as an inevitable expansion of the environmental agenda (Elkington 1997, 2004). He and his colleagues felt that the social and economic dimensions of the agenda, flagged by the Brundtland Report, would have to be addressed in a more integrated way for real environmental progress to be made. Because Elkington mainly worked with business, the new approach would have to resonate with business brains, which is precisely what the TBL did. In the simplest terms, the TBL model focused corporations not just on the economic value they add, but also on the environmental value and social value they add – or destroy.

The TBL model became a success within business. Businesses were introduced to a 'win-win-win' business strategy, which they didn't find in the Brundtland Report. The TBL model became so popular that it started to pop up in non-business studies as well, and the TBL model is now in many cases used interchangeably with sustainable development. Thus, the concept of sustainable *business* development has misleadingly been mixed up with the original concept of sustainable development. Whereas the former is based on the particular needs of business, the latter is based on ideas and principles given in the Brundtland Report.

Indeed, a solid economic bottom line is an important goal in business. Independent and prosperous businesses are an important part of a well-functioning society. But there might be a world of difference between business goals and the overall goals of a society. Thus, in the broader context of global sustainable development, economic growth should not be considered as a goal in itself as it is in the TBL model and, misleadingly, as it is in an increasing number of studies of sustainable development.

Nevertheless, it is important to acknowledge that although notions of economics – for example the level and distribution of gross domestic product – do not belong to the extra prima characteristics of sustainable development, they can still be used as an indications of how the extra prima characteristics are fulfilled.

---

business and NGO's) are jointly working towards a common goal (for example, sustainable development).

Clarification No. 3: Strong vs. Weak Sustainability

A little more than a decade ago, Victor (1991)[4] remarked that one of the contributions that economists have made to the sustainable development debate has been the idea that the depletion of environmental resources in the pursuit of economic growth is similar to living off capital rather than profit. Victor defines sustainable development as the maximum development that can be achieved without running down the capital assets of a nation, which are its resource base. Included in the resource base are man-made capital, natural capital, human capital, and moral and cultural capital. There are, however, differing views regarding the relation between these types of capital.

Turner (1993) argues that the spectrum of views ranges from one he calls 'very weak sustainability' to one he calls 'very strong sustainability.' Turner traces these two opposing positions to the techno-optimists and their techno-centric perspective (very weak sustainability), and the deep ecologists and their eco-centric perspective (very strong sustainability), respectively.

The rule in very weak sustainability (VWS) is that the overall stock of capital assets should remain constant over time. This rule allows, however, for the reduction of an asset as long as another capital asset (or assets) is increased to compensate for such a reduction. Thus, every reduction of natural capital must be offset by an increase in some other form or forms of natural capital or man-made capital.

Weak sustainability (WS) represents a slight modification of VWS. The implication of this modified sustainability thinking seems to be that there is a need for the formulation of a sustainability constraint which will impose *some degree* of restriction on resource-using economic activities. Such restriction would not result from concern for the ecosystems themselves; rather it would result from concern for the ecosystems' ability to meet human needs. Thus, even though there would be some restrictions, there would still be a high degree of substitutability between all forms of capital resources. Both the weak and very weak versions of sustainability are consistent with declining levels of natural capital as long as other forms of capital are substituted for.

Those advocating strong sustainability (SS) claim that just protecting the overall capital is insufficient; rather they claim that natural capital must also be protected because some *critical* natural capital cannot be replaced by other forms of capital. The rationale for this strong view is based on a combination of factors: the uncertainty about ecosystem functions, the irreversibility of some components of natural capital if damaged and the aversion felt by many people about environmental degradation.

The very strong sustainability (VSS) perspective concentrates on the scale of human development relative to global carrying capacity. According to this view, when human development reaches global carrying capacity, no forms of natural capital are substitutable. Thus, there are absolute limits to human development.

The approach we take is based on an understanding of sustainable development in the strong sustainability (SS) sense.[5] Like Tengström (1999) suggests, good

---

4   The work of Victor (1991) is quoted from Turner (1993).

5   According to Daly (2005), the SS view is in line with most ecological economists who suggest that natural and man-made capital are more often complements to each other rather

arguments exist to support claims that there is (critical) natural capital that cannot be replaced by other natural capital or by man-made capital. Certain ecosystems and the global climate are examples of such natural capital. We do not, however, advocate the VSS approach because it implies the primacy of safeguarding long-term ecological sustainability over the safeguarding of other extra prima characteristics, which is not consistent with our understanding of sustainable development.

The Sustainable Development Area

The previous section identified the extra prima characteristics, which characterize sustainable development. The visual representation of the satisfaction of minimum/maximum levels of these characteristics is called 'the Sustainable Development Area' (SDA). The SDA can be used to assess the sustainability of current and future development paths and to discuss the trade-offs between the three extra prima characteristics.

The SDA's construction is based on two fundamental ideas developed in this book. First, the extra prima characteristics have precedence over the prima and secunda characteristics. Second, there is no hierarchy between the three extra prima characteristics. As long as generally accepted minimum/maximum requirements for all three characteristics are fulfilled, a development path must be judged to be sustainable.

The SDA is constructed using a xy diagram (figure 2.2). The x axis represents extra prima characteristic number two, satisfaction of basic human needs. The y axis represents the detrimental effect of human actions on extra prima characteristic number one, ecological sustainability. The third extra prima characteristic, inter- and intra-generational equity, cannot be measured in this xy diagram. However, the diagram can be used to visualize differences across countries regarding the other two characteristics. Next, suitable indicators for measuring achievement of the extra prima characteristics must be found. Below is an example of how this can be done:

An Indicator of Long-term Ecological Sustainability – the Ecological Footprint

We have chosen to use ecological footprint as an indicator of the detrimental effect of human actions on ecological sustainability. The term 'ecological footprint' describes a method of synthesising the overall environmental impact of a given population in a given year.[6] The population can be the global population, the population of a country, or even an individual. A population's ecological footprint represents the amount of the Earth's biological productivity required to produce the resources consumed by and assimilate the wastes generated by it (WWF 2004). Thus, a population's ecological footprint is the total area required to produce everything that it consumes (for example food, furniture, fabric and energy), assimilate its waste, and give space

---

than substitutes for each other.

6   The concept of ecological footprints was developed and quantified by William Rees and Mathis Wackernagel in the early 1990s as an elaboration of the 'carrying capacity' concept (Wackernagel and Rees 1996).

for its infrastructure. Humanity consumes resources worldwide, so humanity's ecological footprint can be thought of as the sum of all ecological footprints on the globe. The Earth's total biological productive area represents the natural environment available for exploitation by humanity. If the global population's ecological footprint exceeds the Earth's biological productive area, long-term ecological sustainability is threatened.

Using ecological footprint as the *sole* indicator of long-term ecological sustainability might seem controversial. It could be argued that monitoring progress toward a complex challenge like achieving ecological sustainability should not be reduced to checking a single indicator. Indeed, there are other methods that are claimed to be good indicators of long-term ecological sustainability. They and ecological footprint have shortcomings.[7] However, the relationship between peoples' consumption practices and the Earth's biological productive area makes ecological footprint perhaps the most valuable tool in assessing long-term ecological sustainability for three reasons: First, ecological footprint as a concept includes a wide range of current major environmental issues.[8] Second, the method used to measure it fits well with the notion of strong sustainability because it explicitly posits limits on the use of the Earth's biological productive area. Third, ecological footprint reflects inter- and intra-generational equity requirements. Present and future generations should have an equal share of the Earth's total biological capacity; that is, they should have equally-sized ecological footprints. Therefore, we regard ecological footprint as a good indicator of long-term ecological sustainability.

An Indicator for the Potential of Satisfying Basic Needs: Gross Domestic Product PPP

We have chosen to use an indicator of national wealth to measure the extent to which basic human needs are satisfied. Gross domestic product (GDP) is the total value of goods and services produced annually within a country's borders. A common measure of the standard of living is per capita GDP, which is calculated by dividing a country's GDP by its population. To compare nations' standards of living, one generally expresses GDP numbers in a common currency. However, using exchange rates when making these comparisons can give a misleading picture of standard of living. Rather, one should identify a basket of ordinary consumer goods, calculate its price in each country using the country's local currency, and finally find the exchange rates as the ration of these prices. The resulting exchange rate is called Purchasing Power Parity (PPP); applying it to per capita GDP yields a measure which can be used to compare the economic wealth of nations.

However, some argue that GDP PPP is an inadequate indicator of living standard (Daly 2005; Hanley et al. 2001). First, GDP is a measure of the economic output of

---

7   See Holden (2004) for a review of EF's shortcomings and limitations.

8   However, ecological footprinting only includes consumption and emissions that require land areas in some form. Important environmental issues relating to emissions of heavy metals, persistent organic and non-organic materials, and radioactive substances are therefore not included.

the whole economy; it does not necessarily measure an individual's living standard. Second, factors such as construction standards, education standards, access to public services, and the extent of pollution are not reflected in GDP. Third, per capita GDP does not take into account inequalities in wealth distribution. Fourth, using the PPP exchange rate for income comparisons might be misleading either because countries put different values on the same goods or because the goods used in the indices vary from country to country, or both. Therefore, GDP *is* an inadequate indicator of living standard.

However, one should remember that the extra prima characteristic of sustainable development is about *basic human needs*, not about living standards, wellbeing, quality of life or other concepts that entail aspirations for a better life. We could alternatively use the Human Development Index (HDI) to indicate whether basic human needs are met.[9] The HDI measures a country's average achievement in each of three basic dimensions of human development: life expectancy at birth, adult literacy rate and per capita GDP PPP. However, replacing per capita GDP PPP with HDI does not alter our analysis, simply because the two measures are strongly correlated (Hanley et al. 2001; Martinez Alier 2006). Thus, it can be argued that a country with a high per capita GDP PPP, distributed fairly among its inhabitants, can provide basic human needs and even increase its inhabitants' living standard.

Defining the SDA

To define the SDA, we must determine a generally accepted maximum level of ecological footprint and a minimum level of GDP PPP.

The World Bank classifies countries into three groups according to *income*: high income (a per capita GDP PPP of more than US$ 9,386 in 2003), middle income (US$ 766–9,385) and low income (US$ 765 or less). Correspondingly, UNDP (2005) classifies countries into three groups according to *human development* – high, medium and low – according to their levels on the HDI index. For 2003 the per capita GDP PPP of countries with medium human development was US$ 4,474. We take the view that the measure of the middle group in both these classifications reflects the minimum requirement a country must meet to ensure the basic human needs of its inhabitants. Thus, we argue for the use of a per capita GDP PPP to satisfy basic human needs of more than US$ 5,000 in 2030. Moreover, the requirement of intra-generational equity implies that the differences in per capita GDP PPP across countries and across individuals within a country should not be too great.

What would be the maximum allowable per capita ecological footprint to safeguard long-term ecological sustainability? First, a strong sustainability requirement implies that demands on the Earth's biological capacity cannot be excessive. Excessive demands on the Earth's biological capacity not only violate the long-term ecological sustainability requirement but also most likely prevent future generations from

---

9   Due to the limitations of GDP as an indicator of living standard (human development), the Human Development Indicator (HDI) was introduced by the United Nations in 1990 (UNDP 1990). The HDI is now being published annually for more than 175 countries (UNDP 2005).

meeting their needs, thus violating inter-generational equity requirements. Second, intra-generational equity requirements imply that each individual is entitled to an equally-sized ecological footprint, which means that the Earth's biological capacity should be shared equally by its population.

WWF (2006) estimated that the ecological footprint was 2.2 global hectares per capita in 2001.[10] However, the biological capacity of the Earth's biologically productive area in 2001 was only 1.8 global hectares per capita. Therefore, in 2001, humanity's ecological footprint exceeded global biological capacity by 0.4 global hectares per capita – a staggering 21 per cent. To achieve an average ecological footprint of 1.8 global hectares per capita would require that the present OECD per capita ecological footprint (6.4 hectares in 2003, WWF 2006) be cut by 72 per cent. In fact, according to UNDP, only countries presently characterised by 'low human development' meet the 1.8 hectare requirement.

However, the Earth's biological capacity as estimated by WWF includes only one-quarter of its surface. The remaining three-quarters of the Earth's surface, including deserts, ice caps, and deep oceans, support, according to WWF, comparatively low levels of bioproductivity, too dispersed to be harvested. These are, however, areas *potentially* suited for biological production and moreover areas that could be used for production of non-organic renewable energy (that could replace fossil fuels thus reducing CO_2 emissions). Therefore, we claim that a less demanding goal can be justified: Long-term ecological sustainability requires that the global per capita ecological footprint be less than 3.0 global hectares. Rather than directly referring to the Earth's biological capacity, this goal is based on a target calling for the per capita ecological footprint in OECD countries by 2030 to be half that of 1990. The former president of the Club of Rome, Ricardo Diez Hochleitner (1998), argues that halving the OECD countries' resource use, which in fact means halving their ecological footprint, closely relates to the challenges of sustainable development. This view is supported by a number of researchers (Weizsäcker et al. 1998; van Dieren 1995; Meadows et al. 1972, 1993; Høyer 2000).

Similar recommendations can be found regarding three specific components making up the main part of the ecological footprint: energy consumption, CO_2 emissions and material use. First, concerning per capita energy consumption, the Brundtland Report sees no other alternative for the 21st century than a 50 per cent fall in per capita energy consumption (based on 1990 levels) in industrial countries: 'The Commission believes that there is no other realistic option open to the world for the 21st century' (WCED 1987, 174). Second, based on data from the International Panel on Climate Change, Åkerman (2005) estimates that a stabilization of CO_2 concentrations in the atmosphere at 450 ppm will constitute a sustainable path. This estimate implies that 1990 levels of global CO_2 emissions should be cut by 37 per cent by 2050 and 70 per cent by 2100 (ibid.). However, since global CO_2 emissions have continued to rise since 1990, global CO_2 emissions by 2050 must be 42 percent lower than present levels (ibid.). Third, several authors have called for halving

---

10 The ecological footprint is measured in global hectares. A global hectare is 1 hectare of biologically productive space with world average productivity (WWF 2004).

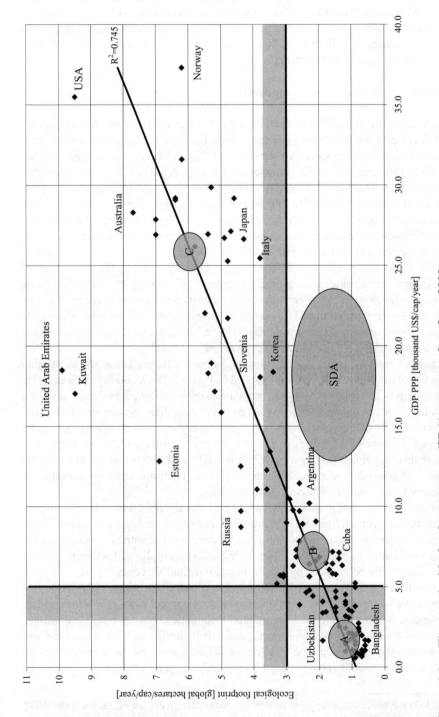

Figure 2.2   The sustainable development area (SDA) – country data from 2002

present material resource use to achieve sustainable development (Schmidt-Bleek 1994; Wackernagel and Rees 1996; Weterings and Opschoor 1992).

Taken together, the above suggest that the per capita ecological footprint in OECD countries in 2030 must be 50 per cent of the 1990 one to be compatible with long-term ecological sustainability requirements.

Different Challenges Country-by-Country

Figure 2.2 shows the global status with respect to sustainability by plotting data for 118 developed and developing countries. Data for ecological footprint comes from World Wide Fund for Nature's *Living Planet Report* (WWF 2004), whereas data for GDP PPP comes from the International Energy Agency's 2005 report on *Key World Energy Statistics* (IEA 2005).[11] The maximum level of ecological footprint and the minimum level of GDP PPP are indicated by a horizontal and a vertical line, respectively. The SDA is defined as the south-east quadrant satisfying the maximum and minimum requirements discussed above. A regression line indicates a linear relation between the ecological footprint and GDP PPP.

Six important points can be made from figure 2.2. First, the main goal of all national sustainable development strategies, as set forth by the extra prima characteristics, should be to enter the SDA. Any policy measure that does not aim at placing a country in the SDA cannot be characterised as part of a sustainable development strategy. Once inside the SDA, a country can start to focus on the *prima* characteristics of sustainable development.

Second, sustainable development would imply different strategies, depending on which category – A, B or C (as labelled in figure 2.2) – a country finds itself in. For countries in category A, as are most developing countries, the main goal of a sustainable development strategy would be to improve their economies. Most likely, as indicated by the regression line, this would imply an increase of their per capita ecological footprint. Countries in category B should promote policy measures that ensure that they hold their position within the SDA and concentrate on fulfilling the prima characteristics of sustainable development. The imperative for countries in category C is to reduce their ecological footprint.

Third, for countries in category C, which includes all OECD countries, sustainable development primarily means reducing their per capita ecological footprint. True, there are large variations in the footprints of developed countries. Getting into the SDA would require substantial effort by the USA, Australia and Kuwait, whereas less effort would be required by Korea, Japan, Italy and Slovenia.

Fourth, even though figure 2.2 represents a country-by-country comparison, the figure can also form the basis for a sustainable development strategy *within* countries or regions. Some countries face substantial inequalities between inhabitant groups. Intra-generational equity requirements mean that the inequalities in income and human development should be levelled out. Thus, sustainable development within such countries would require that the least affluent parts of their populations be

---

11 WWF uses 2001 data, whereas IEA uses 2003 data. In the rest of this book, the WWF and IEA data will be referred to as 'year 2002 data.'

allowed to increase their ecological footprints. Most likely this increase would come at the expense of their more privileged countrymen.

Fifth, the figure reveals anomalies in the data such as comparing Japan and Australia which are equal in per capita GDP PPP but differs substantially in per capita ecological footprint. However, a discussion of these anomalies is beyond this book's scope. Rather, such comparisons could be a topic for further research.

Sixth and finally, the figure lends little support for the Environmental Kuznets Curve (EKC) hypothesis. The EKC hypothesis states that as per capita income grows, environmental impacts rise, hit a maximum and then decline (Hanley et al. 2001). This implies an 'inverted U-shape.'[12] Thus, the EKC hypothesis is based on the idea that economies can grow their way out of environmental problems. Wilfred Beckerman exemplifies this position: 'The only way to attain a decent environment in most countries is to become rich' (Beckerman 1994).[13] However, there is very little in figure 2.2 that indicates an inverted U-shape. Rather the regression line indicates that per capita ecological footprint increases steadily as per capita GDP PPP increases. Thus our data is in line with other studies that have found evidence against the EKC hypothesis: Cole et al. (1997) find no EKC for transport; Horvath (1997) discovers that continually rising energy consumption correlated with increases in per capita income in 114 countries; and Holtz-Eakin and Selden (1995) find that environmental impacts do not hit a maximum until per capita income is at a level that is unachievable even in developed countries, and that therefore EKC is of no relevance. There are, however, empirical studies that *support* the EKC theory. Most of these regard a single pollution or ambient quality measure related to local and regional pollution (Hanley et al. 2001).

In conclusion, a sustainable development strategy for developed countries must meet three challenges:

- Reducing their yearly per capita ecological footprints below 3.0 global hectares in accordance with the long-term ecological sustainability and inter-generational equity requirements.
- Increasing living standards above medium HDI (corresponding to a per capita GDP of US$ 5,000 PPP) for their poor inhabitants through *national* redistribution of wealth in accordance with the basic human needs and the intra-generational equity requirements.
- Increasing living standards above medium HDI (corresponding to a per capita GDP of US$ 5,000 PPP) for people in poor countries through *global* redistribution of wealth in accordance with the basic human needs and the intra-generational equity requirements.

For developing countries, sustainable development primarily means providing increased access to basic human needs even though this results in larger per capita

---

12 The EKC theory is named after Simon Kuznets, who in 1955 hypothesised an inverted U-shape between the equality of income distribution and income levels. A similar relationship is often claimed to exist between income level and environmental quality by proponents of the EKC hypothesis (Hanley et al. 2001).

13 Quote from Hanley et al. (2001, 129).

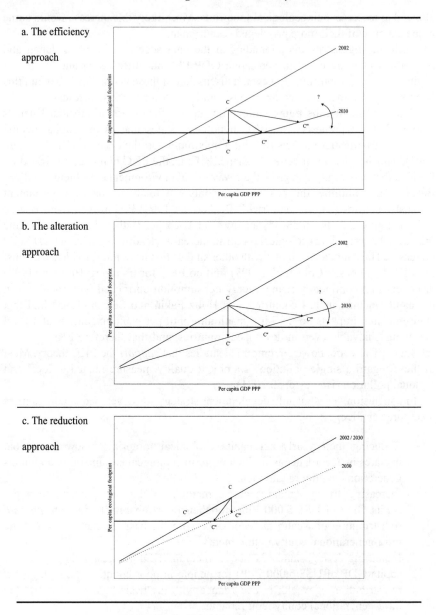

Figure 2.3   The main approaches for achieving sustainable development in developed countries

Note: Point C shows a typical OECD country in 2002, and C', C" and C'" show the possible outcomes of each approach under different growth scenarios for 2030.

ecological footprints. Preferably, this will come as a result of a global redistribution of wealth from developed countries to developing countries.

How Can Developed Countries Enter the SDA?

Developed counties can take one or a combination of three possible approaches to halve their per capita ecological footprints by 2030: the efficiency approach, the alteration approach and the reduction approach. The question of which approach (including concrete pathways or policy measures) is likely to be more successful is treated in chapters 8–9. Here, we merely outline the principles of the three approaches and reflect on their possible implications.

According to the efficiency approach there is a need to develop new technologies that increase the eco-efficiency of production and consumption; for example, introducing more fuel-efficient cars, and increasing productivity in food production. According to the alteration approach there is a need to change our consumption patterns; for example, using public transport instead of cars, and eating vegetable proteins instead of meat. According to the reduction approach, neither the efficiency approach nor the alteration approach offers the necessary reductions in ecological footprints. Rather, it posits that there is an urgent need to decrease the total consumption.

The implications of the three approaches are illustrated in figure 2.3, where the 2002 line is the estimated regression line from figure 2.2. Point C in figure 2.3 shows per capita GDP PPP and per capita ecological footprint for a typical OECD country in 2002. The 2030 line in figure 2.3 indicates a new linear relationship between per capita GDP PPP and per capita ecological footprint in that year. The new 2030 line reflects the assumptions affiliated with the three approaches: a major increase in eco-efficiency in the efficiency approach; a major change of consumption patterns in the alteration approach; and a reduction in GDP PPP in the reduction approach.

The efficiency approach (figure 2.3a) suggests that, given unchanged GDP PPP and consumption patterns, the use of more eco-efficient technology leads a country into the SDA (C'). The alteration approach (figure 2.3b) suggests that, given unchanged GDP PPP and technological levels, changed consumption patterns lead a country into the SDA (C'). The reduction approach (figure 2.3c) suggests that, given unchanged technological levels and consumption patterns, reduction in GDP PPP leads a country into the SDA (C').

Figures 2.3a and 2.3b show the partial effects of the efficiency and alteration approaches. Certainly, technological developments and changes in consumption patterns do not take part in a vacuum. Future growth in GDP PPP must be considered. Thus, whether the two approaches lead a country towards C' (no growth), C'' (weak growth), or C''' (strong growth) is an open question. Furthermore, proponents of the reduction approach are concerned that the positive impacts on the ecological footprint promised by proponents of the other two approaches are based on highly exaggerated assumptions. Rather than supporting the optimistic assumptions portrayed by the 2030 lines in figures 2.3a and 2.3b, the reduction approach suggests that the 2030 lines are more likely to run as indicated by the dotted line in figure 2.3c.

Thus, the only way to enter the SDA (C") would be to reduce future per capita GDP PPP below present levels. Even maintaining the present GDP PPP level (C"') would not reduce ecological footprints sufficiently.

Summary

The concept of sustainable development is in danger of becoming everything; it extends in so many directions and includes so many objectives that it is of little guidance for policy makers. With reference to the Brundtland Report, we suggest that sustainable development is primarily a matter of accomplishing three main objectives: safeguarding long-term ecological sustainability, satisfying basic human needs, and promoting inter- and intra-generational equity. The prima characteristics of sustainable development, for example respect for nature's intrinsic value, encouragement of public participation, and fulfilment of peoples' aspirations for an improved standards of living, must be subordinated to the extra prima characteristics.

As indicated by the SDA, a visual representation of the fulfilment of the extra prima characteristics, sustainable development means different challenges for different countries and groups of people. The challenge for developed countries is above all to reduce per capita ecological footprints to safeguard long-term ecological sustainability. For most developing countries, sustainable development means improving living standards for their inhabitants even if this would increase their per capita ecological footprints.

There are three approaches available for developed countries to enter the SDA: the efficiency approach, the alteration approach, and the reduction approach. The appropriateness of each approach depends on future technological developments, on the degree of future alterations of present consumption patterns and on future economic growth. Most likely, no single approach can lead developed countries into the SDA; rather, a combination of the three approaches seems necessary.

Chapter 3

The Sustainable Mobility Area

Conventional approaches to mitigating transport's environmental impacts have taken observed and projected transport trends as givens and have sought to assess the environmental impact of these developments ex-post. This approach has led to important efficiency gains and has helped to reduce certain environmental and health risks stemming from the transport sector. It has not – and likely will not – however, lead us towards meeting long-term environmental objectives. (OECD 2000)

The three extra prima characteristics of sustainable development, as described in chapter 2, should logically be adapted to transport to achieve sustainable mobility. Constructing and defining a new concept, 'the sustainable mobility area' (SMA), will be central to achieving it.

The 1987 Brundtland Report is the point of departure for discussing sustainable mobility here as it was for discussing sustainable development in chapter 2. The sustainability aspects of mobility (or transport) were not a separate theme in the report; however, three references were made to them. The first was made in the report's overview where faulty transport policies and transport practises were referred to as causes of environmental problems (WCED 1987, 10). The second was made in the report's chapter on energy where transport was referred to as a major source of three environmental problems caused by burning fossil fuels: climate change due to increased CO_2 emissions, increased local air pollution in cities and industrial areas, and amplified acidification (ibid., 172). The third reference was made in the report's chapter on urban challenges, which focused on urban crises in the developing world. Due to lack of power, resources and trained staff, few city governments in the developing world can 'provide their rapidly growing populations with the land, services and facilities needed for an adequate human life: clean water, sanitation, schools and transport' (ibid., 238). Thus, although the Brundtland Report did not treat the problematic relation between transport and sustainable development as a separate theme, it was well aware of it.

Since the presentation of the Brundtland Report, however, this relation has received greater attention. First, the 1992 UNCED meeting, its documents and follow-up mechanisms (all parts of the 'UNCED process') have put transport and sustainable development at the forefront of the sustainability debate.[1] Second, many

---

1 United Nations Conference on Environment and Development (UNCED), Rio de Janeiro, 3–14 June 1992, also known as the Earth Summit. Resulting documents were: Agenda 21, the Rio Declaration on Environment and Development, the Statement of Forest Principles, the United Nations Framework Convention on Climate Change and the United Nations Convention on Biological Diversity. Follow-up mechanisms were: the Commission on

international institutions – for example, the Organisation for Economic Co-operation and Development (OECD), the World Business Council of Sustainable Development (WBCSD), the World Bank and the European Union – have developed policy documents on sustainable mobility. Third, many research projects on sustainable mobility have been carried out due to the report. Taken together, the UNCED process, the policy documents of international institutions and the research projects have contributed to what now must be considered as a large and rich literature on sustainable mobility. This includes literature that uses terms like 'sustainable transport', 'sustainable transportation', and 'sustainable transport system'. Despite this variety in terminology, the reviewed literature essentially discusses the same topic, sustainable mobility, which I mentioned in chapter 1.

This chapter consists of four parts: The first presents a review of the literature on sustainable mobility including international policy documents and research projects. The second constructs and defines the SMA – which is an adaptation of the 'sustainable development area' to the transport sector – and moreover, shows three different approaches for developed countries to enter the SMA. The third part presents three policy orientations that could be applied to lead a developed country into the SMA. Finally, the fourth part outlines a typology of sustainable mobility, from which I derive six hypotheses on sustainable mobility. I study the merits of these six hypotheses in chapters 4–7 and moreover develop fourteen theses in chapter 8 to investigate their feasibility.

A Review of the Sustainable Mobility Literature

This review focuses on studies which deal explicitly with sustainable mobility, which means that the review represents *a first-level theorizing* on sustainable mobility. There are many-times more studies that do not explicitly deal with sustainable mobility, but that nevertheless deal with certain important aspects of it. These studies, which include discipline-specific studies within technology-orientated environmental studies, sociology, psychology and planning research, are reviewed in chapters 4–7 and represent *a second-level of theorizing* on sustainable mobility. It should be mentioned, however, that no sharp distinction exists between studies in the first-level theorizing presented here, and studies in the second-level theorizing presented in chapters 4–7. Indeed, they all belong to the wider interdisciplinary discourse on sustainable mobility.

The first-level literature review reveals that the perception of the sustainable mobility concept has changed since it first appeared in the 1992 *EU Green Paper on the Impact of Transport on the Environment* (CEC 1992). For example, mainstream interpretations of the concepts 'sustainability' and 'mobility' are different today from what they were fifteen years ago. Moreover, current literature draws on more scientific disciplines than the early literature did.

Sustainable Development (CSD), the Inter-agency Committee on Sustainable Development, and the High-level Advisory Board on Sustainable Development.

Therefore, to show how the perception of the concept has evolved, the studies are presented chronologically in three periods: the early years (1992–1993), the intermediate years (1993–2000) and the later years (2000–2005). A detailed analysis of the main characteristics of studies in each period – as well as the reason for presenting them according to three specific periods – is given after the presentation of the studies.

The Early Years (1992–1993)

...planners should be turned to the task of "trip degeneration" – reducing the length and number of motorized trips. (Adams 1992, 332)

The European Commission was among the first to respond to the 'transport and sustainable development challenge' by coining the term 'sustainable mobility' in its 1992 *Green Paper on Transport and Environment* (CEC 1992). The term was a response to the Commission's call for the integration of sustainable development principles into all EU policies. More specifically, the term was presented as a strategy-based global framework that would integrate transport into overall patterns of sustainable development. Thus, sustainable mobility became the new imperative for the EU's Common Transport Policy: 'The new framework set out strict environmental standards for all modes of transport, for quality standards on pollution, for encouraging environment-friendly modes, and for the promotion of guidelines for infrastructure and the development of urban transport' (Banister et al. 2000, 62). The Green Paper was mainly concerned with the environmental impacts of transport. Moreover, it seriously called for a reduction in transport volume, which was regarded as a major obstacle to achieving sustainable mobility.

In a report entitled *Modifying our volume of traffic: the primary route to sustainable transport*, three British transport researchers argue that reducing the total transport volume should be the primary concern in transport policy (Goodwin et al. 1992).[2] They recommend the use of tolls as means to match transport demand to transport supply. Their arguments rested on their claim that environmental costs are real economic costs and that environmental benefits have real economic value.

In a paper entitled *From Growth to Equity and Sustainability: Paradigm Shift in Transport Planning?* Masser et al. (1992) analyse European transport's future by establishing three alternative scenarios. The first scenario is characterized by high-tech and market-economy orientations, which in content were similar to the political ideas of many Conservative governments in Europe at that time. The second scenario shows the impact of policies that aim to reduce social inequality. If a conflict arises between such policies and economic growth, considerations of equal access and equity are supposed to have priority. The third scenario is based on goals such as quality of life and environmental concern. If a conflict arises between these two goals and economic growth, a slower rate of economic growth are supposed to have priority.

---

2   The works by Goodwin et al. (1992) and Masser et al. (1992) are cited from Tengstrøm (1999).

In *Travel Sickness: The Need for a Sustainable British Transport Policy*, Roberts et al. (1992) call for a coherent transport policy for Great Britain. The book's first section identifies targets needed to be met to achieve a particular quality of life. Much of it is devoted to environmental targets, which are seen as having a direct impact on quality of life. The second section analyses ways of achieving these targets. The third section examines particular means of transport and their contributions to achieving the targets. Walking and cycling are given pride of place, closely followed by public transport by bus and rail. In the third section's last chapter, John Adams discusses how to move towards a sustainable transport policy. His key issue concerns reducing the demand for motorized transport: 'The challenge now is to reverse the process by which we have become dependent on an unsustainable level of mobility. The skills of transport planners should be turned to the task of 'trip degeneration' – reducing the length and number of motorized trips' (Adams 1992, 332).

Whitelegg (1993) emphasizes, in a book entitled *Transport for a Sustainable Future. The Case for Europe*, that there can be no understanding of sustainability at any level other than global. This means including the third world in all discussions of transport policy and the environmental impact of transport. Sustainability includes an equity dimension; therefore, a sustainable world cannot be built upon current inequitable consumption patterns. Hence, Whitelegg suggests that sustainability looks strange if we accept present levels of car ownership and use in the West but not in developing countries. Whitelegg attributes unsustainable transport to the increasing number of cars and lorries: 'The car and the lorry are symbolic of the central problem of unsustainability. Their incorporation into behavioural and land-use structures and their role in extending the daily commute, the trip to the shops and the area served by warehousing and distribution companies, is at the core of understanding sustainability' (ibid., 10). He argues that sustainability is nonsense if it depends on reducing emissions at a rate which cannot keep up with the increasing number of cars and lorries. He thus rejects all arguments that the problems will be solved by means of conventional or alternative technology: 'There is (as yet) no such thing as a "green" car' (ibid., 9). Therefore, he recommends a phased reduction in our dependence on motorized transport, which implies an urgent need for behavioural changes to reduce transport patterns and volumes.

In a book entitled *Transport, the Environment and Sustainable Development*, Banister and Button (eds, 1993) give an overview of environmental policy with regard to transport. They primarily consider cost elements which do not fit into normal market regimes. Thus, they focus on the main transport sector contributor to environmental pollution – burning non-renewable fossil fuels for road and air transport. They identify these two modes as those in which consumption has grown fastest. Banister and Button present five means of reducing resource use and pollution. First, in economics they advocate the greater use of pricing, especially precisely targeted pricing to tackle transport's negative environmental impacts. They present several economic instruments: differentiated taxation (promoting unleaded gasoline), carbon tax (combating global warming), subsidies (encouraging public transport modes), and marketable permits (reducing a particular polluting substance). Second, they discuss land-use planning and particularly the European Commission's favouring of (at that time) the high-density compact city (CEC 1990).

The Commission argues that the compact city minimizes land use and is more energy efficient than the dispersed city because it implies shorter journey lengths and better public transport systems. However, Banister and Button argue that traffic congestion might worsen and therefore cause both higher fuel consumption and more emissions. Third, they discuss whether there is a limit to what transport technology can contribute to achieving sustainable mobility. For example, new technology, like the electric car powered by electricity produced from fossil fuels, may well reduce emissions of one pollutant, but end up causing increased emissions of other pollutants. Fourth, they relate the effects of means such as technological improvements, economic instruments and land-use policies to the continuous growth in travel volume; these means may only delay major (difficult) decisions regarding transport volume. Fifth, Banister and Button focus on individual actions. The principle of sustainable development requires changes in attitudes from those based on high consumption and increasing use of non-renewable resources towards those based on maximizing the efficiency of resource use and maximizing awareness of the environmental consequences of individual actions. Finally, it is also notable that they mention, albeit only briefly, non-work-related travel and increased leisure-time travel.

The Intermediate Years (1993–2000)

> ...the Community has neither the power nor the means to set limits on traffic in cities or on the roads... (CEC 2001, 14).

The EU Commission published a document in 1993 on the future development of the Common Transport Policy: *A Global Approach to Construction of a Community Framework for Sustainable Mobility* (CEC 1993). However, the changes in perspectives and understanding compared to those in the 1992 Green Paper are substantial (Høyer 2000); for example, the need for fundamental changes in transport patterns and reductions in transport volume, as set out in the 1992 Green Paper, is no longer at issue. To the extent that reduced levels of mobility are prescribed, the prescriptions are limited to congestion and excessively high (intensive) concentrations of pollution in urban areas and other local pressure points. Thus, achieving sustainable transport is a matter of reducing *traffic intensity* rather than transport volumes (ibid.).

This trend continues in EU documents on sustainable mobility in 1998 (CEC 1998) and 2001 (CEC 2001). These documents introduce the following buzz phrases: 'improving efficiency and competitiveness', 'liberalizing market access', 'ensuring fair and efficient pricing' and 'improving external effectiveness.' Addressing transport volumes is no longer considered appropriate: 'A simplistic solution would be to order a reduction in the mobility of persons and goods and impose redistribution between modes. However, this is unrealistic as the Community has neither the power nor the means to set limits on traffic in cities or on the roads or to impose combined transport for goods.' (ibid., 15). Indeed, this is a major shift from the main message presented in the 1992 Green Paper: 'Fiscal and economic incentives as well as general and selective restrictions on access to infrastructure can contribute [...], as well as reduce the demand for transport' (CEC 1992).

In this period, several supranational institutions begin to struggle with the concept of sustainable mobility. In *Sustainable Transport: Priorities for Policy Reform*, the World Bank (1996) identifies some generally applicable principles and best practices as the basis for a sustainable transport policy. The Bank sees a number of challenges ahead for transport: increasing access to and affordability of transport, responding to growing aspirations for improved transport quality as incomes increase, and reconciling the increased availability of the private automobile and road freight movement with the maintenance of a tolerable environment. The simultaneous achievement of long-term economic, environmental and social sustainability is the key to meeting these challenges.

The World Bank sees economic sustainability, which involves making the best use of available resources and maintaining physical assets, as the basis on which environmental and social sustainability can be founded. The first challenge to be faced in achieving economic sustainability is to create and maintain a competitive market-based transport sector. The second challenge is to introduce economically efficient charges in general, and such charges for the use of road infrastructure in particular.

Regarding environmental sustainability, the World Bank sees two challenges. The first is to understand the mechanisms through which environmental and ecological impacts emerge, the values which society places on them, and potential remedial actions, so that manageable high-priority issues, such as road safety and some air pollution problems can be addressed immediately. The second challenge is to find ways of integrating the less critical but widely dispersed environmental concerns within economic incentive structures. Direct charges for congestion and pollution are preferred, but these mechanisms require further development. In their absence, policies on public transport fares and on-road user charges must be complementary, urban structure and transport planning must be integrated and physical demand management must also be used to compensate for pricing deficiencies. The appraisal of rail and non-motorized transport should involve a rigorous assessment of their potential environmental advantages.

Regarding social sustainability, the World Bank also sees two challenges. The first is to design general transport policies focused on the poor, which involves providing adequate transport to work, eliminating impediments to non-motorized transport, mobilizing the informal sector's potential and eliminating gender biases in transport planning and provision. Poor rural areas may best be helped by emphasizing accessibility, rather than high service quality, in infrastructure provision, and by enhancing local participation in supply and labour-based infrastructure construction and maintenance. The second challenge is to mitigate the unwanted social effects of economic reforms in the sector. This will involve managing problems created by spatial and occupational dislocation.

The OECD acknowledges that current transport trends pose severe challenges to achieving sustainable development. They claim, furthermore, that of all human activities, transport may present the greatest challenges to achieving sustainable development. In response to these challenges, the OECD initiated the *Environmentally Sustainable Transport* (EST) project in 1994 (OECD 2000, 2002b). Since then, future visions, strategies and best practices of sustainable transport have been on OECD's agenda. The first two phases of the four-phase EST project established a definition of EST and selected criteria for its attainment (phase 1), and constructed EST scenarios (phase 2) (Gilbert 2002). Six criteria were selected: CO_2, NO_x, VOXs, particulates, noise and land use. Three scenarios were developed for 2030 (that differentiated from the business-as-usual (BAU) scenario): EST_1, EST_2 and EST_3. Each scenario used different assumptions regarding technological progress and transport activity level. Although all three EST scenarios met the EST criteria, the first two scenarios appeared to be too extreme. The EST_1 scenario seemed to involve unacceptable economic costs. And the EST_2 scenario seemed to involve unacceptable social costs. Accordingly, the research team decided that further work should be confined to assessing how the EST_3 scenario might be attained, and to comparing the EST_3 and the BAU scenario. It is important to note that the EST_3 scenario differs from the BAU scenario in two ways: It implies greater technological progress and less transport activity than the BAU scenario.

In its *Mobility 2030 Report*, the WBCSD sets out a vision of sustainable mobility and ways to achieve it (WBCSD 2004). The Council, representing a coalition of 175 international companies, believes that it is essential to their companies' long-term interests that mobility become sustainable. In December 1992, the United Nations Commission on Sustainable Development (UNCSD) was created to ensure effective follow-up of UNCED. In UNCSD's ninth session, in 2001, transport was discussed within the framework of sustainable development. United Nations Environmental Programme (UNEP) promotes through its *Mobility Forum* the development of sustainable mobility strategies. Considering these institutions' commitments, there can be no doubt that the concept of sustainable mobility is in vogue and will remain so for a long time.

Also, in these intermediate years, many research projects emerged, of which the most important are presented here. The POSSUM[3] consortium, formed by a group of European researchers in 1995, published their work in *European Transport Policy and Sustainable Mobility* in 2000 (Banister et al. 2000). It argues that there is a need for a fundamental rethink about EU transport policies and priorities so that real progress can be made towards sustainable mobility. In the POSSUM project, 'backcasting', a particular kind of scenario methodology, was used to show desirable ways to achieve sustainable mobility. The backcasting methodology results in policy scenarios that systematically combine *strategic* policy elements (that is, 'technology' and 'decoupling') and *contextual* elements (that is, transport-external elements that have a large long-term impact on transport, such as the spread of green values and lifestyles). Then, each policy scenario prescribes some policy measures, policy packages and policy paths that will meet 2030 sustainable mobility goals. The prescribed policy measures are life-style orientated, market orientated, regulation orientated, and infrastructure- and public-transport orientated. The POSSUM project researchers do not underestimate the complexity and difficulty of achieving sustainable mobility. Nevertheless, their conclusions are rather optimistic. They believe that sustainable mobility is achievable within Europe, provided that strong

---

3   Policy Scenarios for Sustainable Mobility.

action is taken at various levels of government and provided that such action is supported by the many actors within the process.

In *Critical Mass*, Whitelegg (1997) argues that a sustainable transport system is one that focuses on reducing the long-term environmental impacts of transport that damage global life-support systems. He presents some policies that should be given top priority if a sustainable transport policy is to be developed, such as developing land-use policies that reduce the need to travel, limiting access by traffic to urban areas, emphasising accessibility rather than increased personal mobility, facilitating a move away from fossil fuel dependence, changing to slower forms of transport (especially cycling and walking) and encouraging the public to change their personal travel behaviour.[4] Whitelegg also argues that equity is an important component of sustainability. Transport policies should therefore be concerned with reducing the inequalities in consumption of finite resources that exist between the developed and the developing world, and between individuals and groups in society. This strategy includes a transfer of clean transport technologies, or the resources necessary to produce them, to developing countries.

In *Towards Sustainable Transport Planning*, Haq (1997) assesses the range and effectiveness of planning approaches to transport and the environment within the EU. Britain and the Netherlands were chosen because of their very different approaches to transport – the British approach being more road-based, while the Dutch approach is more multi-modal. Case studies of a transport corridor in each country are used to discover the extent to which national policy influences and directs transport planning. Using the case studies, Haq outlines an integrated target-led, environmental-based approach to transport planning. His approach contrasts policies which have lacked both integration with other modes and specific targets. Moreover, his approach compares policies which have been reactive to transport problems and thus have dealt with them piecemeal. He concludes that the implementation of target-led transport planning based on concepts such as strategic environmental assessments and corridor studies will be increasingly necessary to deal with transport growth and to achieve a sustainable transport system.

In his book *Towards Environmentally Sustainability?* Emin Tengström (1999) performs a comparative study of Danish, Dutch and Swedish transport policies. Tengström focuses on four policy options for achieving sustainable mobility: reducing speed on the entire road net, increasing the use of carbon-neutral and carbon-free fuels, stabilizing present motorized transport volumes for individual mobility and reducing private car use. Tengström maps the sociopolitical basis for each policy options. First, he claims that the core group comprises people who are environmentally concerned. Many are members of environmental organisations which have expressed views that support the four suggested policy options. Second, he claims that quite a few citizens can be expected to support the policy options if their feelings of being caught in a social dilemma are addressed by policymakers. Some who suffer from cognitive dissonance concerning their car use could also be expected to support the policy options if they were deeply convinced of the negative effects of an unsustainable transport system. Finally, Tengström claims

---

4   For a full list of recommended policies, see Whitelegg (1997, 111–112).

that democratic societies confronting 'the sustainability transition' must revise their transport policies in such a way. This transition leans heavily upon the involvement and commitment of ordinary citizens.

In his PhD thesis *Sustainable Mobility – the Concept and its Implications*, Karl Georg Høyer (2000), identifies seven categories of measures for promoting sustainable mobility: reductions in mobility, reductions of infrastructure provision, transfer between different modes and means of transport, increased load factors, use of alternative energy sources, increased energy efficiency and reduction of polluting emissions. Høyer uses a ladder with seven rungs as a metaphor for these categories. He claims that the higher we ascend this ladder (reduced mobility represents the top rung), the closer we get to the core of the sustainable mobility concept. Based on theoretical and empirical analyses, he argues that the limitations of 'technical fix' strategies (that is the ladder's bottom three rungs) make them unfit as major sustainable mobility strategies. On the contrary, sustainable mobility requires considerable reductions in transport volumes and substantial changes in mobility patterns. In the long run, he argues, there would probably be room for neither private car transportation nor airplane transportation.

The Later Years (2000–2005)

> Transport research can be viewed as a prime example of a research field in which the promotion of an interdisciplinary research approach is needed. (Black and Nijkamp 2002a, xii)

In this period it is increasingly acknowledged that achieving sustainable mobility requires more than just enhanced knowledge about technological solutions. At the *Social Change and Sustainable Transport (SCAST) Conference* at the University of California in Berkeley, sponsored by the US National Science Foundation and the European Science Foundation, focus was set on research challenges regarding social change and sustainable transport. Transport research was viewed as a prime example of a research field in which the promotion of an interdisciplinary research approach is needed (Black and Nijkamp 2002a). In the Conference's manifesto, a Research Triangle identified interesting research themes on social change and sustainable transport (Geenhuizen et al. 2002). The corners of this triangle represent behaviour, policy and technology (level 1). Where the corners intersect – that is, between behaviour and policy, policy and technology, and technology and behaviour – a second category, emerging themes, can be found (level 2). Finally, a third category comprises themes that relate to all three corners in an integrated way (level 3). All three categories together, according to the manifesto, sufficiently cover research in transport fields relevant for social change and sustainable transport.

According to Wachs (2002) the solutions towards sustainable mobility are found in the technology corner. In fact, Wachs does not see much hope for behaviour changes to reduce transport, simply because so many other societal trends tend to increase rather than reduce travel. He particularly questions the role of land-use and transportation planning. He argues that in 2050, land-use and transportation planners will not consider the relationship between urban form and travel to be as significant as we do today because eventually those issues will be uncoupled. Thus, less air pollution and greater energy efficiency may well continue to be more a result of changes in technology than results of changes in urban form, and 'in the future people may not even associate those issues with urban form; nor will they remember that anyone ever did' (ibid., 25).

In comparing the transport systems of North America and Europe, and those continent's governments' approaches to achieving sustainable mobility, Wegener and Greene (2002) make two interesting points. First, they argue that North American governments (the US in particular) believe that the 'rebound effect,' whereby energy efficiency improvements are negated by increased transport activity, is small. The small rebound effect explains why these governments mainly emphasises technological solutions to achieve sustainable mobility. Second, they argue that the European governments, on the other hand, have more faith in the planning system and moreover, that countries with the strongest interventionist planning systems have been the most successful in containing sprawl. (In Europe, reversing sprawl is regarded as a prerequisite for achieving sustainable mobility.)

Janelle and Beuthe (2002) discuss sustainable transport in the broad context of globalization and the changing world economy. They claim that despite the significant role of transport as an agent in globalization, transport is largely ignored in research on globalization. Yet there is a mutual vulnerability of dependence that underlies both globalization and transportation. Janelle and Beuthe identify four important challenges which have relevance for achieving sustainable mobility. First, the expense of linking transportation and communication infrastructure systems limits their feasibility mostly to places along high-density transport corridors linking major urban agglomerations. Though such development might eventually reduce the transport needs of people living in such agglomerations, it might lead to regional inequalities like reduced accessibility for people living and working away from the corridors. Second, as argued by Ivan Illich (1974) in his classic essay *Energy and Equity*, the development of new, energy-intensive transport systems inevitably marginalizes older but still functional systems. In this sense, new transport systems may limit the accessibility of those who cannot afford to make use of them or who lack the technical skill or physical health to function in this new transport environment. Moreover, new, energy-intensive transport systems have in many instances caused old public bus and rail transport systems to be marginalized by increased automobilization. Third, although globalization often is equated with bringing the world together, it still creates distance in the sense that, Janelle and Beuthe argue, it intensifies the demand for transport to support a more spatially extensive production and distribution system. Consequently, goods and people move greater distances. Also, 'thin transport flows' seem to increase, because customization of production and transport often requires more trips and the use of smaller carriers. Ultimately, this increases energy demands. Finally, the declining significance of state enterprises, laws, standards and regulations (due to privatization) potentially reduces the priority given to issues like equity in access to transport and avoiding environmental impacts. Rather, private enterprise gives top priority to issues such as market share, market penetration and return on investment.

In their book *Barriers to Sustainable Transport,* Rietveld and Stough (2005) summarize the work in the STELLA-STAR network.[5] In their book's first chapter, they emphasize that institutional barriers impede sustainable transport: 'There can be little doubt that the primary barriers to sustainable transport are institutional. Certainly, there are technical and operational barriers to the creation of infrastructure and the vehicles that use it, but most of these are well understood over short and intermediate time horizons and involve fairly routine actions for implementation once institutional impediments are overcome' (ibid., 1). Institutions, according to them, are the rules and rule structures that guide public and private action. Institutions can be both formal and informal; they are the rule of the 'game' and as such, they describe how society operates and is maintained. Organisations, on the other hand, which differ from institutions, are the agents that act and thus 'play the game'. Based on Williamson (1994), they identify institutions as being of four types. The first type, informal institutions, has deeply embedded values, norms, practices and traditions. These institutions are powerful conditioners of behaviour, but generally change very slowly. However, when an informal institution does change, it may change rapidly and profoundly. The second type, formal institutions, has codified statutes, constitutional provisions, laws, regulations and high-level administrative orders. Formal institutions may change more quickly than informal ones, but tend to be stable for fairly long periods (decades) unless their environments change radically. The third type, governance institutions, has rules (minor laws, administrative orders, regulations and policy directives) that either maintain or change how governments and related organisations conduct business and direct transactions with other actors and agents. Here institutional change occurs frequently, often in years rather than decades. The fourth type of institution comprises the diverse actions and behavioural patterns of multiple actors in environments ranging from government agencies and private firms to non-profits. Because of the diversity, these institutions change almost continuously.

Stough and Rietveld argue that understanding these four types of institutions provides ways to identify and understand the forces that guide behaviour in specific transport contexts. Understanding them also provides ways to identify and even define efficiency, effectiveness, equity problems and policy intervention strategies. Based on these four types of institutions, they offer a number of institutional issues (categorized by short-, medium- and long-term time horizons) in sustainable transport. Some examples are the Kyoto Agreement, international agreements on taxation, barriers to efficient pricing, consumer preferences for unsustainable lifestyles, land-use variances and managing land-use and zoning codes. Finally, they

---

5   Initiated in January 2002, STELLA-STAR network focuses on common issues in transatlantic transport research through five work groups. The network addresses five major areas which have been identified as critical fields of interest for a transatlantic thematic network in the transportation field. Group 5 have decided to focus on institutional barriers to sustainable transport. STELLA (Sustainable Transport in Europe and Links and Liaisons with America) is a Thematic Network of the European Commission's 5th Framework Programme for Research and Development. STAR is the North American sister thematic network (Sustainable Transportation Analysis and Research), which is supported by the National Science Foundation and Transport Canada.

make three important comments on methodological and data issues in institutional analyses. First, due to the richness and complexity of institutional variables, there is a need for softer (that is, qualitative) data than those quantitative variables typically used in traditional transport analyses. Second, and related to their first comment, the methodologies used in institutional analyses are broader than those typically used in mainstream transport studies. This opens up for in-depth case studies and loosely structured policy-maker interviews, scenario analyses, qualitative modelling, focus group interviews and historical interpretive analyses. Third, and related to both their first and second comments, whenever institutions are an object of study in transport research, the focus is more interdisciplinary. The interdisciplinary approach includes, in addition to engineering and economics, fields such as political economy, sociology, psychology, social psychology, anthropology and history.

Gorham (2002) addresses car dependence as a *social* problem. Clearly, strong car dependence in most developed countries is a major cause of their unsustainable transport patterns. Gorham proceeds from two extreme paradigms that seek to explain the phenomena of car dependence. On the one hand: 'Inappropriate land use, poorly designed suburban development patterns and the absence of transportation alternatives render individuals and households slaves to their cars. A coalition of forces – including car manufacturers, road-building lobbies, suburban tract-housing developers, land speculators and unscrupulous politicians – has been imposing these inappropriate land uses on the rest of society, who are then forced into choices they would rather not make, locking them into a dependence on their cars' (ibid., 107). Thus, according to this view, households are victims of constraining land-use choices made by powerful interests. On the other hand: 'Land use or urban form as it has developed in the outlying areas of metropolitan regions over the past several decades has simply been the result of market mechanisms, the collective output of many individual choices about where and how to live or locate by households and firms seeking to maximize their private utility' (ibid., 107). Thus, sprawl results from a well-functioning market mechanism of supply and demand. Gorham criticises these two opposing paradigms for not adequately addressing the question of car dependency. Focusing on cities' form as the sole or even primary source of car dependence is inadequate. Yet to suggest that car dependence is simply a lifestyle choice made by free-willed economic units maximizing their utility is equally inadequate. Thus, he argues that the paradigms do little to advance an understanding of car dependency and its causes, or to advance an understanding of how to measure, avoid, and reverse it. In trying to define car dependence, Gorham suggests that it has three distinct components. The first component is physical-environmental dependence. The built environment – including urban form, regional structures, and the distribution of activities within these structures, and the nature and status of collective transport modes – influences car dependency. The mentioned factors cause an individual or household without a car to feel cut off from social activities, friends, family, businesses, shops and work. The second component is psychosocial dependence. Emotional and behavioural associations with the car render the individual reluctant to alter his car-dependent behaviour. The third component is circumstantial dependence. The activities in which a household regularly engages render it car dependent. This car dependence is unrelated to urban development patterns, and psychological and social projections onto the car. It is not, however, unrelated to the economic activity in an area and the particular requirements of an individual's lifestyle. Gorham stresses that the three components of car dependence interact significantly. Consequently, they open up for a more thorough understanding of why car dependence has become a major characteristic of life in most developed countries.

Sandqvist (2002) offers some hope for the future, stating that there are signs showing that young people are less car dependent. She begins by describing three stages of mobility: the romantic stage (in which very few people can afford a car, but still dream of having one), the transitional stage (an in-between stage in which most families own a car), and the final stage, in which car ownership no longer is a dream, but rather is regarded as a necessity. According to Sandqvist, most countries in Western Europe are in the transitional stage, whereas the US is mostly in the third stage, along with most of Canada and Australia. Based on a large Swedish survey, Sandqvist finds support for the idea that young adults (who usually have grown up with a family car) seem less attracted to the idea of car ownership. They are more concerned with the environmental drawbacks of cars and less eager to obtain a driver's licence. Taking this evidence seriously, she claims that perhaps transport history in Sweden (and other West European countries) might take a different course from that in the US; thus, total car dominance may not be inevitable.

Gatersleben and Uzzell (2002) present a social-psychological model for sustainable transport. Based on a survey of households in the borough of Guilford (UK), they analysed the travel patterns of people living in the town centre, people living in the suburban areas outside the town centre, and people living in rural areas outside the town. They found that those living in the rural areas use less public transport and use their cars more often than those who live in urban areas. This is not surprising and in line with much other research in this field. However, they also found that people who live in rural areas use their cars more often than others, even for very short trips. Furthermore, rural dwellers walk significantly less than people living in urban areas and in suburban areas. The authors argue that these results cannot be explained merely by differences in travel distances or differences in transport provision; rather, they argue, social-psychological factors should be sought. Their analyses suggest that three factors influence people's willingness to change their transport patterns. First, people's willingness to change is related to how much they feel that their personal car use contributes to transport problems (responsibility). Second, people's willingness to change is related to how much they feel that changes in their travel behaviour will help to solve such problems (self-efficacy). Third, people's willingness to change is related to how much they believe others are willing to help solve such problems (trust). Thus, when developing policy measures that aim at changing travel mode choice, physical planning measures should be accompanied by communication strategies that focus on: (i) increasing knowledge of the costs and benefits of different travel modes, (ii) increasing feelings of responsibility for the problems and (iii) increasing mutual trust, and (iv) control over the solutions.

Feitelson (2002) introduces three types of environmental equity analyses (which, he argues, often are missing in studies on sustainable transport) that can be formulated in the transport context. The first type involves comparing populations exposed to transport-generated environmental problems to unexposed populations. The purpose of such analysis is not merely to identify who is affected by environmental problems, but also to analyse systemic differences by studying both those affected and those unaffected. The second type of analysis concerns the distributional implications of policies advanced to address transport-generated environmental problems. Building limited-access highways through low-income neighbourhoods might reduce congestion. However, the people living in those neighbourhoods suffer from more pollution and moreover, have less access to the highways. The third type of analysis identifies transport's impact on environmental equity concerning land use, urban form and activity patterns. Nevertheless, it is acknowledged that transport policies often have environmental benefits as well as costs. Hence, an environmental equity analysis of such policies should include the distribution of both benefits and costs.

Tillberg (2002) seeks to determine whether residential location still is a factor in total distance travelled. Thus, she analyses how total distance travelled by car differs between households living in the countryside and in town. This aspect is interesting from an energy standpoint, as it is often claimed that counterurbanization leads to increased car dependence. She focuses especially on recreational trips because they now account for 53 per cent of total kilometres travelled in Sweden. Her study suggests that city households travel substantially more for recreational purposes than country households.

Salomon and Mokhtarian (2002) oppose a widely accepted truism in traditional transport research: 'Travel is a derived demand.' However, they claim that there are some indications to support the idea that people travel for other reasons than performing activities at their destinations. In particular, two forms of travel raise doubts about the derived-demand assumption. The first is joyriding in which travel itself is the activity. The second is excess travel that is embedded within routine trips to work, shopping, and leisure activities. Thus, they suggest that some people have an intrinsic urge to travel for travel's sake; they do not travel to perform an activity at their destination. Specifically, the authors identify the following factors as important to understanding individual's travel and mobility: one's general affinity for travel (travel liking), the amount one travels (objective mobility), one's view of the amount travelled (perceived mobility) and one's satisfaction with the amount travelled (satisfaction). Individuals who want to travel more than they do are considered 'deprived' and individuals who want to travel less are considered 'surfeited'. The rest are considered to be 'in balance'. According to the authors, individuals who feel surfeited are likely to welcome reduction-related policies, whereas the rest likely will not. If those who feel balanced or deprived are large enough in number, their reluctance to react positively to reduction-related policies, that is, to travel less, might offset the reduction in travel by the surfeited group. Based on empirical data from the US, they found a clear difference of satisfaction with short- and long-distance travel. Whereas a majority are likely to feel surfeited about their short-distance travel (less than 100 miles one way), a majority feels deprived about their long-distance travel. Thus, people have a strong affinity for more long-distance travel, which most likely is long-distance leisure-time travel. Indeed, these findings represent a serious challenge to policies seeking to motivate people to travel less.

Anable (2002) claims that transport policy has tended to focus on commuting journeys within urban areas, and that it has approached traffic problems in rural areas and off-peak leisure travel with less urgency. The fact that 40 to 50 per cent of travel distance in most western countries is leisure travel raises serious doubts about the appropriateness of this focus. However, according to Anable, there is a clear lack of knowledge about 'leisure travel' because the term is not yet clearly defined. Moreover, leisure travel trends are poorly documented and therefore we have no deep understanding of the factors influencing discretionary travel behaviour. The factors influencing the decision-making process for leisure travel tend to be different from those influencing, say, decision-making for commuting. Knowledge about these factors is crucial to any policy that aims at reducing the environmental consequences of leisure travel. Anable presents a list of characteristics of leisure travel, which forms the basis for a better understanding of these travels.[6] The psychology of leisure indicates that in this sphere individuals experience freedom from obligations. However, it is questionable that leisure travel fits into the notion of travel as derived demand. Anyhow, Anable suggests that in light of the characteristics he lists, leisure travel may be less influenced by such factors as accessibility and price elasticity as is assumed or proven to be the case concerning other travel types. Instead, in leisure travel psychological issues linked with the expression of identity and practical issues concerned with the timing of decision-making and journeys take precedence.

Black and Nijkamp (2002a) point at two important technological changes that give reason for optimism regarding the achievement of sustainable transport: fuel cell cars and hybrid cars, which both promise increases in fuel efficiency by a factor of two or three. They argue, however, that we should not forget that transport growth in the developing world may absorb any fuel or emissions savings from these new technologies. There are also social changes occurring that are less favourable to solving the sustainability problem. One change is the great increase in air travel in general and tourism in particular. Another change is that consumer choice regarding car purchase presently is at odds with sustainability; consumers demand sport utility vehicles rather than small and energy-efficient cars. Black and Nijkamp suggest that the problem of sustainable transport will not be solved solely by a technology approach or by a policy approach; rather, both approaches are needed. They are quite certain that people must be willing to try new technologies and, in some cases, even give up some of their present mobility.

In *Transportation: A Geographical Analysis*, William Black (2003) discusses the implications of promoting sustainable transport. With reference to the Brundtland Report, he defines sustainable transport as 'satisfying current transport and mobility needs without compromising the ability of future generations to meet their needs' (ibid., 317). Black argues that it is doubtful whether achieving sustainable transport will be very pleasant or satisfying. Indeed, sustainability would be at its highest when transport and travel are at or near some minimum level. Black doubts that either developed or developing nations are willing to voluntary move toward a sustainable transport system. Sustainable transport seems to be wrapped up in some idea of potential mobility that is seen as fundamental to their economic well-

---

6   A full list of the characteristics can be found in Anable (2002, 187).

being. Consequently, according to Black, an index of sustainable transport and potential mobility (STPM) is necessary, which he defines as 'travel and transport that minimize the negative impact on the environment and the human health and welfare, and utilize minimum amounts of non-renewable resources in the presence of comparable economic levels that enable mobility' (ibid., 318). Black arrives at the following index for STPM:

$$STPM = GDP - \frac{VKT + FUEL}{2}$$

Where GDP is gross domestic product (representing potential mobility), VKT is vehicle kilometres of travel and FUEL is total gasoline and diesel fuel use by the transport sector (VKT and FUEL represent sustainable transport). All variables are converted to per capita figures and standardized. Each variable has a mean of 50 and a standard deviation of 10, except for STPM. If a nation has an average value of 50 for each of the variables, the value obtained for the index will be 0. Black considers this to be a desirable value that indicates that the level of potential mobility is relatively the same as travel and fuel use. Black has calculated STPM for 104 areas, including the states of the United States, most of the OECD nations and some developing nations. In general, the areas fall into three groups: 1) Countries of the developing world have low negative values (less than -10), reflecting low levels of potential mobility. These countries should be allowed to increase GDP in the future, while retaining the higher scores on their VKT and FUEL measures; 2) Developed countries of the OECD and Europe have scores that fall for the most part between -10 and +10. This is a desirable range; 3) The states of United States tend to have a high positive value (greater than +10), indicating unsustainable transport. Whereas the scores for the OECD and Europe are desirable, it is questionable whether these countries' transport can be considered to be sustainable. The STPM represents a pragmatic method without explicit reference to long-term ecological sustainability goals Contrary to Black's assertion that Europe has balanced potential mobility and sustainable transport, most studies regard Europe's present transport to be unsustainable.

In their book *Sustainable Mobility: Renewable Energies for Powering Fuel Cell Vehicles*, Edinger and Kaul (2003) outline their perception of the challenges to achieving sustainable mobility. Their work is based on three fundamental principles of sustainability: the maintenance of the natural capital stock (inspired by ecological economics), justice between today's and future generations in terms of satisfying human needs, and constant or eventually increased wealth. To achieve sustainable mobility, they recommend taking action in three areas: enhancing the efficient use of limited resources, starting the transition to using renewable resources and introducing new concepts for mobility services to decelerate the increase in individual mobility. Edinger and Kaul argue that all these areas must be assessed for their social and economic feasibility: 'Concepts fail when there is no public support, and capital is wasted if approaches are not cost-effective' (ibid., 14). In their book, however, they concentrate on the first two areas; they scrutinize the transition from fossil fuels to renewable resources, and new propulsion technologies allowing more efficient use of both fossil and renewable resources. For road transport, Edinger and Kaul distinguish between two paths that should be followed in parallel. First, advanced internal combustion engines with direct injection, vehicles built of lightweight materials, advanced motor management, hybrid drive systems, and improvements in aerodynamics and rolling resistance, can increase energy efficiency. Second, new drive systems may be introduced in future vehicles. The most promising drive system is the fuel cell, which has the potential to increase 'well-to-wheel' energy efficiency. (See chapter 4 for an explanation of the concept 'well-to-wheel'.) The authors strongly recommend a shift towards hybrid and fuel-cell propulsion to achieve sustainable mobility. This shift must be coordinated with a corresponding fuel-source shift towards fuels from renewable energy sources. Renewable fuel production such as hydrogen from electrolysis using renewable electric power, and methanol from biomass could be viable.

In a recent paper in *Transportation Research Part D*, Åkerman (2005) focuses on sustainable air transport. He argues that if present trends continue, air transport might have an adverse environmental impact of similar magnitude to car transport's by the mid-21st century. By way of backcasting, three images of sustainable air travel in 2050 are outlined. The images are assessed as to whether they achieve a sustainable level of carbon dioxide emissions, which, according to Åkerman, demands carbon dioxide concentration in the atmosphere be stable at 450 parts per million. Due to the difficulties in assigning the overall reduction goal to air transport, two levels are presented: a lower level implying air transport CO_2 emissions at a constant share of total emissions and a higher level implying a doubled share. The lower level implies a 42 per cent reduction in emissions compared to the 2000 level, whereas the higher level implies a 15 per cent increase in emissions compared to the 2000 level. Åkerman concludes that a high-speed propeller aircraft, with a cruise speed which is 20–25 per cent lower than that of a conventional turbofan aircraft, entails a 56 per cent cut of CO_2 emissions per passenger kilometre compared to 2000. Furthermore, he argues that if this technology trajectory is combined with development characterized be a weakened emphasis on economic growth, and less hectic lifestyles, even the most demanding target levels may be achievable.

In his most recent book, *Unsustainable Transport*, David Banister (2005) argues that seven basic objectives must be met if transport is to conform to the goals of sustainable development:

- Reduce the need to travel.
- Reduce the absolute levels of car use and road freight in urban areas.
- Promote more energy-efficient modes of travel for both passengers and freight.
- Reduce noise and vehicle emissions at source.
- Encourage a more efficient and environmentally sensitive use of the vehicle stock.
- Improve safety of pedestrians and all road users.
- Improve the attractiveness of cities for residents, workers, shoppers and visitors.

Banister argues that the objectives would tackle the problems of congestion, air pollution, noise, safety, degradation of urban landscapes, the use of space and global warming. Furthermore, he argues that land-use and planning strategies have a clear potential to reduce the need to travel, and that both transport and land-use policies will help reduce the absolute level of car use and promote the use of more environmentally friendly transport. Banister considers targets and standards to be important tools to tackle noise and emissions at source. Finally, he suggests that road safety and the attractiveness of cities can also be addressed by transport and land-use policies, and by the application of targets and standards.

Sustainable Mobility: An Evolving Concept

This literature review shows that since the European Commission launched the 'sustainable mobility' concept in its 1992 Green Paper on Transport, there has been a steady increase in the number of books, articles and reports about sustainable mobility. Therefore, there now is a large and rich literature on this field. Because most indicators show that transport continues to grow more unsustainable year-by-year, the number of books, articles and reports is likely to increase, too.

Three important lessons can be learned from this literature review. First, it shows that the focus of mainstream literature on sustainable mobility has changed during the last 15 years. Surely, there have always been some studies that deviated from the mainstream studies. Nevertheless the review gives one a good idea of how the typical understanding and interpretation of the sustainable mobility concept have changed since the early 1990s.

Second, there are six dimensions by which sustainable mobility is typically understood and interpreted. The review shows that there have been significant changes within the following six dimensions: transport's impacts, EU policy focus, travel categories, scientific disciplines, methodological approaches and types of research questions.

Third, it shows that the typical understanding and interpretation of sustainable mobility cluster into three generations of studies: the early years (1992–1993), the intermediate years (1993–2000) and the later years (2000–2005). Between these generations changes occurred in the mainstream studies' understanding and interpretation of the concept, which is shown in figure 3.1.

Such changes occurred in the dimension concerning transport's impacts. Whereas most studies of sustainable mobility carried out in the early 1990s focused solely on transport's environmental impacts, later studies also focused on societal, economic and distributional impacts.

There were also changes in the EU policy-focus dimension. Apparently, the Brundtland Report's recommendation for a reduction in per capita energy consumption led to an emphasis on reduced transport volume in the 1992 EU Green Paper. Also, some EU countries in the early 1990s supported reduced consumption in general and reduced transport in particular. The emphasis on reduced transport volume is, however, a long-gone idea. Indeed, the 2001 EU White Paper on European Transport Policy does not support the idea of reduced transport volume, nor does

Dimension	First generation of sustainable mobility studies [1992–1993]	Second generation of sustainable mobility studies [1993–2000]	Third generation of sustainable mobility studies [2000–2005]
Transport's impacts	environmental impacts	+ societal impacts (quality of life)	+ economic, distributional impacts (equity)
EU policy focus	reductions in transport volume (global consumption)	transport intensity (local pollution)	+ congestion, quality of life, safety, accessibility, competitiveness
Travel categories	production travel (work)	+ reproduction travel (non-work travel by car)	+ leisure-time travel (including long-distance travel by car and plane)
Scientific disciplines	environmental engineering, transport geography, transport economy	+ sociology	+ psychology, social psychology, anthropology, political science, history (interdisciplinary)
Methodological approaches	environmental impact assessment, quantitative modelling, regression analysis	+ scenario building, scenario analysis	+ case studies, in-depth interviews, qualitative modelling, institutional analysis, historical interpretive analysis
Types of research questions	'Is' transport sustainable?	'When' is transport sustainable?	+ 'How' must we change to achieve sustainable mobility? 'Why' do we fail to achieve sustainable mobility?

'+' indicates that the focus of the previous generation is broadened to included the marked item.

Figure 3.1   Three generations of studies on sustainable mobility

the EU apparently have either the means or the desire to support it. Thus, the 1993 EU transport policy represented a change in focus from one that recommended a reduction in overall transport volume to curb global resource consumption and pollution to one that recommended a reduction in transport intensity to reduce local pollution. Moreover from 2000 on, the focus on reduced local pollution has been accompanied by calls for reduced congestion, increased competitiveness and improved quality of life.

Moreover, changes took place in the dimension concerning travel categories. Vilhelmson (1990) distinguishes between three categories of travel: production travel (travel to work and school), reproduction travel (travel to shop and nursery school) and leisure-time travel (travel to recreational activities, on holidays and to visit friends and relatives). Whereas most sustainable mobility studies in the early 1990s assessed only the impacts of production travel, studies in the late 1990s also assessed the impacts of reproduction travel. After 2000, studies began assessing the impacts of the staggering growth in leisure-time travel by car and plane. Hence, the focus of sustainable mobility research evolved as follows: in the early 1990s it was exclusively on production travel, during the late 1990s it was broadened to include reproduction travel and finally after 2000 it was broadened further to include leisure-time travel too.

Furthermore, changes occurred in the dimension concerning scientific disciplines. Since 2000, research on sustainable mobility has gradually included new disciplines and is today becoming more interdisciplinary. This is quite different from the situation 15 years ago when transport engineers, transport geographers and transport economists dominated the field. During the 1990s, a number of sociological studies were carried out, and from 2000 the sociological studies were accompanied by historical, political scientific, psychological and anthropological studies.

Changes also occurred in the methodological approaches dimension. Studies in the early years were mainly based on environmental impact assessments, quantitative modelling and regression analysis. During the intermediate years, studies based on scenario building and scenario analysis grew in popularity. When sociologists, psychologists and others fully entered the sustainable mobility research field around 2000, a broad spectrum of scientific methods began being used, such as case studies, in-depth interviews, qualitative modelling, institutional analyses and historical interpretive analysis.

Finally, there were changes in the research questions dimension. In 1992 and 1993 a number of studies were occupied with '*is*' questions like, 'Is the present transport pattern sustainable?' and 'Is present the transport trend sustainable?' According to most studies, the answer to both questions has been 'no.' Therefore, the '*is*' questions are no longer asked within mainstream sustainable mobility research.

After 1993, another type of question emerged: '*When* is transport sustainable?' Studies differed substantially in the approaches they took to answer this question, of which the most prominent are mentioned in this book's introduction: the development of new and more efficient conventional transport technology, the use of alternative fuels, the promotion of an efficient and affordable public transport system, the encouragement of environmental attitudes and awareness and the use of sustainable land-use planning.

At the beginning of this century, a new type of question appeared in the literature on sustainable mobility: 'How can changes which lead towards sustainable mobility be achieved?' Questions under study typically include: 'How can a hydrogen infrastructure be implemented?', 'How can people be convinced to buy hydrogen cars (or other "clean" cars)?' and 'How can consistency between green attitudes and sustainable travel behaviour be increased?' These were soon followed by a related type of question, which acknowledged that actual changes for achieving sustainable mobility seemed conspicuous by their absence: '*Why* do we not manage to change our unsustainable mobility pattern?' This leads to the larger question: 'Why do we travel?' Apparently, research has not been paying this larger question the attention it deserves. Anable (2002) argues that the problem is that researchers rarely ask 'why' questions like 'Why are people willing to wait in line for hours in their cars to enter our national parks, or to drive for hours to reach a heritage site, walk two hundred metres, buy an ice cream, and go home?' (ibid., 187). Indeed, adequately answering such questions is crucial to achieving sustainable mobility. Clearly, to answer 'how' and 'why' questions requires methodological approaches that are unknown to traditional engineering-based transport research. One must understand why people travel, which requires methodological approaches found within political science, sociology, social psychology, psychology and anthropology.

Thus, the mainstream research on sustainable mobility has experienced a gradual evolution from asking the original 'is' questions in the early 1990s, to 'when' questions in the late 1990s, and finally to asking the present prevailing 'how' and 'why' questions.

A Brief Comment

A brief comment seems highly necessary at this point. Researches conducting third-generation research on sustainable mobility are in danger of including too much in it and thus reducing it to nothing. For example, as I mentioned in chapter 2, 'sustainable development' is about to become a term that includes everything and therefore risks becoming meaningless. Correspondingly, 'sustainable mobility' could end up meaning everything that is desirable in society and hence, end up being meaningless too. Therefore, it would end up as mere rhetoric with little guidance for policy makers.

One should therefore not lose sight of the fact that sustainable mobility, like sustainable development, is *something*. For sustainable mobility researchers, this means adapting the three extra prima characteristics of sustainable development to the transport sector. Logically, this leads to three extra prima characteristics of sustainable mobility, which in turn lead to the SMA and the challenges to get there for both developed and developing countries.

From the Extra Prima Characteristics of Sustainable Development to the SMA

Chapter 2 presented the extra prima characteristics of sustainable development and the sustainable development area (SDA). This section adapts these concepts to the transport sector.

The three extra prima characteristics of sustainable mobility (SM) are:

- Extra prima SM characteristic 1: Sustainable mobility demands that impacts of transport activities must not threaten long-term ecological sustainability.
- Extra prima SM characteristic 2: Sustainable mobility demands that *basic mobility needs* be satisfied. Basic mobility needs entail accessibility to appropriate means of transport to meet basic human needs, like travel to work

and other vital private and public services (WCED 1987, 238). Thus, basic mobility needs are not goals in themselves, but rather a necessary means to accomplish the goal of meeting basic human needs.

- Extra prima SM characteristic 3: Sustainable mobility demands that inter- and intra-generational *mobility equity* be promoted. Mobility equity does not necessarily mean equity in mobility outcome (actual kilometres travelled); rather, mobility equity means that everyone should have access to a specified minimum level of mobility.

The SMA visually represents the achievement of minimum/maximum levels for the three extra prima characteristics. The SMA can be used to assess the sustainability of current and future development paths and to discuss the trade-offs between the three extra prima characteristics. In this section I will construct and define the SMA, which includes finding appropriate indicators as well as goals for each extra prima characteristic.

The construction of the SMA is based on two fundamental ideas. First, there is a clear hierarchy amongst various characteristics derived from sustainable development; the three extra prima characteristics shown above have precedence over the prima characteristics. Second, there is no hierarchy amongst the three extra prima characteristics. Thus, as long as generally accepted minimum/maximum requirements for all three extra prima characteristics are fulfilled, a development path must be judged to be sustainable.

The SMA is constructed using an xy diagram (figure 3.2), following the same logic used in constructing the SDA. The x axis represents extra prima characteristic number two, satisfying basic transport needs. The y axis represents the detrimental effect of transport on extra prima characteristic number one, safeguarding ecological sustainability. The third extra prima characteristic – inter- and intra-generational mobility equity – cannot be explicitly measured in this xy diagram. However, the diagram can be used to visualize inequalities across countries, and within countries, with respect to the first two extra prima characteristics.

Constructing and defining the SMA involves two steps. The first (constructing) is to find suitable indicators for the three extra prima characteristics. The second (defining) is to determine generally accepted maximum and minimum levels (goals) for each indicator. Below is an example of how these indicators can be constructed and defined.

Safeguarding Long-term Ecological Sustainability

I have chosen per capita energy consumption as an indicator of the first extra prima characteristic of sustainable mobility. There are two reasons for this choice: First, a large amount of data on energy consumption for transport is readily available, whereas data on ecological footprint for transport is not. (Ecological footprint was used as an indicator of the first extra prima characteristic of sustainable development.) Moreover, calculating energy consumption from travel-survey data requires considerably less supplementary data than does calculating the ecological footprint. Second, data on energy consumption for transport shows strong correlation with data on ecological footprints (IEA 2005; WWF 2004) and is therefore also a good indicator for long-term ecological sustainability. In fact, the importance of focusing on energy consumption as an indicator of overall ecological sustainability was acknowledged already in the Brundtland Report, because all types of energy consumption – renewable and non-renewable alike – cause a large spectrum of environmental impacts and thus cause a threat to long-term ecological sustainability (WCED 1987, 59). Thus, I regard energy consumption as a key indicator for long-term ecological sustainability. The goal which all countries should aim for is the Brundtland Report's low-energy scenario; the specific goal for the EU is given later in this chapter.

Satisfying Basic Mobility Needs

I have chosen per capita travel distance by motorized transport as an indicator of the second extra prima characteristic of sustainable mobility. There are two reasons for this choice: First, per capita travel distance tells to what extent people are mobile in a modern world. A high level of travel distance indicates that people have sufficient mobility to meet their basic transport needs, whereas a low level indicates otherwise. Second, data on yearly travel distance shows strong correlation with data on gross domestic product (GDP) (Banister 2002; Black 2003; Schafer 1998; WBCSD 2001, 2004; IEA 2002b). As already indicated in chapter 2, a high per capita GDP indicates a country's potential to provide basic needs – including mobility needs – to its inhabitants.

It is, however, problematic to use yearly travel distance as an indicator of a country's potential to ensure basic transport needs, simply because the basic transport-needs concept is highly context dependent. Indeed, people living in remote areas are likely to travel farther to meet their basic needs than people living in densely populated cities. Nevertheless, access to a certain amount of motorized transport is a necessity for most people; therefore, I regard yearly per capita travel distance as a key indicator for a country's ability to meet basic transport needs.

Yet finding the minimum level of mobility needed to meet basic transport needs is problematic due to the context dependence mentioned above. However, as a starting point for discussing such a minimum level, a rough estimate of a minimum level of mobility is presented here. First, a minimum level of GDP PPP to meet basic needs is in chapter 2 estimated to be $US 5,000 (corresponding to UNDP's medium human development). Second, the ratio between GDP PPP and yearly travel distance has been estimated to be 0.7–0.9 (Banister 2002; Black 2003; Schafer 1998; WBCSD 2001, 2004; IEA 2002b). Thus, a minimum per capita mobility level sufficient to meet basic transport needs would be 3,500–4,500 km yearly (approx. 11 km per capita daily). Indeed, people having access to mobility above this level would most probably be able to meet their basic transport needs.

Promoting Inter- and Intra-generational Mobility Equity

Inter-generational equity requires that future generations be able to meet their needs. Although we do not know these future needs, it is unlikely that future generations' needs can be met without safeguarding long-term ecological sustainability. Thus, promoting inter-generational equity and safeguarding long-term ecological sustainability are essentially the same thing.

Hence, inter-generational mobility equity requires that per capita energy consumption for passenger transport be below the maximum requirement derived from the Brundtland Report's low-energy scenario. Intra-generational mobility equity, on the other hand, requires that per capita travel distance available to all be above the minimum requirement. Moreover, public transport should meet the minimum requirement of present and future low-mobility people because they are generally unable to afford a car.

Thus, inter- and intra-generational mobility equity require that a country's (or a region's) per capita levels of energy consumption and travel distance be within the SMA. Moreover, both require that inequalities in per capita energy consumption and per capita travel distances be small – even in societies which meet everyone's basic mobility needs. However, more important than minimizing inequalities in outcome (that is, actual travel distance) is ensuring that everyone at least has the possibility to meet their basic mobility needs.

Different Challenges Country-by-Country

Figure 3.2 shows the relation between per capita energy consumption for passenger transport and per capita travel distance. The figure adapts figure 2.2 in chapter 2 to the transport sector; it reflects two strong correlations: between energy consumption for transport and the overall ecological footprint, and also between yearly travel distance and GDP PPP. The SMA is defined as the south-east quadrant where the maximum and minimum requirements discussed above are met.

Figure 3.2 serves two purposes: First, it shows that a country's main challenge is to enter the SMA in order to achieve sustainable mobility. Moreover, the figure is a powerful visualisation of the general relation between energy consumption and travel distance. Second, it is a basis for discussing various approaches that developed countries can take to achieve sustainable mobility. The general principles are outlined in the next section, whereas chapter 9 analyzes how the EU can enter the SMA.

Four important issues are revealed by figure 3.2. First, the main goal of all national sustainable mobility strategies, as set forth by the extra prima characteristics, should be to enter the SMA. Furthermore, policy measures that do not aim at placing a country in the SMA cannot be part of a sustainable mobility strategy. Once inside the SMA, a country can start focusing on the prima characteristics of sustainable mobility (derived from the prima characteristics of sustainable development).

Second, the appropriate sustainable mobility strategy depends on which category – A, B or C (as shown in figure 3.2) – a country finds itself in. For countries in category A, as are most developing countries, the main objective of a sustainable mobility strategy would be to increase access to basic transport needs. Most likely, this would imply an increase of yearly travel distance and, as indicated by the figure, a corresponding increase in energy consumption. Countries in category B should promote policy measures that ensure they remain within the SMA, and should concentrate on fulfilling the prima characteristics of sustainable mobility. Countries in category C, as are all OECD countries, must, in accordance with the Brundtland

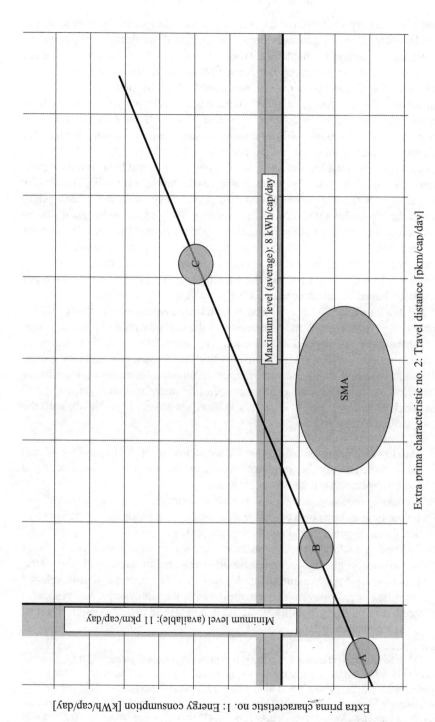

Figure 3.2   The Sustainable Mobility Area (SMA): EU goals for 2030 are indicated in the figure

Report's low-energy scenario, reduce their per capita energy consumption to 50 per cent or less of the 1990 level to meet long-term ecological sustainability requirements (see also the discussion in chapter 2). True, amongst developed countries there are large variations in per capita energy consumption for passenger transport. Thus, getting into the SMA would require substantial effort by high-mobility OECD countries like the US, Australia and Canada, but considerably less effort by low-mobility OECD countries like Japan, Italy and Austria. If for example the high-mobility and the low-mobility OECD countries were to aim at the same level of per capita energy consumption – that is 50 per cent or less of the 1990 OECD levels – this would mean that the high-mobility OECD countries would have to reduce their energy consumption by some 70 per cent, whereas the low-mobility OECD countries could get away with merely maintaining their present level of energy consumption. However, high-mobility OECD countries would probably be very reluctant to accept a large percentage reduction in energy consumption if low-mobility OECD countries would merely have to maintain their current energy consumption. Therefore, I assume that the goal of halving per capita energy consumption is uniformly distributed throughout all OECD countries. For the EU, the energy goal would be 8 kWh per capita daily (based on an estimated 16 kWh per capita daily in 1990[7]).

Third, the figure can also form the basis for a sustainable mobility strategy *within* countries or regions. Indeed, in some countries the mobility levels between groups vary substantially. Intra-generational equity requirements mean that achieving sustainable mobility within such countries would require that low-mobility groups be allowed to increase their per capita energy consumption for transport. Most likely this increase would come at the expense of their high-mobility countrymen.

In conclusion, for *developed* countries, achieving sustainable mobility entails the following three challenges:

- Halving their energy consumption for passenger transport (to 8 kWh/cap/day) in accordance with the long-term ecological sustainability requirement and the inter-generational equity requirement.
- Increasing mobility for their low-mobility groups (to 11 km/cap/day available by public transport) in accordance with the basic transport-needs requirement and the intra-generational equity requirement.
- Increasing mobility for low-mobility groups in *developing* countries in accordance with the basic transport-needs requirement and the intra-generational equity requirement. Moreover, it is important that developed countries supply developing countries with the knowledge and resources needed to increase mobility while remaining at the lowest possible level of energy consumption.

---

7   Data for 1990 travel distances (in 1,000 mio pkm/year): passenger cars = 3,139; powered two-wheelers = 126; buses and coaches = 369; trams and metros = 42; railways = 268; inland navigation = 28; planes (domestic and intra-EU) = 157; planes (extra-EU) = 382, sources: EC (2004), author's estimates for extra-EU flights based on EC (2006). Data for fleet-average specific energy consumption (kWh/pkm): passenger cars = 0.412; powered two-wheelers = 0.287; buses and coaches = 0.189; trams and metros = 0.195; railways = 0.212; inland navigation = 0.780; planes (domestic and intra-EU) = 0.647; planes (extra-EU) = 0.518.

This books deals with only the first two challenges. However, the third is not less important than the first two, and should therefore not be forgotten in a sustainable mobility strategy.

For developing countries, achieving sustainable mobility entails increasing access to motorized transport even though this results in larger per capita energy consumption. However, it is extremely important that this path include transport policies that ensure increased accessibility at the lowest possible level of energy consumption – for example, transport policies based on sustainable land-use planning and improved public transport systems. If developing countries were to adapt the US transport pattern, they would likely consume four times as much energy per capita than they would if they were to adapt the European transport pattern (Kenworthy and Laube 2002a).

The Main Approaches for Entering the SMA in Developed Countries

The literature review reveals three main approaches for developed countries to enter the SMA: the efficiency approach, the alteration approach and the reduction approach.[8]

The efficiency approach for achieving sustainable mobility suggests that the environmental problems caused by transport can be reduced and moreover that the lack of accessibility for low-mobility groups can be relieved by developing more efficient technology.[9] The efficiency approach can be divided into two main sub-approaches: (i) the use of new, conventional technology and (ii) the use of alternative technology. The new, conventional technology approach seeks *incremental* improvements in *existing* transport technology such as: advanced internal combustion engines with direct injection, energy-efficient hybrid-drive systems, improved catalytic converters, reduced vehicle weight using lightweight materials, advanced motor management, improved aerodynamics, reduced rolling resistance and low-sulphur diesel. The alternative approach seeks to implement *fundamentally new* transport technology such as introducing new fuels (biofuels, hydrogen) and drive systems (fuel cell), and promoting new public transport systems.

The alteration approach recognizes the urgent need to fundamentally change present transport patterns. Accordingly, the prevailingly transport pattern, dominated by the car and plane, must be changed into one based on collective forms of transport, namely an affordable well-functioning public transport system.[10] Such a public transport system would lead to increased use of buses, trains and trams – which are all more energy efficient than cars and planes – and therefore reduced

---

8   These three approaches are presented in chapter 2 within the broader discussion on entering the SDA in developed countries.

9   The concept 'technology' is here used in a broad sense; it includes the use of both 'hard technology' (like developing more efficient vehicle technology and fuels) and 'soft technology' (like developing more efficient transport logistics). Moreover, more efficient technology could be implemented in all parts of the transport system: motorized transport, transport infrastructure and the energy system.

10   True, travel by plane is also a collective form of transport. However, its high energy consumption per passenger kilometre makes travel by plane comparable to travel by car.

use of cars and planes. Moreover, an affordable well-functioning public transport system would increase accessibility for low-mobility groups. Also, the alteration approach comprises the idea of substituting walking and cycling for motorized travel. However, there is a danger that improved public transport could lead to less walking and cycling because cyclists and pedestrians might find public transport more attractive. Nevertheless, the alteration approach strongly supports increasing the use of public transport and non-motorized transport and correspondingly supports reducing the use of cars and planes.

The reduction approach for achieving sustainable mobility does not question the importance of improved efficiency and increased alteration. Indeed the latter two approaches would, according to the reduction approach, offer some reductions in energy consumption. However, these reductions are not large enough to meet sustainable mobility's energy goal. Moreover, continuous transport growth negates any reductions in energy consumption achieved by implementing new technology and altering transport patterns. Thus, present transport volume must urgently be decreased – except for those whose basic transport needs are not met – or at least transport growth trends must be changed.

In everyday terms, the three approaches can be characterized respectively as: 'travel more efficiently,' 'travel differently' and 'travel less'.

However, substantial grey areas exist between the approaches; in practical policy the three approaches will likely overlap. On one hand, a sustainable mobility policy could combine elements from the approaches; in fact, a sustainable mobility policy *must* combine the three approaches, which will be shown in chapter 9. Thus, although an efficiency-based policy approach *mainly* applies measures that increase efficiency, it could also include measures from the alteration and reduction approaches. Similarly, a reduction-based policy approach would *mainly* apply measures that reduce transport volumes, yet it could also include measures from the efficiency and alteration approaches. On the other hand, a particular measure could belong to more than one approach. For example, an electric bus consumes less energy per vehicle kilometre which means it is more energy efficient than a conventional diesel-fuelled bus; therefore, introducing an electric bus might be characterised as an element of the efficiency approach. However, introducing an electric bus could also be characterized as an element of the alteration approach because its introduction also aims at increasing public transport use. Nevertheless, each approach reflects its *main* area of interest; furthermore, differentiating between the three approaches for achieving sustainable mobility facilitates analysis. Thus, three approach-based hypotheses for promoting sustainable mobility can be formulated:

- *The efficiency hypothesis*: Above all, promoting sustainable mobility means increasing energy efficiency in the transport system by using new, conventional and/or alternative technology.
- *The alteration hypothesis*: Above all, promoting sustainable mobility means altering present car- and plane-based transport patterns into patterns dominated by the use of buses, trains and trams through improving the public transport system.

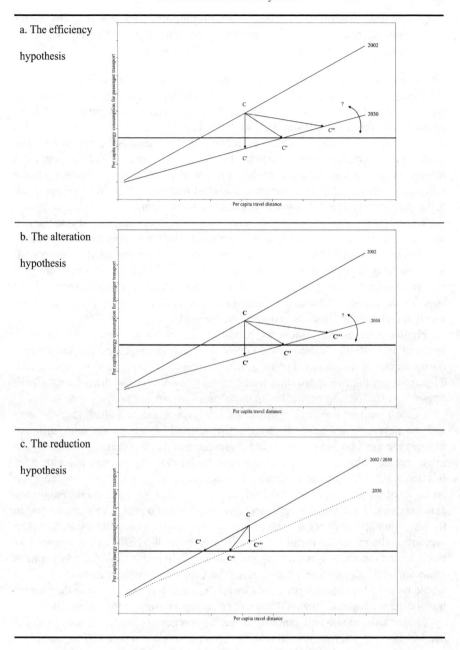

Figure 3.3   The three approach-based hypotheses for sustainability mobility for developed countries

- *The reduction hypothesis*: Above all, promoting sustainable mobility means reducing overall transport volumes by reducing the need or the desire for travel.

The implications of these three hypotheses are illustrated in figures 3.3a–c where the 2002 line is the estimated regression line from figure 2.2. Point C in figure 3.3 shows a typical OECD country's per capita travel distance and per capita energy consumption for passenger transport in 2002. The 2030 line in figure 3.3 indicates a *new* linear relationship between per capita travel distance and per capita energy consumption for passenger transport. The new 2030 line reflects assumptions affiliated with the respective approaches: a major increase in energy efficiency in the efficiency approach, a major change of transport patterns in the alteration approach and a reduction in travel distance in the reduction approach.

The efficiency approach (figure 3.3a) suggests that, given unchanged yearly travel distance and transport patterns, more energy-efficient transport technology leads the country into the SMA (C'). The alteration approach (figure 3.3b) suggests that, given unchanged yearly travel distance and technological levels, changing transport patterns lead the country into the SMA (C'). The reduction approach (figure 3.3c) suggests that, given unchanged technological levels and transport patterns, reducing yearly travel distance leads the country into the SMA (C').

Figures 3.3a and 3.3b show the partial effects of the efficiency and alteration approaches. Certainly, technological developments and changes in transport patterns do not occur in a vacuum. Future growth in travel distance must be considered. Thus, whether the two approaches lead a country towards C' (no growth), C'' (weak growth), or C''' (strong growth) is an open question.

Other important points to consider are the level of technological developments and the degree of alteration in transport patterns. If for example, more efficient engines are put into larger, faster and more comfortable cars, energy consumption might not be reduced. Or if we continue to travel more by car and plane than by bus and train, the alteration effect would in fact be negative. These are the main concerns of proponents of the reduction approach – that the assumptions are highly exaggerated in the efficiency approach regarding technological developments and in the alteration approach regarding changes in present transport patterns. Rather than supporting the rather optimistic scenarios portrayed by the 2030 lines in figures 3.3a and 3.3b, the reduction approach suggests that the 2030 lines are more likely to run as indicated by the dotted line in figure 3.3c. Thus, the only way to enter the SMA (C'') would be to reduce present per capita travel distance. Even maintaining the present travel distance (as in C''') would not reduce energy consumption sufficiently.

The actual outcome of employing each approach, or rather of employing a combination of approaches, should be empirically investigated. The empirical investigations must establish reliable estimates of future developments in transport technology and the degree of future alterations in transport patterns. Furthermore, accurately forecasting transport growth is necessary. The SMART model presented in chapter 9 shows how this can be done for the EU.

The Policy Orientations

The Dutch economist Jan Tinbergen formulated in the 1950s what has become known as the 'Tinbergen rule'. Simply stated, the rule is that for every independent policy goal there must be a complementary independent enabling policy instrument (Turner 1993). Consequently, the goal of sustainable mobility must be accompanied by policy instruments which facilitate its fulfilment.

The different policy instruments cluster into *policy orientations*. By policy orientation, I understand the generic rationale which usually can be found behind different policy measures (Banister et al. 2000). Three main policy orientations can be identified:

- Policy orientation aiming at voluntarily changing behaviour through information.
- Policy orientation aiming at changing behaviour through regulation.
- Policy orientation aiming at developing new technology.

The main prerequisite for achieving sustainable mobility, according to an information-orientated policy, would be the voluntary transformation of individuals' transport patterns – or lifestyles. The basic elements of these transformed lifestyles are increased awareness and subsequently more positive attitudes about achieving sustainable development in general and sustainable mobility in particular. Changing behaviour through regulation, on the other hand, would only minimally contribute to the growth of sustainable lifestyles. Thus, governments and businesses would primarily issue public information about transport's negative impacts and give guidance on reducing them. Moreover, governments and businesses would launch awareness campaigns that increase people's positive attitudes towards sustainable mobility.

On the contrary, regulation-orientated policies would suggest that the authorities should regulate behaviour by setting up standards and norms (like minimum vehicular emissions and maximum speed limits), by applying land-use planning (like densification and mixed development) and by providing improved public transport and public infrastructure (like lowering fares for buses, trains and trams). The basic rationale for regulation-orientated policies is that individuals cannot be trusted to voluntarily comply with the requirements of sustainable mobility; rather, they need to be pushed in the right direction by regulation that makes the preferred behaviour more attractive.

Technology-orientated policies rely heavily on the development and implementation of new and improved technology as prerequisites for sustainable mobility. It is acknowledged that many of transport's negative impacts result from using inappropriate technology. Correcting this situation requires the development of new technology that does not have the same negative impacts. The basic rationale behind technology-orientated policies is that the development of new technology needs public support, including innovation strategies, generous government funding schemes of R&D and large-scale demonstration programmes.

POLICY ORIENTATIONS

Approaches		Information	Regulation	Technology
	Efficiency	Adapt to the use of more energy-efficient transport technology (e.g., buying smaller and less powerful cars).	Regulate the use of more energy-efficient transport technology (e.g., national emissions standards for vehicles, inspection and maintenance programs and the retirement of grossly polluting vehicles).	Develop more energy-efficient transport technology (e.g., public funding of R&D and large-scale demonstration programmes).
	Alteration	Adapt to the use of more energy-efficient modes of transport (e.g., increase the use of public transport and non-motorized travel).	Regulate the use of more energy-efficient modes of transport (e.g., lowering fares for public transport and increasing frequency and punctuality).	Develop new technology for more energy-efficient modes of transport (e.g., AGV(i), MAGLEV(ii) trains and Smart Cards(iii)).
	Reduction	Reduce travel demand through increasing positive environmental attitudes (e.g., information packages and awareness campaigns).	Reduce travel demand through land-use planning (e.g., dense and concentrated housing development, and mixed land use).	Reduce travel demand through the development of information and communication technology (e.g., attractive forms of mobile conferences and telecommuting).

(i) AGV=Automatically Guided Vehicles. (ii). MAGLEV=Magnetically Levitated Trains; a form of transport that suspends, guides and propels vehicles via electromagnetic force. (iii). Information technology will probably have profound effects on public transport options. Smart Card technology may considerably enlarge possibilities for customers to pay for transport options in a flexible way, implying new possibilities and roles for public transport operators.

Figure 3.4   A typology for sustainable mobility

In practical policy these policy orientations are not as clearly defined and separated as indicated above. There are grey zones in which the orientations overlap. Furthermore, there is, as indicated by the SCAST triangle (Geenhuizen et al. 2002), a close interplay between the measures that belong to each main policy orientation. For example, new and improved technology must be developed (by applying technology-orientated policies). Moreover, the technology must be implemented, either by the individuals' voluntary adaptation to it (by applying information-orientated policies) or by the authorities' regulation of behaviour (by applying regulation-orientated policies).

A Typology for Sustainable Mobility

Based on the three main approaches and the three main policy orientations for achieving sustainable mobility, a typology for sustainable mobility can be constructed (illustrated in figure 3.4).

The figure shows a number of paths – a combination of approaches and policies – which potentially reduce energy consumption and increase accessibility and thus promote sustainable mobility in developed countries. Each path's appropriateness must, however, be treated as hypothesis rather than fact and the proposed outcome of each path must be subjected to thorough empirical investigations (which is done in chapters 4–7). The question that must be answered is: 'Does the suggested path lead to sustainable mobility?' The literature review shows that there are four prominent paths in which new technology, public transport, green attitudes and land-use planning, respectively, play dominant roles.

The Role of New Technology

The use of new technology requires that three actions be taken. First, the technology must be developed, presumably as a result of private and public innovation programmes, R&D schemes and large-scale demonstration programmes. Second, it must be made available to the users, either by enforcing law or by applying incentives (a mixture of information packages, awareness campaigns and economic measures like incentives, taxes and subsides). Third, it must be adapted by the users, either because they are forced to do so or because they find it more attractive.

Indeed, the problems occurring when new technology is to be made available to and subsequently adapted by users are significant. However, the main focus here is on the development of new technology. Certainly, the new technology must be proven to comply with sustainable mobility requirements before it is implemented.

I have chosen to focus on three parts of the broad transport-technology sphere: energy source, fuel and vehicle drive train. These three parts are interrelated and together they form energy chains (explained in chapter 4). I consider both new, conventional energy chains and alternative energy chains. Thus, the following two hypotheses can be formulated regarding how new technology can be used to achieve sustainable mobility:

- *The new, conventional energy chain hypothesis*: Sustainable mobility requires that new, conventional energy chains (energy source, fuel and vehicle drive train) be developed to reduce energy consumption for passenger transport.
- *The alternative energy chain hypothesis*: Sustainable mobility requires that alternative energy chains (energy source, fuel and vehicle drive train) be developed to reduce energy consumption for passenger transport.

The Role of Public Transport

The hypothetical role of public transport in achieving sustainable mobility is twofold. First, an improved public transport system is assumed to increase accessibility for low-mobility groups. Moreover, an improved public transport system could have mode-switching impacts, which simply means that people who usually travel by car will find it more attractive to use public transport. Second, increased use of public transport – for example as a result of an improved public transport system – is assumed to reduce energy consumption for passenger transport. However, this assumption rests heavily on how much public transport use increases and moreover, on how much total passenger transport volume increases. Therefore, the actual effect of increased public transport use on energy consumption must be clarified by way of scenario analyses. Thus, the following two hypotheses can be formulated regarding the role of public transport in achieving sustainable mobility:

- *The improved public transport hypothesis*: Sustainable mobility requires that public transport systems be improved to increase accessibility for low-mobility groups and moreover, to encourage mode switches.
- *The increased use of public transport hypothesis*: Sustainable mobility requires that the use of public transport be increased to reduce energy consumption for passenger transport.

The Role of Green Attitudes

Agenda 21[11] urges that individual values and attitudes that support sustainable consumption in general be reinforced: 'Governments and private sector organizations should promote more positive attitudes for achieving sustainable consumption through education, public awareness programmes and other means' (Agenda 21, chapter 4.26).

Indeed, whatever the preferred path for achieving sustainable mobility, it is unthinkable to proceed without some kind of willing participation by individuals. Even in cases where regulation-orientated policies have been implemented, there is almost always some degree of freedom left to the individual. Therefore, achieving sustainable consumption ultimately depends on choices taken by individuals: New, more efficient technology must be purchased, a shift towards more sustainable mobility patterns must be freely chosen and reductions in transport volume must be voluntary. Thus, individuals' developing positive values and attitudes towards

---

11 Agenda 21 is the action plan from the 1992 UNCED meeting in Rio de Janeiro.

sustainable development is necessary for achieving sustainable mobility in industrialized countries.

The hypothetical relation between green attitudes and sustainable mobility is based on the rationale that individuals try to avoid attitude-behaviour inconsistency; simply put, they want to do what they regard to be right. Therefore individuals holding green attitudes try, to a greater extent than non-greens, to reduce their energy consumption for transport, either by travelling less or by travelling by public transport. Thus, the following hypothesis can be formulated regarding the role of green attitudes in achieving sustainable mobility:

- *The green attitude hypothesis*: Sustainable mobility requires that more environmentally responsible (or simply 'green') attitudes be encouraged to reduce energy consumption for passenger transport.

The Role of Land-use Planning

Within planning research it is commonly assumed that the way we form the built environment – that is, land-use planning – has consequences for individuals' transport patterns and demands. On one hand, land-use planning can facilitate an improved public transport system, which in turn increases accessibility for low-mobility groups and, moreover, encourages mode switches away from car use. On the other hand, land-use planning can reduce transport demand, which in turn reduces energy consumption for transport. Either way, land-use planning is a potentially important means to achieve sustainable mobility.

However, some dispute the claim that land-use planning is an important means to reduce energy consumption for transport. According to Boarnet and Crane (2001), this claim must still be treated as a hypothesis rather than as a fact; therefore, according to them, the relation between land-use planning and individuals' transport patterns and demands should be regarded as a subject for research. Furthermore, they argue that such research should give empirical evidence to support the claim that land-use planning influences travel behaviour. Thus, the following hypothesis can be formulated regarding the role of land-use planning in achieving sustainable mobility:

- *The land-use planning hypothesis*: Sustainable mobility requires that land-use planning be changed to increase accessibility for low-mobility groups and moreover, to reduce energy consumption for passenger transport.

Summary

This chapter starts with a literature review that shows how the typical understanding and interpretation of the concept of sustainable mobility have changed since it first appeared in the 1992 EU Green Paper on Transport and Environment. The sustainable mobility concept has evolved from one characterised by a single-disciplinary approach with a focus on environmental issues, everyday-travel and transport-volume issues in the early 1990s, to the present one characterised by a multi-disciplinary approach with an additional focus on social issues, leisure-time travel and transport-intensity issues. Moreover, mainstream research on sustainable mobility has experienced a gradual evolution from the original 'Is transport sustainable?' questions in the early 1990s, to 'When is transport sustainable?' questions in the late 1990s, and finally to the present prevailing 'How can transport be made sustainable?' and 'Why are we not succeeding in making transport sustainable?' questions.

This chapter then defines the extra prima characteristics of sustainable mobility; the definition is based on adapting the extra prima characteristics of sustainable development to the transport sector. In turn, based on these extra prima characteristics of sustainable mobility, the SMA is constructed; it is defined by maximum per capita energy consumption and minimum per capita available travel distance by public transport. The SMA shows that achieving sustainable mobility represents different challenges country-by-country: The main challenge for developed countries is to reduce average per capita energy consumption for transport, which can be done by means of an efficiency approach, an alteration approach or a reduction approach. Moreover, developed countries should increase accessibility for their own low-mobility groups. The main challenge for developing countries is to increase access to motorized transport even though this results in larger per capita energy consumption.

The chapter also presents three main policy orientations for achieving sustainable mobility: The first is an information-orientated policy, which is based on a voluntary transformation of individuals' lifestyle due to individuals' increased awareness and more positive environmental attitudes. The second is a regulation-orientated policy, which acknowledges that individuals cannot be trusted to comply with the requirements of sustainable mobility and therefore need to be pushed in the right direction by facilitation that makes the preferred behaviour more attractive. The third is a technology-orientated policy, which relies on the development and implementation of new and improved transport technology.

Finally, this chapter constructs a typology for sustainable mobility, from which six hypotheses for achieving it are formulated with reference to the roles of technology, public transport, green attitudes and land-use planning.

This concludes the description of the book's foundation. In the next part, chapters 4–7 present four case studies regarding the roles of technology, public transport, green attitudes and land-use planning in achieving sustainable mobility.

PART II
The Case Studies

Chapter 4

The Roles of New Conventional and Alternative Technologies

We cannot solve our problems with the same technology we used when we created them.
(Albert Einstein)

'Yes, my friends,' said Cyrus Harding. 'I believe that water will one day be employed
as fuel, that hydrogen and oxygen which constitute it, used singly or together, will
furnish an inexhaustible source of heat and light [...] There is, therefore, nothing to fear.
[...]Water will be the coal of the future.'
'I should like to see that,' observed the sailor.
(Jules Verne: The Mysterious Island 1874)

This chapter assesses the roles of new conventional and alternative technologies
in achieving sustainable mobility. Under examination are two hypotheses: the
hypothesis that suggests new conventional energy chains (energy source, fuel and
vehicle drive train) will reduce energy consumption for passenger transport, and the
hypothesis that suggests alternative energy chains will reduce energy consumption
for passenger transport.

Researching sustainable mobility technology is a large and complex field which
involves asking two questions: Which technology can make transport sustainable?
How can this technology be implemented on a large scale?

The second question is more difficult to answer despite the fact that new
conventional and alternative technology is being implemented already; for
example, a small number of hydrogen fuel-cell vehicles are currently running in
demonstration projects worldwide. Although the users of such vehicles generally
report that their technical performance is satisfactory, there nevertheless remain
difficult implementation issues which need to be addressed: How can automobile
manufacturers be persuaded to build millions of hydrogen-powered cars? How can
national governments be persuaded to spend large amounts of money to supply the
necessary infrastructure? How can the public be persuaded to buy these vehicles?
However, technology implementation is outside the main scope of this book, although
it is discussed briefly in part III.

Answering the question about which technology can make transport sustainable is
less difficult because it involves finding the optimal combination of vehicle concept,
fuel and energy source – the energy chain – that satisfies long-term ecological
sustainability requirements. One approach is the new conventional technology
approach which seeks incremental improvements in various parts of existing energy
chains, such as producing low-sulphur diesel and developing more efficient diesel

Energy chain type	Energy source	Fuel	Vehicle's drive system
Elements of the conventional technology approach	Raw oil	Petrol and diesel [i]	Internal Combustion engine (ICE)[v]
Elements of the alternative technology approach	E.g. biomass, hydropower, natural gas [ii]	E.g. CNG/LNG [iii], hydrogen, electricity [iv]	E.g. fuel cell, electric engine
An example of the purely conventional energy chain	Raw oil	Petrol	ICE
An example of the purely alternative energy chain	Biomass	Hydrogen	Fuel cell
An example of a hybrid energy chain	Biomass	Bio diesel	ICE
Another example of a hybrid energy chain	Raw oil	Diesel	Fuel cell

(i) Including 'cleaner' versions of petrol and diesel
(ii) Although hydropower and natural gas are well-established conventional energy sources in some sectors (for example, heating houses and technical appliances), they are considered as alternative energy sources for producing fuel for transportation.
(iii) CNG=Compressed natural gas. LNG=Liquefied natural gas.
(iv) Strictly speaking, electricity is not a fuel. However, within the discussion of alternative fuels, it is regarded as one.
(v) Including petrol-electric and diesel-electric hybrids

Figure 4.1   A typology for transport energy chains

engines. The alternative technology approach, on the other hand, seeks to implement fundamentally new technology into one or more parts of energy chains, such as the introduction of biomass-based hydrogen and the introduction of new drive systems for vehicles.

Figure 4.1 gives examples of the elements that are parts of the new conventional and alternative technology approaches, respectively. Whereas the new conventional technology approach is limited to combining raw oil–based petrol or diesel and an internal combustion engine (ICE), the alternative technology approach includes a large number of energy chains. The difference between conventional and alternative energy chains, however, is not sharp because a specific energy chain may well include elements from both conventional and alternative technology. Consequently, there are three types of energy chains: purely (existing) conventional energy chains, purely alternative energy chains and hybrid energy chains.

The purely conventional energy chains consist of conventional technology in all parts and are of two types: raw oil–based petrol in an ICE and raw oil–based diesel in an ICE. Recently, attempts have been made to label cleaner forms of petrol and diesel (for example, lead-free petrol and low-sulphur diesel) as alternative fuels. However, cleaner forms of petrol and diesel are examples of incremental improvements of existing energy chains, and as such are considered to still be elements of conventional energy chains.

The purely alternative energy chains consist of alternative technology in all parts. A large number of such energy chains can be constructed. Those which include biomass (energy source), hydrogen (fuel) and fuel cells (drive system) have been given much attention recently.

The hybrid energy chains consist of both conventional and alternative technology, meaning that elements of the conventional energy chain are substituted by alternative technology elements. Examples are ICEs fuelled by biomass-based diesel or fuel-cells fuelled by raw oil–based diesel. Also, hybrid energy chains include those energy chains where a single element of the chain, for example the drive system, consists of both conventional and alternative technology: the petrol-electric hybrid and the diesel-electric hybrid vehicles. One could argue, however, that hybrid vehicles represent an incremental improvement of existing technology. In fact, the series hybrids use only petrol or diesel as a fuel; the electricity is produced on board. Therefore, hybrid vehicles are simply more energy-efficient conventional cars, which is why we consider them to be part of conventional technology. Examples of purely conventional energy chains, purely alternative energy chains and hybrid energy chains are given in figure 4.1.

The preferred methodological approach to answering the 'Which fuel?' question is a well-to-wheel analysis (WTW), which includes comparisons of several energy chains. (The two concepts, WTW and energy chain, will be explained in the next section of this chapter).

This chapter focuses on 16 core energy chains which are selected to reflect recent developments in both conventional technologies (building advanced ICEs and hybrids) and alternative technologies (building fuel-cell drive systems and promoting fuels such as natural gas, hydrogen, and biomass). In addition, two energy chains are included that reflect the situation today, giving a total of 18 energy chains. They are selected to reflect European conditions; that is, they are based on raw material and vehicle technologies that are most prominent in the European discussion of future fuels. The results from the energy chain analyses are, however, to a large extent also valid for both non-European developed countries and developing countries. Moreover, the analyses are based on technologies that can be made commercially available by 2010 and broadly implemented by 2020.

This chapter has three sections: The first gives a brief history of alternative fuels, several of which have been introduced during the last 25 years. The second presents a well-to-wheel analysis of the 18 energy chains. The third presents an analysis of the ecological footprints of these 18 energy chains.[1]

Alternative Fuels

Alternative fuels in transport have a long history. The first pilot projects were launched some 30 years ago. Generally, they were not part of an environmental discourse, but rather were mostly focused on issues of national security involving fuel supplies. During the last decade there has been a renewed focus on alternative fuels in transport. This time they are very much integrated in a global discourse on sustainable development.

The modern environmental discourse dates to the early 1960s when the American biologist Rachel Carson and others focused on pollution problems in nature caused by the extensive use of pesticides. However, throughout the Western World energy problems would very soon become an integral part of the environmental discourse. In Norway it started in the late 1960s with environmental movement protests against hydropower schemes. However, three international events dating to the early 1970s would have a greater influence on the discourse's development.

The first event was the 1972 publication of the book *The Limits to Growth* (Meadows et al. 1972) by The Club of Rome. It highlighted absolute limits to future global growth regarding the exploitation of non-renewable natural resources such as fossil fuels. This issue gave rise to a type of understanding described by the term 'limited resources,' as a distinct category from 'limited sinks' (absorption capacity). Limits to global emissions of CO_2 represent an example of the latter. It was soon apparent that the Club of Rome was right about the absolute limits to future global growth regarding fossil fuels. The second event was the 1973 oil crisis. Although in the public debate it was referred to as an energy crisis, it was actually caused by an oil embargo imposed by the major Arab oil producers. In several countries gasoline was rationed; for instance, Norway prohibited the use of private cars during weekends, and Norwegians skiing on highways became a symbol of the crisis. The third event was the nuclear power debate, which in fact was more like a series of events. Nuclear power was intensely debated from the early 1970s in most Western countries. Even in Norway with its rich hydropower resources, planning for nuclear

---

1 The well-to-wheel and ecological footprint analyses are both based on research carried out within the program 'Systems for Implementation of Hydrogen Energy in the Transport Sector', a strategic research program at Western Norway Research Institute (Holden 2003).

power was launched; however, as a result of the debate it was ultimately discontinued by the Parliament.

All three events brought into focus the need to develop alternative, renewable energy resources and technologies. Solar, wind, and wave power, bio energy, and heat pumps based on geothermal sources soon became integral parts not only of the public energy debate, but also of governmental energy development plans. Energy scenarios – based on renewable resources – were drawn up in almost every country, and substantial efforts were put into R&D. A prominent American researcher at that time, Amory Lovins, summarised this in his 1977 book Soft Energy Paths: Toward a Durable Peace (Lovins 1977). But the paths (technologies) he described covered only a limited area. His soft energy technologies were mainly alternatives to large-scale nuclear and fossil-fuel power plants; they were alternatives for stationary energy consumption. The soft paths for mobile energy consumption, energy consumed for transport, were for the most part not described in his book or elsewhere. For instance, when the Research Council of Norway in 1979 summarised the status of R&D on alternative energy resources and the demands on those resources, the technologies described were stationary ones for producing heat and electricity (Holter et al. 1979).

However, there was at the time some R&D on alternative energy for the transport sector. Early in the 1970s an ambitious French program was launched involving both battery-powered and hydrogen fuel-cell-powered cars. However, it failed after a short time (Callon 1999). In 1979 Brazil launched its extensive program to develop ethanol as fuel for automobiles. The ethanol was produced solely from domestic biological resources (sugar cane and sugar beets). In Norway a pilot program for using methanol in private cars was launched in the early 1980s. The methanol used in the Norwegian program had a fossil base, but there were prospects that it could be produced from biological resources. But all these early efforts in the transport sector were largely independent from the dominant discourse on the environment and alternative energy. Furthermore, their origins were only loosely tied to the oil crisis, and moreover, alternative energy in transport was almost entirely considered as a matter of increasing national security in fuel supplies.

This situation has however changed greatly since the late 1980s due to a new and intense focus on the need to develop alternative energy resources and technologies in the transport sector. Not only has this focus become an integral part of the current environmental and energy discourses, but it has also even come to dominate them. The term used in these discourses is no longer 'soft energy paths,' but rather 'sustainable energy systems,' which includes energy for mobile purposes as a crucial part. Issues related to the development of alternative energy in the transport sector are thus integrated into the much wider discourse on sustainable development (Høyer 2000).

Such a link was not always evident. The total volume of transport was not a topic in the Brundtland Report (WCED 1987), nor was it highlighted in the common global action plan – Agenda 21 – from the follow-up World Summit in Rio in 1992. To the extent transport related problems were taken up directly, they were considered as traditional problems of intensity, that is, too many cars concentrated in one place – primarily in the fast growing mega-cities of developing countries. But the indirect relations would soon become pressing issues. The Brundtland Report itself emphasised the importance of environmental and climate problems caused by extensive use of fossil-based energy, and the need to both reduce energy consumption in rich countries and achieve a substantial transition to renewable energy to solve these problems. Transport is the societal sector most fundamentally dependent on fossil-based energy. In every country – rich or poor – transport is almost entirely dependent on it. Historically in the West since the Second World War, the fossil-fuel society and the mobile society have grown as Siamese twins. Separating them is particularly challenging because they have grown together for so long (Høyer 2000). That growth has been very great indeed. While in many countries in the post-industrial era energy use in stationary sectors has remained stable or declined, in most countries energy use for transport has continued to grow, not only for passenger transport but also for freight transport.

The discourse on soft energy paths began around 1970, while the discourse on sustainable energy systems began around 1990. Regarding transport, both in Norway and in the UK, the rule of doubling prevailed during this 20-year period; energy consumption for all transport doubled, energy consumption for all passenger transport doubled, the number of private cars doubled, and the average kilometres travelled per individual doubled (Høyer 2003). Against this background the understanding of transport problems changed; instead of being understood as problems of intensity – local pollution in urban areas – as they were understood around 1970, they came to be understood as problems of volume – energy consumption and regional and global pollution – around 1990. As the review in chapter 3 shows, however, after 2000 the pendulum has swung back to the focus on intensity.

A Well-to-Wheel Analysis

The overriding issue in a WTW analysis is how alternative fuels compare with each other and with the conventional fuels regarding the environmental consequences of their use. However, a number of questions and methodological issues need to be addressed before one can make such comparisons systematically and fairly.

Questions that must be clarified include: Which fuels are included in the analysis and what are the criteria used to select them? What is the time frame of the analysis? What kind of vehicle category and what kind of driving cycle should be the basis for the analysis? Which environmental impacts are included in the analysis? Methodological questions that must be clarified include: Which method is applied? What are the demarcations of a study's boundaries? Which data sources have been used?

Assumptions

The first assumption regards the selection of a trustworthy time frame for the analysis, which is crucial when comparing energy chains. To compare existing energy chains, which use present technology, with alternative energy chains would be unfair because the latter include immature technology which needs further development. Thus, we have selected 2010 as a point of reference, which means that well-known, but not yet fully developed, technologies are included in the analyses. Given the proper incentives, these technologies could be commercially available by 2010, and broadly applied by 2020. Choosing 2010 as the basis for the comparison establishes a fair and trustworthy time frame, striking a balance between two conditions: the need to allow sufficient time for the components of the alternative energy chains to develop their full potential, and the need to avoid time frames that are so far into the future that the results of any comparisons would be solely based on speculation.

The second assumption regards which vehicle category and driving pattern (driving cycle) to consider. Here we have chosen the private car in combined city and highway driving. The reason for choosing the private car is twofold: First, the available data on private cars is better, both in terms of quantity and quality. Most recent studies about alternative fuels have concentrated on the private car, leading to high quality data from a large number of sources.[2] Second, the private car plays an important role in transport volume and environmental consequences. In Norway, about 50 per cent of the fuel used in the transport sector, and 50 per cent of CO_2 emissions and more than 80 per cent of emissions of CO from the transport sector are caused solely by private cars (Statistics Norway).

The third assumption regards which environmental impact categories to include in the analysis, which is a matter of balancing different needs. On one hand, a comparison of energy chains should be based on as many impact categories as possible, including various indicators within each category. There is no limit to the number of indicators that can be included in one specific analysis as long as data with sufficient quality are available. On the other hand, however, in practice there is a need to limit the number of impact categories and their indicators. Nevertheless, it is important that the included categories reflect the most important aspects regarding the issue of environmental sustainability. Thus, we have included three main impact categories in the analyses: (i) energy consumption, (ii) emissions of greenhouse gases (with the indicator CO_2 equivalents made up from data on CO_2, CH_4 and N_2O[3]), and (iii) emissions of substances that lead to poor air quality and other negative environmental consequences locally and regionally. In the last category, NOX is used as an indicator. Even though there certainly are other important impact categories – for example land use for producing fuels – it is our opinion that the three categories, and the selected indicators, give a good first picture of the overall environmental consequences connected to alternative fuels. (In the next section land use for producing fuels is included in the ecological footprint analysis.) Taken together the three categories reflect three important issues related to long-term environmental sustainability: energy consumption, emissions of greenhouse gases and emissions of pollution locally and regionally.

---

2   Our estimates are based on emissions and energy consumption measurements of the New European Driving Cycle (NEDC). The US data sources generally used the US FTP-75 driving cycle; these data are used for comparing the data from the European studies.

3   The Global Warming Potential (GWP) for each gas is as follows: $CO_2 = 1$, $CH_4 = 23$ and $N_2O = 296$. The GWP applies to a time span of 100 years (IPCC 2001).

Methodology

During the last two decades it has been common practice to use a life cycle perspective to compare the environmental consequences of products and services. Thus, the life cycle perspective – and the related analytical methods – has developed as an integral part of the sustainable development discourse. A life cycle perspective implies that the environmental consequences related to a product, or service, are analysed from the time raw materials are extracted until the time that waste is deposited. Therefore, no product can any longer be assessed solely on the consequences of its use. Thus, assessing the responsibility of those who produce products becomes more complex. Since the late 1980s there have been attempts to develop standardised methods, based on the life cycle perspective, for carrying out analyses. It is common to call such analyses life cycle assessments.

Life cycle assessments of fuels are commonly referred to as well-to-wheel analyses (WTW). As indicated by the term, all processes should be assessed from the well all along the energy chain that ends at the vehicle's wheels. A WTW analysis is often divided into two parts: The first is called well-to-tank (WTT) and the second is called tank-to-wheel (TTW). Whereas WTT includes all the phases from feedstock production to filling the vehicle's tank, TTW includes all the systems and processes that convert the energy stored in the fuel to mechanical energy at the wheels. There are three good reasons for distinguishing between the two parts – WTT and TTW – in a WTW analysis: First, the environmental impacts from the use of fuel (TTW) in the vehicle make up such a large share of the total environmental impact (WTW) that it is necessary and important to keep them separate. Second, these environmental impacts quite often occur where people live and are therefore particularly important regarding serious human health problems. The third reason is related to the separation of types of data sources. Data for WTT processes can be collected from the energy companies and governmental regulations that are developed for the energy sector in particular. Data for TTW processes can, on the other hand, be collected from the automobile industry and corresponding regulations.

WTW analysis is a methodology which analyses the processes (the energy chain) from the feedstock site to the vehicle. It is common to include six processes in an energy chain: (i) feedstock production, (ii) feedstock transport, (iii) fuel production, (iv) fuel distribution, (v) refuelling and finally (vi) end use. While the first five processes constitute the WTT part, the sixth process, end use, constitutes the TTW part. A WTW analysis does not include energy consumed or emissions generated in manufacturing the vehicles and constructing transport infrastructure.

Data and Sources

A WTW analysis demands an enormous amount of data which is collected from many and widely varied sources. Our analyses are based on:

- A comprehensive WTW study by Massachusetts Institute of Technology (Weiss et al. 2000).
- Two large WTW studies by General Motors Corporation: one North American

study reflecting American conditions (General Motors 2001a; General Motors 2001b) and one European study reflecting European conditions (General Motors 2002).

- A WTW study by Ecotraffic (Ecotraffic 2001).
- A WTW study by Western Norway Research Institute and Norwegian Institute of Technology (Western Norway Research Institute and National Institute of Technology 2002).

Preferably, data on TTW fuel consumption and emissions should be collected from laboratory tests, using a dynamometer to measure, according to a standardised procedure, fuel consumption and emissions. Alas, most of the data included in this analysis is based on vehicles that are not yet fully developed (or that exist only on a drawing board), which obviously rules out the dynamometer. Therefore, rather than being measured, fuel consumption and emissions must be estimated, either by Expert Groups or by using computer simulations. The four studies above have used various computer programmes to simulate, or estimate, consumption and emissions data.

The Energy Chains

It is possible to construct many energy chains for study. Creative combinations of feed stocks, fuels, production processes and power trains could easily lead to the construction of hundreds of energy chains. For example, the General Motors study referred to above includes more than 200 chains, and the Ecotraffic study includes almost 100. There is, however, good reason to limit the number of energy chains because too much detailed information could mask the message.

We have used the following criteria for choosing energy chains in this analysis:

- The energy chain must be based on a feedstock that is available in large quantities in Europe.
- The energy chain must be based on technology that is likely to be commercially available by 2010 or no later than 2015. Exceptions in this particular context can only be made for energy chains that have very great, long-term potential and that currently are the subject of substantial R&D efforts.
- The energy chain must have the potential to offer major improvements in environmental impact compared to present conventional chains, that is raw oil–based petrol and diesel chains.
- The energy chain must have the potential to substitute more than 10 per cent of the existing fuel market.

Energy chains meeting the above criteria total 16, all of which are based on estimated (simulated) data for the year 2010. In addition, two energy chains are included that reflect the situation in 2000, giving a total of 18 energy chains which are shown in table 4.1.

Table 4.1   Energy chains included in the WTW and EF analyses

No.	Feedstock	Fuel [i]	Power train [ii]	Year	Abbreviation
(1)	Raw oil	Petrol	Conventional	2000	PETROL-CONV
(2)	Raw oil	Diesel	Conventional	2000	DIESEL-CONV
(3)	Raw oil	Petrol	Conventional	2010	PETROL-CONV
(4)	Raw oil	Petrol	Hybrid	2010	PETROL-HYB
(5)	Raw oil	Diesel	Conventional	2010	DIESEL-CONV
(6)	Raw oil	Diesel	Hybrid	2010	DIESEL-HYB
(7)	Natural gas	CNG	Conventional	2010	NG-CNG-CONV
(8)	Natural gas	CNG	Hybrid	2010	NG-CNG-HYB
(9)	Natural gas	LNG	Conventional	2010	NG-LNG-CONV
(10)	Natural gas	LNG	Hybrid	2010	NG- LNG-HYB
(11)	Natural gas	GH2	Fuel cell	2010	NG-GH2-FC
(12)	Natural gas	LH2	Fuel cell	2010	NG-LH2-FC
(13)	Hydropower	El	Battery	2010	HP-EL-BATT
(14)	Hydropower	GH2	Fuel cell	2010	HP-GH2-FC
(15)	Biomass (wood)	Methanol	OBR + Fuel cell	2010	BIO-MET-FCOBR
(16)	Biomass (wood)	Methanol	Conventional	2010	BIO-MET-CONV
(17)	Biomass (wood)	Ethanol	OBR + Fuel cell	2010	BIO-ET-FCOBR
(18)	Biomass (wood)	Ethanol	Conventional	2010	BIO-ET-CONV

(i) CNG = compressed (gaseous) natural gas; LNG = liquefied natural gas; GH2 = (compressed) gaseous hydrogen; LH2 = liquefied hydrogen; El = electricity.

(ii) The power train consists of three separate parts: the energy converter (to convert from chemical or electrical energy to mechanical energy (e.g. an internal combustion engine or a fuel cell), the energy transmission device (e.g. a mechanical or electrical drive train) and the energy storage device (e.g. a battery). Conventional = conventional internal combustion engine. Hybrid = internal combustion engine + electric motor (in parallel). OBR = on-board reformer. All fuel cells are hybrid (fuel cell + electric motor).

Results of WTW Analyses

The results from the WTW analyses are presented below. Two important points should be made regarding these results:

First, while there is almost a consensus regarding the performance of IECs, hybrids and electric vehicles, there is not yet a consensus regarding the performance of fuel cells. There are wide-ranging assumptions regarding energy efficiency (and consequently the energy consumption and footprint size) of fuel cells when operating under real driving conditions. The data vary from a low estimate of just over 23 per cent (Ecotraffic 2001) up to a high estimate of over 40 per cent (General Motors 2002). The differences reflect uncertainty regarding the performance of a fuel cell in a vehicle driven under real driving conditions. Therefore, we use high and low estimates for the fuel cell option – 11a is based on the low-efficiency fuel cell, while 11b includes a high-efficiency fuel cell. We have used low energy efficiency for

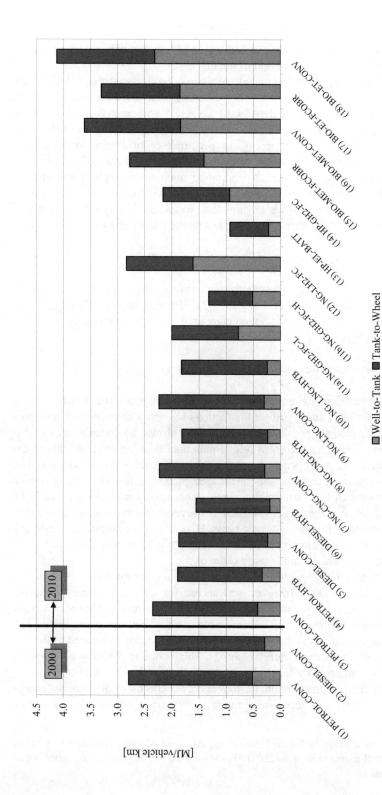

Figure 4.2 Well-to-wheel energy consumption for conventional and alternative energy chains (passenger car under mixed driving conditions)

all other energy chains that include a fuel cell implying that only energy chain 11b mirrors the most positive assessment of the fuel cell.

Second, the energy chain that includes what may be considered as a 'full electric vehicle' (energy chain 13) is somewhat different than the other energy chains. At present the performance of the electric vehicle – for example, driving range, acceleration and maximum speed – is inferior to that of the vehicles in the other energy chains. The key to increasing the performance of electric vehicles is to improve battery performance. Alas, although a variety of advanced batteries are under development, a breakthrough leading to mainstream applications of fully electric vehicles does not appear likely (OECD 2004). Nevertheless, this energy chain is included in the analyses to show the advantages it may offer. Great care should however be taken when comparing it with the other energy chains.

Energy Consumption: Conventional Energy Chains 2000–2010

Over the next decade energy consumption in conventional energy chains could be reduced by more than 30 per cent (figure 4.2). The high energy efficiency of the diesel engine makes it a favourite option compared to the petrol engine, both in ICE vehicles and in hybrids.[4]

Energy Consumption: Conventional and Alternative Energy Chains 2010

Energy chains based on natural gas as both a feedstock and a fuel (energy chains 7–10) would not offer any significant reductions in energy consumption compared to the energy reductions possible from conventional raw oil–based energy chains (energy chains 3–6). This picture would remain unchanged even if the natural gas were converted into hydrogen for use in a fuel cell (energy chains 11a and 12). The most important reason for this unchanged picture is that the energy needed to produce hydrogen from natural gas would substantially raise the level of WTT energy consumption in these energy chains. However, using the most optimistic data for fuel cell energy efficiency (energy chain 11b), it seems reasonable to estimate that WTW energy consumption could be reduced by 15 per cent compared to the best conventional energy chain (energy chain 6).

Electric cars operating on hydropower-based electricity (energy chain 13) consume the least energy. However, widespread use of such vehicles would be impractical due to the limitations already mentioned. If hydropower-based electricity is used to produce hydrogen which is then used in a fuel-cell car (energy chain 14), the WTW energy consumption would not offer any reduction compared to the raw oil–based petrol alternative (energy chain 3). This is due to the substantial rise in WTT energy consumption when producing the hydrogen through electrolysis.

Regarding energy consumption, the four energy chains based on biomass (energy chains 15–18) share one thing in common – they have a higher WTW energy

---

4   There are indications that the future energy efficiency of a petrol engine will get close to that of a diesel engine (Ecotraffic 2001). We do not, however, expect this to happen within the next ten years.

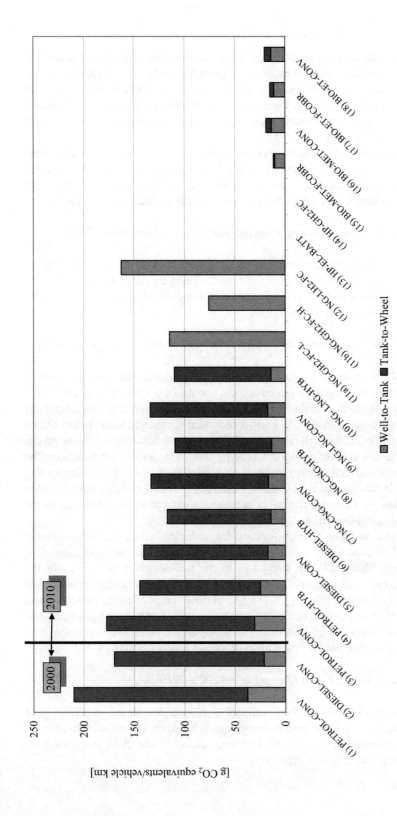

Figure 4.3   Well-to-wheel CO$_2$ equivalent emissions for conventional and alternative energy chains (passenger car under mixed driving conditions)

consumption than all other alternatives. True, biomass fuel cells (energy chains 15 and 17) perform better than biomass ICEs (energy chains 16 and 18), but all the biomass chains nevertheless increase WTW energy consumption compared to all the other energy chains. This is because it takes about two energy units of biomass to produce one unit of methanol or ethanol. No viable technology exists that will improve this significantly.

To sum up, none of the alternative energy chains based on natural gas, hydropower-based and biomass offer reductions in WTW energy consumption which exceed those offered by conventional raw oil–based energy chains. The only alternative energy chain which does is that which includes the high-efficiency fuel cell.

Emissions of Greenhouse Gases: Conventional Energy Chains 2000–2010

As was the case for energy consumption, there seems to be large potential for reducing emissions of greenhouse gases over the next ten years by using new conventional technology (figure 4.3). Hybrid versions of petrol and diesel vehicles will be major contributors to reducing such emissions.

Emissions of Greenhouse Gases: New Conventional and Alternative Energy Chains 2010

For 2010, all alternatives to the conventional petrol-driven car (energy chain 3) imply reductions in greenhouse gas emissions: about a 20 per cent reduction from the diesel alternative (energy chain 5), and a 25 per cent reduction from the natural gas alternatives (energy chains 7–10). Further reductions compared to the petrol-driven car seem possible if a fuel cell running on hydrogen from natural gas is used: 35 per cent using the low-efficiency fuel cell (energy chain 11a) and 55 per cent using the high-efficiency fuel cell (energy chain 11b). However, it is worth mentioning that diesel hybrids (energy chain 6) and low-efficiency fuel cell vehicles (energy chain 11a) offer equally large reductions in greenhouse gas emissions compared to the conventional petrol-driven car.

Thus, there are many opportunities for reducing emissions. Considerable reductions, however, are possible only in energy chains that use non-fossil feed stocks (energy chains 13–18). Compared to the well-to-wheel emissions for the petrol-driven car (energy chain 3), the biomass-based alternatives offer reductions of some 90 per cent (energy chains 15–18). Use of diesel engines during collection and transport of the raw biomass causes the small amounts of greenhouse gas emissions from biomass energy chains. Elimination of nearly all emissions seems possible only for the energy chains that are based on hydropower (energy chains 13–14).

NO_x *Emissions: Conventional Energy Chains 2000–2010*

The results from the well-to-wheel analyses of NO_x emissions are generally quite promising (figure 4.4). Compared to energy chains based on the present conventional technology (energy chains 1–2), all 16 energy chains in the 2010 scenarios offer substantial reductions in NO_x emissions.

Table 4.2   An overall assessment of the environmental impacts of 16 energy chains in 2010

No.	Energy chain [i]	Energy	CO_2-eqv	NO_x	Total [ii]
1	(11b) NG-GH2-FC-H	1	6	2	9
2	(14) HP-GH2-FC	8	1	1	10
3	(8) NG-CNG-HYB	3	7	6	16
4	(10) NG- LNG-HYB	4	8	7	19
5	(11a) NG-GH2-FC-L	7	9	3	19
6	(15) BIO-MET-FCOBR	12	2	5	19
7	(6) DIESEL-HYB	2	10	12	24
8	(7) NG-CNG-CONV	9	11	8	28
9	(16) BIO-MET-CONV	15	4	10	29
10	(17) BIO-ET-FCOBR	14	3	14	31
11	(5) DIESEL-CONV	5	13	13	31
12	(9) NG-LNG-CONV	10	12	9	31
13	(12) NG-LH2-FC	13	15	4	32
14	(18) BIO-ET-CONV	16	5	11	32
15	(4) PETROL-HYB	6	14	15	35
16	(3) PETROL-CONV	11	16	16	43

(i) See table 4.1 for details about the energy chain acronyms. The electric vehicle is not included in the table. Data is based on a passenger car under mixed driving conditions.
(ii) Total shows the overall rank of a particular energy chain.

NO_x Emissions: Conventional and Alternative Energy Chains 2010

However, a comparison of the 16 energy chains in the 2010 scenarios shows that the conventional energy chains using petrol and diesel from raw oil (energy chains 3–6) have the highest emissions.[5] All other energy chains (energy chains 7–16) have lower emissions except, due to high NO_x emissions at the production site, the biomass-based ethanol chains (energy chains 17–18).

Discussion of the WTW Results for 2010

To assess the overall impact, it is necessary to synthesize the impacts of the 2010 energy chains in all three categories: energy consumption, and emissions of CO_2 equivalents and NO_x. This highly problematic task should be carried out with great care. A simple way to make a synthesis is to rank the 16 energy chains within each impact category, and then sum the three rankings into an overall ranking for each chain. The lowest ranked energy chain has the least impact whereas the highest ranked has the most impact. There is no weighting of the relative impact of the individual impact categories. Thus, the overall ranking is ordinal. Results are shown in table 4.2.

---

5   At present a diesel vehicle emits more NO_x than a petrol vehicle. By 2010, however, NO_x emissions from petrol and diesel vehicles are expected to by equal.

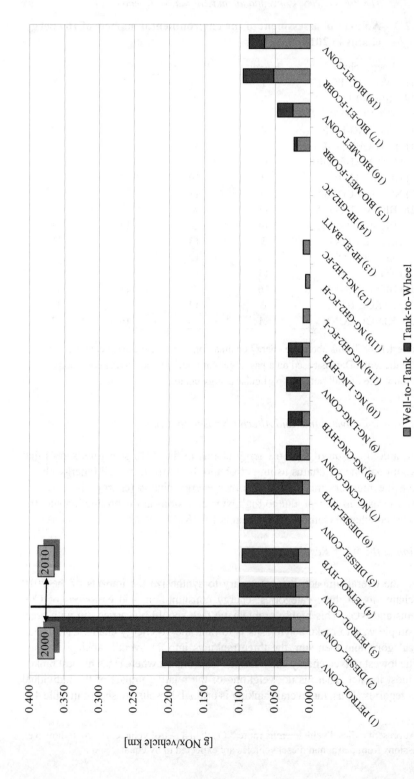

Figure 4.4   Well-to-wheel NO$_X$ emissions for conventional and alternative energy chains (passenger car under mixed driving conditions)

Some important observations can be made from the table. First, the conventional petrol vehicle in 2010 (energy chain 3, called the reference chain) can be found at the bottom of the table because it has the highest overall negative environmental impact. The hybrid version of the reference chain (energy chain 4) does not rank much better. Thus, one can conclude that all energy chains perform better than the reference chain. However, it should be noted that the diesel hybrid (energy chain 6) ranks high in the table because it has low overall negative environmental impact, indicating that substantial reductions in impacts are possible even within the conventional energy chains.

Second, the natural gas–based hydrogen fuel cell chain (energy chain 11b) is ranked highest. This chain has a high-efficiency fuel cell, which reflects a rather optimistic assessment of the fuel cell's potential. However, even the energy chain that has a low-efficiency fuel cell (energy chain 11a) performs well compared to the reference chain. In fact, all natural gas–based energy chains (energy chains 7–11) perform well compared to the reference chain. The exception is energy chain 12, which consumes large amounts of energy and has high emissions.

Third, the non–fossil fuel energy chains (energy chains 14–18) are ranked all over the table. The hydropower-based hydrogen fuel cell chain (energy chain 14) ranks second highest, whereas biomass-based methanol in a conventional ICE (energy chain 18) ranks close to last.

Fourth, no energy chain scores best in all impact categories. Thus, the answer to the question 'Which energy chain (or fuel) is the best?' depends on which impact category one considers most important.

Ecological Footprints of Fuels

The analysis of the ecological footprints of fuels is based on data from the WTW analysis; hence, it uses the same assumptions and methodological clarifications as that analysis. Thus, the analysis of ecological footprints is more of a supplement to the WTW analysis than a substitute for it. Whereas the WTW analysis gives life-cycle data for environmental impact categories (and a very simple synthesis of the overall impacts in table 4.2), the analysis of ecological footprints gives a broader and weighted synthesis of the fuels' overall environmental impacts. (The ecological footprint concept is described in chapter 2.)

The methodology for calculating the ecological footprint is based on the general literature on ecological footprint (for example, Wackernagel and Rees 1996; Chambers et al. 2000; WFF 2004). However, this methodology has yet to be applied to a comparison of fuels; thus, some modifications to the methodology are necessary.

Methodology

A fuel's ecological footprint consists of three components: the area needed for energy production, the area needed to sequester emissions of greenhouse gases, and the area needed for the safe deposit of nitrogen and sulphur. These components are calculated by multiplying the consumption (or emission) by a conversion factor using data from Holden (2003).

The data on the land area needed for energy production are taken from Høyer and Heiberg (1993), Chambers et al. (2000) and Jørgensen et al. (2002). The area required for hydropower is calculated as 0.222 m²/MJ. This includes power plant reservoirs as well as transmission lines. The area needed to produce one MJ of wood is set at 0.518 m2/MJ. The areas needed to extract oil and natural gas are so small compared to the others that I have chosen not to include them. To calculate the ecological footprint (per kilometre driven) of an energy chain, these figures are multiplied by the chain's WTW energy consumption. Thus, the results represent the area necessary to produce the energy required to drive a vehicle one kilometre.

Four greenhouse gases are included (CO_2, CH_4, N_2O and NO_x[6]) which together form CO_2-equivalent emissions, using the Global Warming Potential recommended by the International Panel of Climate Change (IPCC 2001).[7] This analysis uses the CO_2 assimilation method which refers to the necessity of setting aside a forest area for sequestering the CO_2 emissions to prevent CO_2 from accumulating in the atmosphere Wackernagel and Rees 1996. As long as adequate land area is set aside for sequestering, there will be no net emissions of CO_2 to the atmosphere. According to the Norwegian Pollution Control Authority, forests assimilate 1.58 tons of CO_2 per hectare.

Regarding the methods available for calculating footprints for the land area required for the safe deposit of sulphur and nitrogen, critical loads (for acidity) are used to calculate the footprints of sulphur and nitrogen emissions from the energy chains. The critical load of sulphur and nitrogen acidity for an ecosystem can be defined as the level at which deposition of acidifying compounds will cause chemical changes leading to long-term harmful effects on ecosystems and functions (Posch et al. 2001). In the Nordic region the critical load for sulphur, expressed as SO_2 emissions, is 3 kg of sulphur per hectare per year. The corresponding figure for nitrogen, expressed as NO_x, is 1.5 kg of nitrogen per hectare per year.

Results of EF Analysis

Figure 4.5 shows results from the EF calculations. The greenhouse gas component of the ecological footprint is separated into a CO_2 emissions component and a non-CO_2 emissions component.

Conventional Energy Chains: 2000–2010

Conventional technology can potentially reduce the EF substantially by 2010: a 22 per cent reduction can be achieved for petrol cars and more than 35 per cent for diesel cars. The EFs of petrol and diesel cars were almost equal in 2000; by 2010

---

6   CO_2, CH_4 and N_2O are among a large number of gases that have a *direct* global warming potential (GWP). According to the Intergovernmental Panel on Climate Change (IPCC 2001). the direct GWPs are believed to be reasonably accurately (±35 per cent) known. However, there are also gases that have *indirect* effects, for example NO_x. These gases have a GWP through their effect on the production of O_3.

7   The GWP for each gas is as follows: $CO_2 = 1$, $CH_4 = 23$, $N_2O = 296$ and $NO_x = 5$. The GWP applies to a time span of 100 years.

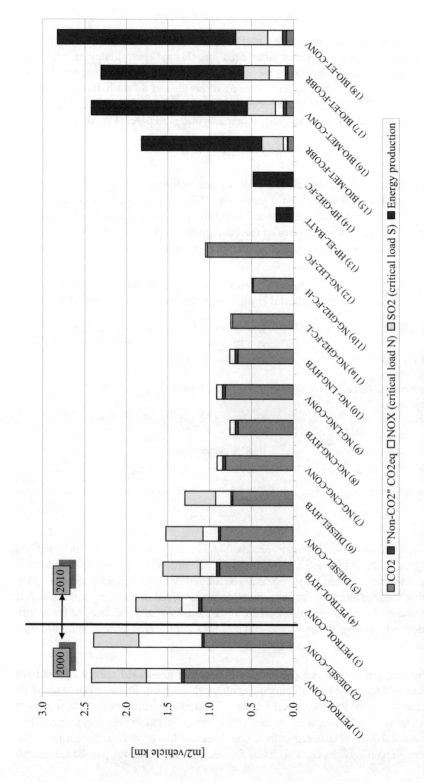

Figure 4.5 The ecological footprints of fuels (passenger car under mixed driving conditions)

diesel cars are expected to have a smaller EF than petrol cars because of tight NO_x emission standards for diesel engines equalling those of petrol engines. However, diesel engines will continue to be more energy-efficient than petrol engines into the next decade. Furthermore, hybrid versions of petrol and diesel ICEs have smaller EFs; for example, compared to the present petrol car, the petrol-electric hybrid has a 33 percent smaller EF and the diesel-electric hybrid a 50 percent smaller EF.

Conventional and Alternative Energy Chains: 2010

Compared to the ecological footprint of the reference energy chain (that is conventional raw oil–based petrol used in an ICE – energy chain 3) the ecological footprints of the energy chains included in the analysis are clustered into four groups. There are differences in the sizes of the ecological footprints within each group but the differences between the groups seem more important (table 4.3).

Table 4.3   The energy chains sorted into four groups based on their reduction potential compared to the reference energy chain

Energy chain	Ecological footprint compared to the reference energy chain's ecological footprint [i]
The hydropower-based energy chains (13–14)	More than 75% reduction
The natural gas–based energy chains (7–12)	45–75% reduction
The raw oil–based energy chains (4–6)	15–30% reduction
The biomass (wood)-based energy chains (15–18)	0–50% increase

(i) The reference energy chain refers to 2010 energy chain 3 (raw oil – petrol – conventional power train).

The hydropower-based energy chains The energy chain with the smallest ecological footprint is based on hydropower. Compared to the footprint reduction of the reference chain, a huge footprint reduction (by more than 75 per cent) seems possible because there are hardly any emissions involved in the many processes that constitute the hydropower energy chain, and because the land area needed for energy production is relatively small compared to, for example, the area needed for biomass production.

The natural gas–based energy chains The natural gas–based energy chains have considerable potential for reducing the ecological footprint, although not to the same extent as hydropower-based energy chains. The most promising involves an energy chain based on a high-efficiency fuel cell running on gaseous hydrogen produced from natural gas. This energy chain could reduce the ecological footprint of the reference chain by 75 per cent. Even the least efficient natural gas–based energy chain – liquid hydrogen combined with a low-efficiency fuel cell – gives a reduction of almost 45 per cent. Natural gas used in conventional ICEs reduces the ecological footprint by 50 per cent, and as much as 60 per cent in natural gas–electric hybrids. Low NO_x and SO_2 emissions are the main causes for the small ecological footprints of the natural gas–based chains.

The raw oil–based energy chains   There is substantial potential for reducing the ecological footprints with existing fuels. The energy chain which includes a raw oil–based hybrid diesel has an ecological footprint that is over 30 per cent smaller than that of the reference chain, while the hybrid petrol-electric engine cuts the footprint more than 15 per cent.

The biomass-based energy chains   The losers in this analysis are the biomass-based energy chains, such as those using ethanol and methanol produced from biomass, which lead to ecological footprints which are as large as or larger than the reference chain's. An increase of up to 50 per cent could result if ethanol were used in conventional ICEs. An energy chain based on methanol (in combination with a fuel cell) produces a footprint about the same size as that of the reference chain. There are two reasons for these disappointing results: First, producing ethanol and methanol from biomass feedstock requires large amounts of energy. While it takes around 10 per cent of the energy content in raw oil to produce petrol, it takes two energy units of biomass feedstock to produce one unit of ethanol or methanol. Second, biomass feedstock has a very low energy density per unit of land area necessary to produce it.

Summary

The WTW analyses show that, in terms of overall negative environmental impact, all energy chains perform better than the conventional raw oil–based petrol used in an ICE. However, it should be noted that the raw oil–based diesel hybrid has relatively low impact, indicating that substantial reductions in impacts are possible even within the conventional energy chains. No energy chain scores, however, best in all impact categories. Thus, the answer to the question 'Which energy chain (or fuel) is the best?' depends on which impact category one considers most important.

The EF analyses show that energy chains based on hydropower have very small ecological footprints. There is, however, not enough hydropower to support global transport demands. On the other hand, natural gas energy chains, which also have small ecological footprints, are more feasible because natural gas reserves are sufficient to support such demands for several decades. However, natural gas is not a renewable energy resource, and therefore does not fulfil the long-term requirements of a sustainable energy system. Biomass is available worldwide in large volumes and is a renewable resource, but extensive use of it would lead to unacceptable increases in ecological footprints. Therefore, it seems that only a combination of more efficient use of resources, substitution of harmful fuels by less harmful ones, and reductions in transportation volumes will meet long-term sustainability objectives.

Chapter 5

The Role of Public Transport

...shifting the balance between modes of transport [is] at the heart of the sustainable development strategy. (CEC 2001)

The study of public transport's role in achieving sustainable mobility raises two types of questions: Is increased use of public transport sufficient for achieving sustainable mobility? And if it is, how can increased use of public transport be achieved? The latter question is answered in part III, whereas the former question is answered in this chapter.

To illustrate the relation between the increased use of public transport and sustainable mobility, we focus on the environmental strategy of Oslo's Public Transportation Company Ltd. (Oslo Sporveier – OS hereafter). Its strategy includes an assessment of three scenarios for passenger transport in Oslo up to 2016, which are: The private car scenario that assumes all growth in passenger transport will be addressed by increasing private car use; the public transport scenario that assumes growth in passenger transport will be addressed by greatly increasing public transport use; and the sustainability scenario that assumes *reduction* in passenger transport will be achieved by greatly reducing private car use and *simultaneously* greatly increases public transport use, walking and cycling.

In chapter 9, I study public transport's role in achieving sustainable mobility in the EU based on the same scenario methodology developed in the Oslo study. Thus, this chapter's conclusions are also relevant for passenger transport in the EU. However, whereas the Oslo study's scenarios are based on 2016, the EU scenarios in chapter 9 are based on 2030.

Chapter 5 has three sections. The first presents the Oslo study's methodology and the overall passenger transport in 1996, the base year. The second presents the assumptions made in the three 2016 scenarios, and the third section presents the impacts on energy consumption, emissions and land use in the three scenarios.

Methodology

Figure 5.1 shows the three 2016 scenarios and the impact groups. The impact group 'energy' includes energy consumption for passenger transport. The impact group 'emissions' includes CO_2 emissions, NO_x emissions and particle emissions (PM). The impact group 'land use' includes land use for transport purposes. Moreover, the study is restricted to transport within Oslo, whose population is expected to increase from approximately 490,000 in 1996 to almost 600,000 in 2016. Furthermore, the following transport means are included in the analysis: walking, cycling, private car, taxi, bus, tram and metro.

Each scenario makes assumptions regarding the following three variables:

*   Total passenger transport (that is, total passenger kilometres per year).
*   Distribution of passenger transport by the transport means.
*   Average occupancy rate for each transport means.

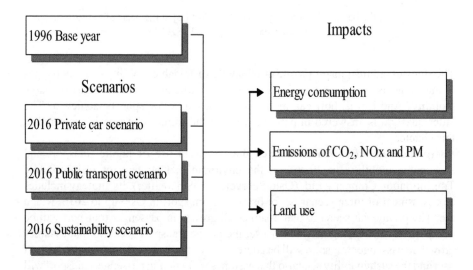

Figure 5.1   The structure of the scenario analyses

Passenger Transport in the Base Year 1996

The main source for calculating total passenger transport was the Planning and Building Department of Oslo Municipality, which continuously collects transport data in connection with their transport planning. At the request of Western Norway Research Institute, the department performed specific calculations based on this data which subsequently were used in the scenarios. In addition, data from passenger transport surveys carried out by OS and the Greater Oslo Local Traffic (Stor-Oslo Lokaltrafikk – SL hereafter), were used.

The following apply to calculating the 1996 total passenger transport, which is shown in table 5.1 (for details, see Andersen et al. 2004):

*   The figures include weekend and holiday travel.
*   The figures for walking and cycling are estimated from the 1990 travel survey for Oslo and cover only Oslo citizens.
*   The passenger transport by private car includes all trips in Oslo. The Planning and Building Department in the Municipality of Oslo estimated the number

of vehicle kilometres driven by private car, based on traffic censuses made at various locations in Oslo.

- The taxi figures are estimated on the basis of statistical material from Oslo Taxi.
- The train figures include trips with SL starting in Akershus (a neighbouring county) and ending in Oslo.
- The bus figures for Oslo cover the bus services of OS including contract driving and SL, and include trips starting in Akershus and ending in Oslo. Other types of bus transport in Oslo, such as the bus to the airport and long-distance express coaches to and from Oslo, are not included.

Table 5.1   Passenger transport in Oslo in 1996

Transport means	Yearly travel distance		Number of trips		Average trip length
	mill pkm	%	mill	%	km
Walking	131	2.9	147	25.8	0.9
Cycling	68	1.5	44	7.7	1.5
Private car (i)	3,280	73.8	219	38.5	15.0
Taxi (ii)	160	3.6	15	2.6	10.7
Bus (iii)	253	5.7	48	8.4	5.2
Train (iv)	173	3.9	9	1.6	20.4
Tram (v)	87	2.0	32	5.6	2.7
Metro (v)	294	6.6	56	9.8	5.2
Total	4,446	100.0	569	100.0	-

(i) An occupancy rate of 1.6 passengers per vehicle is applied. This was based on a census made at the toll ring in Oslo, a travel pattern survey for Oslo in 1990, and the private car survey made by Statistics Norway in 1995.
(ii) An occupancy rate of 1.3 passengers per taxi is applied.
(iii) An occupancy rate of 13.5 passengers per bus is applied.
(iv) An occupancy rate of 32 per cent is applied. This is based on empirical data for local and inter-city train traffic in Oslo (Høyer and Heiberg 1993).
(v) An occupancy rate of 16 per cent for tram and metro is applied, based on analyses performed by OS.

Table 5.1 shows that travel by private cars and taxis accounts for 77 per cent of Oslo citizens' total transport in passenger kilometres. Moreover, the table shows that travel by public transport accounts for 18 per cent of the total transport, whereas walking and cycling together account for 5 per cent. However, the number of trips made with the various means shows a different picture: 41 per cent by private cars and taxis, 25 per cent by public transport and 34 per cent by walking and cycling. Travel by private cars and taxis accounts for a larger share of passenger kilometres than it does for number of trips because the average trip length of travel by cars and taxis generally is longer than the average trip length by public transport, walking, and cycling. Whereas the average trip length for travel by cars and taxis is 10–15 kilometres, the average trip length for travel by public transport, walking and cycling is 1–5 kilometres.

Passenger Transport Scenarios for 2016

The 2016 Private Car Scenario

This scenario uses predictions made in the 1998–2007 National Road and Road Traffic Plan which assumes that 1996–2016 annual growth rate for total passenger transport is 0.9 per cent; thus, total passenger transport increases from 4,446 million passenger kilometres in 1996 to 5,324 million passenger kilometres in 2016.

Moreover, this scenario assumes that *all* growth in total passenger transport will be addressed by private cars and taxis, which means that annual growth rate for transport by cars and taxis is 1.1 per cent. The annual growth rates for transport by public transport, walking and cycling, on the other hand, are 0.0, which means that 2016 passenger transport by these means equals that of 1996. Therefore, travels by private cars and taxis, by public transport, and walking and cycling account for 81 per cent, 15 per cent and 4 per cent of total passenger transport, respectively. Occupancy rates for all means of transport remain at 1996 level, except for travel by private cars, which is assumed to decline from 1.6 to 1.4 persons per car.

The private car scenario presupposes a continuation of today's development in land-use patterns in the Oslo region, with a continued tendency to urban sprawl, as well as suburbanisation on a regional level. This development stems from a continuation of the policies of expanding the road system and parking facilities.

The 2016 Public Transport Scenario

This scenario assumes that in 2016 1/3 of trips are carried out by public transport, 1/3 by private car, and 1/3 by walking and cycling. This distribution of passenger trips is roughly equal to the present distribution in Copenhagen (Eir 1997). At the same time, this scenario assumes that annual growth rate for total passenger transport equals that in the private car scenario, which means that total passenger transport is 5,324 million passenger kilometres in 2016.

Accordingly, 1996–2016 annual growth rates are as follow: 0.3 per cent for travel by private cars and taxis, 2.8 per cent for travel by public transport and 1.3 per cent for walking and cycling. As a result of these growth rates, travels by private cars and taxis, by public transport, and by walking and cycling account for 69 per cent, 26 per cent and 5 per cent of total passenger transport, respectively. Occupancy rates decline from 1.6 to 1.4 persons per car, increase from 13.5 to 20 passengers per bus, increase from 32 per cent to 38 per cent for trains, and increase from 16 per cent to 22 per cent for trams and metros. The occupancy rate for taxis equals that of 1996.

The public transport scenario presupposes a major increase in public transport infrastructure, which implies establishing new public transport nodes and moreover coordinating through land-use planning the construction of bus, tram and rail stations.

To avoid congestion, nodes will be built where a fast transfer can occur between the commuter buses, using the main arteries to and from Oslo, and the public transport network in Oslo. Furthermore, the scenario presupposes that a 'combined rail system' will be built. This system is based on rail cars that can be used on the national rail tracks as well as on the tram and metro tracks of OS (which operates all the tram and metro lines in Oslo). The introduction of a combined rail system will reduce the need for a major expansion of the bus system. We have, however, no basis for estimating the share of bus traffic that can be transferred to a combined rail system. Finally, the scenario presupposes a strong effort to construct pedestrian and bicycle lanes, with emphasis on ensuring access for walkers and cyclists to important public transport nodes and stops.

The 2016 Sustainability Scenario

This scenario is constructed in two steps. The first assumes that if Oslo's citizens were to achieve sustainable mobility by 2050, the following would need to apply (Høyer 2000, Jahn Hansen et al. 2000; Aall et al. 1997): Passenger transport by cars and taxis would be zero; present level of passenger transport by public transport and walking would be doubled; and present level of cycling would be tripled. The second step estimates 2016 passenger transport by assuming linear transport development for the period 1996–2050. Thus, total passenger transport is reduced from 4,446 million passenger kilometres in 1996 to 4,049 million passenger kilometres in 2016.

Accordingly, 1996–2016 annual growth rates are as follow: -2.3 per cent for travel by private cars and taxis, 2.8 per cent for travel by public transport and 4.7 per cent for walking and cycling. As a result of these growth rates, travels by private cars and taxis, by public transport, and walking and cycling account for 53 per cent, 34 per cent and 12 per cent of total passenger transport, respectively. Occupancy rates equal those of the 2016 public transport scenario.

The sustainability scenario presupposes strong measures aimed at reducing the car transport level and thus the total transport level. These measures emphasize compact land-use planning practices, meaning that severe restrictions would be put on new construction (such as workplaces and car-based shopping centres) on Oslo's fringes. These restrictions would also entail extensive development on brownfield areas within Oslo and the redevelopment of existing roads into housing. Other measures include: a restrictive parking policy, meaning a gradual closing down of central car parks and parking areas connected to major workplace locations, and a new form of land-use policy in relation to existing transport infrastructure (mainly roads and car parks). Instead of building special pedestrian and bicycle lanes, sections of the existing road system would be reserved for bicycles; similarly, there would be a significant increase in the development of special bus lanes on all important transport arteries. Finally, car-free zones would be greatly increased.

Comparison of Passenger Transport in the Scenarios

Table 5.2 shows estimated passenger transport by the various means and total passenger transport for the three 2016 scenarios. Compared to 1996, the 2016 private car and public transport scenarios increase total passenger transport by 20 per cent, whereas the 2016 sustainability scenario reduces it by 9 per cent.

Table 5.2   Passenger transport in Oslo in three 2016 scenarios

Transport means	2016 Private car scenario		2016 Public transport scenario		2016 Sustainability scenario	
	mill pkm	%	mill pkm	%	mill pkm	%
Walking	131	2.5	171	3.2	241	6.0
Cycling	68	1.3	89	1.7	254	6.3
Private car	4,096	76.9	3,505	65.8	2,065	51.0
Taxi	222	4.2	171	3.2	101	2.5
Bus	253	4.8	438	8.2	438	10.8
Train	173	3.2	300	5.6	300	7.4
Tram	87	1.6	147	2.8	147	3.6
Metro	294	5.5	504	9.5	504	12.4
Total	5,324	100.0	5,324	100.0	4,049	100.0

Passenger transport in the three 2016 scenarios is also shown in terms of the number of trips made by each means of transport (table 5.3). The calculation of the number of trips made in each scenario is based on the assumption that average 2016 trip lengths by the various means of transport would remain at 1996 levels.

Table 5.3   Number of trips in Oslo in three 2016 scenarios

Transport means	2016 Private car scenario		2016 Public transport scenario		2016 Sustainability scenario	
	mill	%	mill	%	mill	%
Walking	147	21.2	192	25.6	271	32.6
Cycling	44	6.3	57	7.6	165	19.8
Private car	337	48.6	234	31.2	138	16.6
Taxi	21	3.0	16	2.1	9	1.1
Bus	48	6.9	84	11.2	84	10.1
Train	9	1.3	15	2.0	15	1.8
Tram	32	4.6	54	7.2	54	6.5
Metro	56	8.1	97	13.0	97	11.7
Total	694	100.0	749	100.0	832	100.0

The eight means of transport can be combined into three main categories of transport *modes*:

- Walking and cycling.
- Public transport.
- Private cars and taxis.

The development of passenger transport in the scenarios for these three main categories of transport modes is shown in figure 5.2.

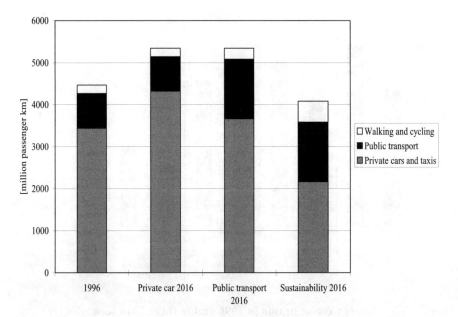

Figure 5.2   Passenger transport in 1996 and in three 2016 scenarios

Impacts

Energy Consumption

Total energy consumption for passenger transport comprises three main components:

- Direct energy consumption ('direct'): Energy consumed for the propulsion of the transport means, that is, end use (corresponding to the Tank-to-Wheel concept – TTW – described in chapter 4).
- Gross direct energy consumption ('gross'): Direct energy consumption plus the energy consumption taking place at all stages from feedstock production to distribution and refuelling (corresponding to the Well-to-Wheel concept – WTW – described in chapter 4).
- Indirect energy consumption ('indirect'): Energy consumed to produce and maintain the transport means and their infrastructures.

The 1996 specific energy consumption factors for direct energy consumption are taken from Holtskog and Rypdal (1997)[1] and the factors for gross direct and indirect energy consumption are taken from Høyer and Heiberg (1993). The assumptions made regarding 2016 factors are given in the table's footnotes. The results of the calculations of the direct and total (gross direct plus indirect) energy consumption are shown in figure 5.3.

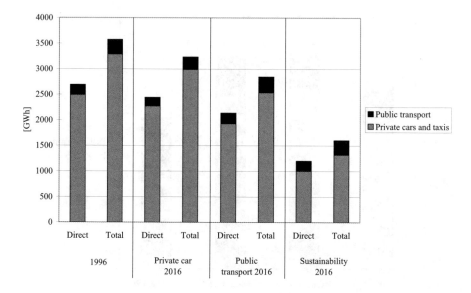

Figure 5.3   Energy consumption in 1996 and in three 2016 scenarios

Private cars and taxis accounted for 92 per cent of energy consumption in 1996. Total energy consumption in 2016 will be lower than 1996 levels by the following amounts: 9 per cent in the private car scenario, 20 per cent in the public transport scenario, and as much as 55 per cent in the sustainability scenario. Although the 2016 scenarios seem to reduce energy consumption, the reasons for their doing so vary. Total energy consumption decreases substantially in the sustainability scenario simply because the scenario presupposes a strong reduction in both total travel and car travel. Furthermore, total energy consumption decreases in the public transport scenario because that scenario presupposes a strong increase in public transport, which is more efficient in terms of per capita energy consumption than private cars. One should notice, however, that *compared* to the 2016 private car scenario, the 2016 public transport scenario offers only a modest 10 per cent reduction. Finally, total energy consumption decreases because they presuppose that growth in the use of private cars in Oslo will be more than compensated for by the improved energy efficiency of the cars.

---

1   Holtskog and Rypdal's factors are based on average national driving patterns; these averages have here been adjusted to reflect Oslo residents' driving patterns.

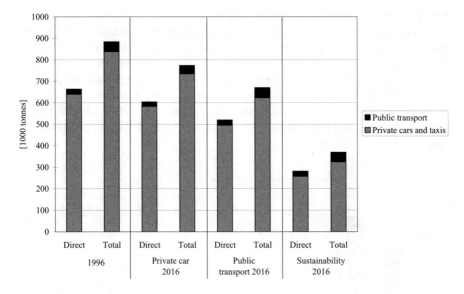

Figure 5.4 CO$_2$ emissions in 1996 and in three 2016 scenarios

CO$_2$ Emissions

The total emissions of CO$_2$ comprise three main components: direct CO$_2$ emissions, gross direct CO$_2$ emissions, and indirect CO$_2$ emissions. The calculations of direct CO$_2$ emissions for cars, taxis and buses are based on the factors for direct specific energy consumption. The following conversion factors are used for converting energy consumption to CO$_2$ emissions: 3.13 kg CO$_2$ per kg petrol, and 3.17 kg CO$_2$ per kg diesel. Rail-based transport (train, tram and metro) in Oslo is all electrified, and thus has no direct CO$_2$ emissions. The factors for gross direct and indirect CO$_2$ emissions are taken from Høyer and Heiberg (1993). The results of the calculations of direct and total (gross direct plus indirect) CO$_2$ emissions are shown in figure 5.4.

In 1996, private cars and taxis accounted for up to 95 per cent of total CO$_2$ emissions from passenger transport in Oslo. In the 2016 private car scenario, the total CO$_2$ emissions from passenger transport in Oslo will be 13 per cent less than in 1996. In other words, improved energy efficiency will more than compensate for the increased use of private cars in the private car scenario. Even greater reductions of CO$_2$ emissions will be achieved in the public transport and sustainability scenarios. These two scenarios will result in reductions of CO$_2$ emissions of 24 and 58 per cent, respectively.

NO$_x$ Emissions

The total emissions of NO$_x$ also comprise three main components: direct NO$_x$ emissions, gross direct NO$_x$ emissions, and indirect NO$_x$ emissions. The factors for direct NO_x emissions in 1996 are based on those used by Statistics Norway (Holtskog and Rypdal 1997). Statistics Norway's factors for national averages have been adjusted to city factors by applying data on different driving patterns from the National Pollution Control Agency (SFT 1993, 1999). Factors for direct NO_x emissions in 2016 are based on the assumption that all cars, taxis and buses would comply with the EURO IV standard. The factors for gross direct and indirect NO_x emissions are based on a study by Høyer and Heiberg (1993). The calculated direct and total (gross direct plus indirect) emissions of NO_x from passenger transport in Oslo are shown in figure 5.5.

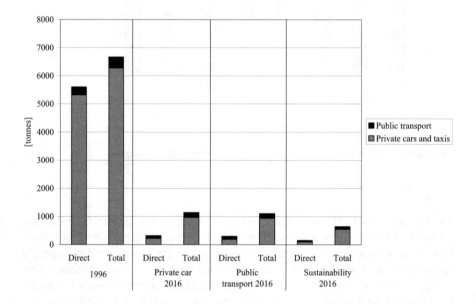

Figure 5.5 NO_x emissions in 1996 and in three 2016 scenarios

Private cars and taxis accounted for 95 per cent of NO_x emissions in 1996. For all three scenarios there is a considerable reduction (94–96 per cent) in the direct emissions of NO_x up to 2016. Technological developments coupled with gradually more stringent regulations on NO_x emissions from vehicles (particularly for private cars) would contribute to this reduction.

Particle Emissions

The calculation of emissions of particles includes direct emissions of PM_{10} and $PM_{2.5}$ –PM_{10} contains all particles less than 10 μm, whereas $PM_{2.5}$ contains all particles less than 2.5 μm. Gross direct and indirect emissions of particles are not included due to large uncertainties connected to the quantification of these components of total particle emissions. This analysis includes five main processes responsible for generating particles:

- Emissions from exhaust: The factors for calculations of particles from exhaust in 1996 are based on those used by Statistics Norway (Holtskog and Rypdal 1997).
- Pavement wear: The calculations of PM_{10} and $PM_{2.5}$ from wear of pavement, mainly from the use of studded tyres, are based on several Norwegian studies (Larssen 1987; Vegdirektoratet 1997; SINTEF 1994; Larssen 1997; Anda and Larsen 1982).
- Tyre wear: The calculations of emissions of PM_{10} and $PM_{2.5}$ caused by tyre wear, that is, particles originating from the tyres, are based on estimates by the California Air Resources Board (CARB 1979).
- Brake wear: The calculations of particle generation from brake lining wear are also based on estimates by the California Air Resources Board (CARB 1979; CARB 1998).
- Grinding of larger particles with subsequent re-suspension in the air: The calculations of PM_{10} and $PM_{2.5}$ from grinding of larger particles with subsequent re-suspension in the air are based on estimates by the Norwegian Institute for Air Research (Larssen 1987).The calculations cover particle emissions from buses, private cars and taxis. Emissions of particles from rail transport are not included, as these are generated by diesel trains, which do not exist in the Oslo region, where all trains are electrified. The factors for calculating emissions of PM_{10} and $PM_{2.5}$ are taken from Andersen et al. (2004). The results of the calculations of PM_{10} and $PM_{2.5}$ are shown in figure 5.6.

Private cars and taxis accounted for 95 per cent of particle emissions in 1996. The total emissions of PM_{10} and $PM_{2.5}$ from passenger transport in 2016 in Oslo will be reduced from 1996 levels in all 3 scenarios. Technological developments and political measures, and more stringent regulations on particle emissions would contribute to this reduction. The reduction would be smallest in the private car scenario, and largest in the sustainability scenario.

Land Use

Considerable land is used in the transport sector. Land use serves as an indicator of land-linked environmental problems, such as reduction of biological diversity, closing down of valuable food production areas and cultural landscapes, and conflicts between users vying to use the same areas. In the analysis two types of land use are distinguished:
   Direct land use:

- Transport artery (road and rail).
- Stations (bus stops, railway stations etc.).

Indirect land use:

- Land tied up due to other land use as a consequence of transport activities (for example, building restriction zones along roads).
- Car parks and other types of parking grounds.

- Land use linked to offices, workshops, etc. for the transport mode.
- Land use linked to production and distribution of energy (for example, water reservoirs and transmission lines for electricity generation and distribution, respectively, petrol stations, etc.).
- Land use linked to maintenance and distribution of transport means (for example, garages and car dealers).

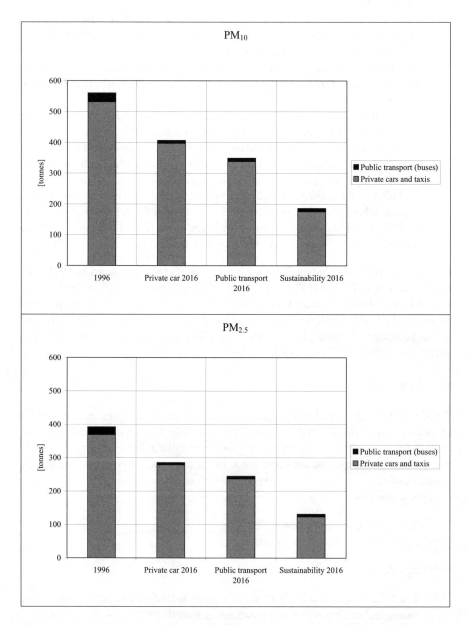

Figure 5.6   PM$_{10}$ and PM$_{2.5}$ emissions in 1996 and in three 2016 scenarios

This analysis covers direct and indirect land use for transport in Oslo. The indirect land use is limited to land areas for car parks and petrol stations, terminals, and depots. The calculations are based on estimates of land use for various transport purposes taken from Andersen et al. (2004).

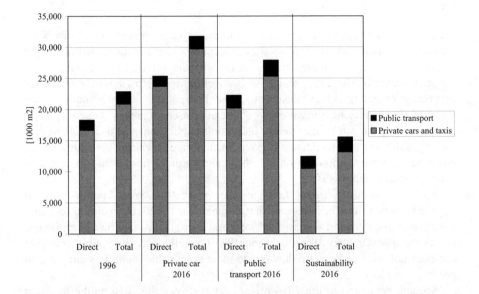

Figure 5.7   Land use in 1996 and in three 2016 scenarios

Private cars, taxis and buses driving in Oslo all use the same roads. For the calculations, the total land use for roads was allocated to each of these transport means based on the vehicle kilometres and the relative size of the transport means. In 1996 the total length of Oslo's tramlines was 40 kilometres. Almost all were double tracks having a width of 6.3 metres. This gives a direct land use of 252,000 m². Private cars, taxis and buses also use about 40 per cent of this, but in the calculations this part of the streets is considered to be exclusively for tram use. The total length of Oslo's metro in 1996 was 78 kilometres. The whole length comprises double tracks with a width of 10.4 metres. This gives a direct land use of 811,000 m². About 15 kilometres of the metro are in tunnels. The metro thus has a direct land use on the surface of 657,000 m². The rail net for trains in Oslo is used for local, regional and international trains. However, data was unavailable for estimating the direct land use of each train type. Instead the calculations are based on an assumption that the land use per passenger kilometre for local trains is similar to the land use per passenger kilometre for the metro. This gives a direct land use of 388,000 m² in 1996. The results of the calculations of the direct and total (direct plus indirect) land use are shown in figure 5.7.

Private cars and taxis account for the majority (91 per cent) of total land use for passenger transport in Oslo. Compared to 1996, the total land use increases by 39 per cent in the 2016 private car scenario and 22 per cent in the 2016 public transport scenario. It decreases by 32 per cent in the 2016 sustainability scenario because use of private cars and taxis is drastically reduced in this scenario.

Summary

This chapter analyses three scenarios for transport development in Oslo in 2016. The three scenarios are: 1) the private car scenario, where all predicted passenger transport growth is to be addressed by greatly increasing private car use, 2) the public transport scenario, where the predicted passenger transport growth is to be addressed by greatly increasing public transport use, and 3) the sustainability scenario, where the *reduction* in passenger transport would be addressed by greatly reducing private car use and at the same time greatly increasing public transport use, walking and cycling. Each scenario estimates impacts in three areas: energy consumption for passenger transport, emissions of CO_2, NO_X and particles from transport, and land use for transport purposes.

Four conclusions regarding the importance of greatly increased public transport use can be drawn from the analyses. First, compared to the 2016 private car scenario, the 2016 public transport scenario reduces total energy consumption and emissions of CO_2 by approximately 10 per cent each. Thus, greatly increasing public transport use does not offer sufficient reductions to meet sustainable mobility's energy goal presented in chapter 3.

Second, compared to the 2016 private car scenario, the 2016 public transport scenario does not offer significant reductions of emissions of NO_X and particles, nor of land use for transport (reductions are typically 5–15 per cent).

Third, the 2016 public transport scenario does not offer substantial reductions of energy consumption, emissions and land use because it does not include additional measures to restrict growth in total transport. Although public transport use is greatly increased in the public transport scenario, most of the growth in passenger transport in this scenario would still be covered by private cars. Thus, advantages offered by the use of energy-efficient public transport modes are negated by a simultaneous strong increase in the use of less energy-efficient private cars.

Fourth, significant reductions of energy consumption, emissions and land use are achieved in the 2016 sustainability scenario because this scenario greatly reduces car use and *simultaneously* greatly increases public transport use. Thus, to achieve sustainable mobility, increased public transport use and restrictions on private car use must be promoted simultaneously.

Chapter 6

The Role of Green Attitudes

> The Commission has completed its work. We call for a common endeavour and for new norms of behaviour at all levels and in the interests of all. The changes in attitudes, in social values, and in aspirations that the report urges will depend on vast campaigns of education, debate, and public participation. [...] To this end, we appeal to citizens' groups, to non-governmental organizations, to educational institutions, and to the scientific community. They have all played indispensable roles in the creation of public awareness and political changes in the past. They will play a crucial part in putting the world onto sustainable development paths, in laying the groundwork for Our Common Future. (WCED 1987, xiv)

This chapter assesses the role of attitudes in achieving sustainable mobility. Under examination is the green attitude hypothesis suggesting that more environmentally responsible (or simply 'green') attitudes will reduce energy consumption for passenger transport.

Agenda 21[1] urges that values and attitudes that support sustainable consumption – for example, environmentally responsible mobility behaviour – must be reinforced: 'Governments and private-sector organizations should promote more positive attitudes towards sustainable consumption through education, public awareness programmes and other means' (Agenda 21, chapter 4.26). Whichever of the strategies mentioned in chapter 3 is ultimately adopted for achieving sustainable development – and thus sustainable consumption – it would be unthinkable to proceed without some kind of willing participation of consumers. New, more efficient technology must be purchased, a shift towards more sustainable consumption patterns must be freely chosen, and reductions in consumption must be voluntary.

Nevertheless, when promoting sustainable consumption strategies it is important to acknowledge conditions in addition to attitudes and awareness. Such conditions include economic incentives (taxes and subsidies), regulations (laws and standards), and physical infrastructures (public transport systems and urban forms), all of which either constrain or enable consumption behaviour. However, conditions must be based on policies that are supported by a majority of consumers. Thus, consumers are called upon not only to promote sustainable consumption through their daily behaviour, but also – as voters – to actively support necessary changes in national policy (Thøgersen 1999). Furthermore, even in cases where regulatory measures have been implemented, there will almost always be some degree of freedom left to the individual consumer. Therefore, achieving sustainable consumption ultimately depends on choices taken by individual consumers (ibid.).

---

1   Agenda 21 is the action plan from the 1992 UNCED meeting in Rio de Janeiro.

Changing unsustainable *household* consumption patterns is crucial to achieving the goal of sustainable development in OECD countries (OECD 2002a; EEA 2005). Thus, 'household consumption' is a key concept in this context. A number of studies point to three distinct consumption categories as the major problem areas: housing, transport and food (Hille 1995; Holden 2001; Lorek and Spangenberg 2001; Aall and Norland 2002). These three categories account for up to 80 per cent of the direct and indirect environmental impacts caused by households. Therefore, any discussion about sustainable consumption must address these consumption categories.

The main concern in this book is travel behaviour. However, in this chapter, travel behaviour is set in a broader household consumption perspective. The relation between various types of household consumption is complex because to some extent they are dependent on each other. Therefore, we have studied the relationships between, on one hand, attitudes and energy consumption for housing, and on the other, attitudes and transport. There are two categories of transport: everyday travel (by all means of transport) and long-distance leisure-time travel (by car and plane). Thus, four energy consumption categories are studied: (i) heating and operating a house, (ii) everyday travel, (iii) long-distance leisure-time travel by car, and (iv) long-distance leisure-time travel by plane. Throughout the chapter, these four energy consumption categories are referred to as 'household consumption.'

The chapter has three sections. The first gives an introduction to attitude theory. The second presents the SusHomes Project, carried out by the Program for Research and Documentation for a Sustainable Society (ProSus) at the University of Oslo (2001–2004). At the core of this project was a household survey in the Greater Oslo Region. A total of 941 individuals responded on their individual and their household's consumption of energy and transport, as well as on family structure, income and housing facilities. The sample included 133 responses by members of the Norwegian Environmental Home Guard (NEHG), making possible a quantitative comparison between the hypothetically 'green' members and the 'not-so-green' non-members. The third section presents the results from a qualitative study of 20 in-depth interviews with households in Greater Oslo and Førde, which is a small, rural Norwegian town. The main focus in this study is to reveal potential mechanisms that activate environmentally friendly behaviour.

Attitude Theory

Some 70 years ago Allport wrote, 'The concept of attitude is probably the most distinctive and indispensable concept in contemporary American social psychology. No other term appears more frequently in the experimental and theoretical literature' (Allport 1935, 798).[2] McGuire (1985) noted that since the 1920s, interest in attitudes has always been substantial, although it has waxed and waned. According to McGuire (1986), however, few will today dispute that attitudes have been a constant, and sometimes paramount, topic of social psychological and consumer research.

---

2   Quoted from Pieters (1988).

The study of attitudes has gained its status in social psychological research and theorizing for several reasons. First, attitudes are thought to serve certain psychological functions for the persons holding them (Pieters 1988). Thus, one of the main functions served by attitudes is that of organizing and structuring a rather chaotic world. Second, and most important for the purpose of this chapter, attitudes are thought to direct and thus to explain and predict behaviour (Fishbein and Ajzen 1975).

At least two research lines can be distinguished in the study of attitudes (Pieters 1988). First, much attention has been focussed on the question of attitude-behaviour consistency. If attitudes do not direct, or at least precede behaviour, then one of the elements of the utility of the attitude concept would be absent. Second, behaviour change via attitude change has been and still is a prominent research line. Both these research lines will be addressed here. The main focus will, however, be on the question of attitude-behaviour consistency.

After Allport's enthusiastic elaboration of the attitude concept, a large number of empirical studies made it clear that orally expressed attitudes do not usually correlate highly with overt behaviour (Ronis et al. 1989). In one of the classics on the absence of consistency between attitudes and behaviour, LaPiere (1934) investigated whether the behaviour of US hotel and restaurant owners was consistent with their self-reported attitudes towards discrimination against ethnic groups. LaPiere's results showed that there was attitude-behaviour inconsistency, and furthermore he expressed doubt as to whether attitude is actually related to behaviour. In a review of 46 studies on attitude-behaviour consistency, Wicker (1969) reported that the typical attitude-behaviour correlation was about 0.2 and that rarely could as much as 10 per cent of the variance in overt behavioural measurements be accounted for by attitudinal data. Thus, he concluded that attitude research is of no use in understanding behaviour. Furthermore, he noted that one of the roads future research could follow was 'to abandon the attitude concept in favour of directly studying overt behaviour' (ibid., 75).

The problem of attitude-behaviour inconsistency has also been analysed in studies of environmentally responsible consumption (Thøgersen 1999). Thøgersen suggests that inconsistencies between expressed attitudes and actual behaviour have a number of negative consequences. First, they reduce the usefulness of attitude research in the environmental field. Why bother to study attitudes if they have no effect? Second, and more seriously, they reduce the producer's faith in the economic defensibility of developing environmentally friendlier products and services. Why bother to spend money to produce environmentally friendly products if nobody buys them? Finally, inconsistencies between expressed attitudes and actual behaviour reduce the effectiveness of political interventions. Why should government bother to issue public information or launch awareness campaigns if there is no possibility to predict the consequences of these interventions?

However, research on attitude-behaviour consistency has made progress since LaPiere's study and Wicker's review. According to Pieters (1988), LaPiere's study is an example of what can be called the first generation of research questions on attitude-behaviour consistency, the 'is' questions. The second generation of research questions deals with the *conditions* under which attitude-behaviour consistency can be observed. Such questions can be called the 'when' questions. Fazio and Zanna stress the importance of such questions, recommending that rather than asking whether attitudes relate to behaviour, one should ask, 'Under what conditions do what kinds of attitudes of what kinds of individuals predict what kinds of behaviour?' (Fazio and Zanna 1981, 165). The third generation of research questions deals with the variables and processes that moderate the relationship between attitude and behaviour. These questions can be called the 'how' questions.

Because of the increased focus on the 'when' and 'how' questions, Pieters (1988) concluded that the study of the relationships between attitudes and behaviour is vibrant. He suggested that optimism in establishing the existence of attitude-behaviour consistency has grown and that many studies have shown that attitudes can and do predict behaviour. Furthermore, he argued that attitude theory is slowly but steadily progressing from the second generation ('when') to the third generation ('how') questions.

In this chapter, the relationship between attitudes and behaviour is discussed in some detail. What exactly is an attitude? What characterises behaviour? Theorists have been generous in providing us with definitions and conceptualisations of attitudes. Reviewing the literature on attitudes and opinions, Fishbein and Ajzen (1972) compiled 500 operational definitions of what an attitude is. They noted that in some studies even several definitions were used. According to Ronis et al. (1989), the term 'attitude' is defined in one of two ways. Either attitude is defined as a predisposition to behave in a certain way, or the relevant behaviour is defined as one component of the attitude itself. The latter way suggests that an attitude consists of several components. In the tripartite model, which was popular in the 1950s and 1960s, attitudes were assumed to consist of three parts: cognitive (knowledge), affective (feeling) and conative (disposition, behaviour). Despite the tripartite model's popularity in textbooks and reviews of attitude literature, the bulk of attitude research and theory focused on the affective component of attitudes (Ostrom 1969).

Pieters (1988) presents two criticisms of the tripartite model. First, there is little evidence that cognitions directly determine behaviour. Second, behaviour (the conative part) cannot be a part of the definition of an attitude, because the relationship between attitude (the affective part) and behaviour is precisely what must be empirically proven. Thus, the term 'attitude' will be used here, in keeping with the definition used by most theorists, to refer to a positive or negative feeling towards a specific behaviour. Possible antecedents, consequences and correlates of an attitude are excluded from this definition.[3]

Not much will be said here about the conceptualisation and definition of behaviour. However, one important point will be made that has implications for promoting sustainable consumption. Fishbein and Ajzen (1975) explain that when studying behaviour, four specification elements can be distinguished: (i) the action, (ii) the target at which the action is directed, (iii) the context in which the action is performed, and (iv) the time at which the action is performed. On the basis of these elements, Pieters (1988) recognises two types of behaviour: *single acts* and *behaviour within categories*. A single act is a specific behaviour where all four

---

3   The term 'lifestyle' is suited to the tripartite model.

specification elements are present. A behaviour category is a set of single acts that are similar in at least one specification element, usually the target. Buying a water-saving showerhead is a single act. This single act can be an element of the behaviour category 'energy saving,' to which other single acts belong, such as turning off lights when leaving a room. In this behaviour category, all single acts are aimed at the same target, energy saving.

This chapter focuses on sustainable household consumption, which must be considered as a broad behaviour category. The four energy consumption categories can be considered as behavioural sub-categories, each covering a large number of possible single acts.

Attitude-Behaviour Inconsistency

Recent failures to understand the relationship between attitudes and behaviour fall into three categories (Ronis et al. 1989; Thøgersen 1999; Pieters 1988): (i) using incorrect measurement methodology, (ii) not taking into account other determinants of behaviour, and (iii) not taking into account processes or factors that moderate the attitude-behaviour relationship.[4] The first two categories are discussed first, because they function as guidelines for the empirical investigations. The third category will be discussed as a part of answering the 'how' questions at the end of this chapter's second section.

Incorrect Measurement Methodology

Attitudes and behaviour can be defined in several ways. In 'attitudes towards sustainable consumption' only the action element is defined. In 'attitudes towards taking the bus to work Monday morning to contribute to sustainable consumption' all four specification elements (action, target, context, and time) are defined. Taking into account the correspondence between the levels of specification, Ajzen and Fishbein (1977) studied attitude-behaviour consistency. They examined 109 studies, which reported a total of 142 attitude-behaviour relationships. The four specification elements (action, target, context and time) comprising attitude and behaviour entities were taken as starting points. They tested the hypothesis that attitude-behaviour consistency can be identified when measurements of attitude correspond in specification elements to measurements of behaviour. Thus a specific attitude was expected to predict a single act, while a global attitude was expected to predict global behaviour.

The results confirmed the hypothesis. When attitudes and behaviour corresponded in specification elements, 'significant attitude-behaviour relations of considerable

---

4 Three additional categories can be added to the list: (iv) methodological problems, such as measurement unreliability, statistics used, behaviour measure distribution, and threshold level (Pieters 1988), (v) incorrect conceptualisation of attitudes (Pieters 1988), and (vi) incorrect conceptualisation of behaviour (Thøgersen 1999). These categories will not be addressed here.

magnitude were found.'[5] This implies that the application of Fishbein's and Ajzen's *principle of correspondence* radically increases the correlation between attitudes and behaviour. A review of attitude-behaviour consistency in the environmental domain by Moisander and Uusitalo (1994) gives further support for this hypothesis. According to them, attempting to explain a specific action in a specific context at a specific time by a general measurement of environmental attitude is a typical, and frequent, example of incorrect specification.

Thøgersen (1999) shows that general attitudes towards environmental issues are of little help in predicting specific actions towards the issues. This does not imply, however, that general attitudes are unimportant. Citing basic principles of action identification as defined by Vallacher and Wegner (1987), Thøgersen suggests that 'a seemingly heterogeneous bunch of visible acts share a common identity in the mind of an actor' (Thøgersen 1999, 10). Hence, studying attitudes toward environmental issues, with the development of change strategies for given behaviour categories in mind, is indeed meaningful. When deciding which option to choose from available action alternatives within a behaviour category, however, people chose the one(s) they find most appropriate under the given circumstances. Hence, general attitudes towards sustainable household consumption is not very predictive of specific actions within that behaviour category (Thøgersen 1999).

Other Determinants of Behaviour

Failure to find attitude-behaviour consistency can be due to the fact that attitude is only one of the factors that influence behaviour. Thus, measuring attitudes alone is not sufficient to predict or explain behaviour. Other factors (determinants) that influence behaviour are important to understanding the attitude-behaviour relationship.

The term 'determinants' does not, as one might suspect, refer to determinism in an absolute sense. Absolute determinism would imply that a single factor (or a group of factors, usually related to social factors external to the individual) solely *determines* behaviour. However, although people are influenced by the social contexts in which they find themselves, their behaviour is not solely determined by those contexts (Giddens 2001). Thus, in this chapter the term 'determinants' is used synonymously with 'factors.' Determinants and factors can describe respondents' individual characteristics as well as features of the social and physical surroundings. In this chapter's data analyses, factors and determinants are replaced by the term 'variables.'

The *Reasoned Action (RA) Theory*, developed by Fishbein and Ajzen (1975), is a suitable starting point for discussing other determinants of behaviour. They argue that most behaviour of interest to social scientists is voluntary. Thus, behaviour can be predicted by analysing intentions. In RA Theory, a behavioural intention is the weighted sum of an individual determinant of behaviour (that is, the individual attitude towards performing the behaviour under study) and a social component (that is, the subjective norm). Thus, the theory specifies the relationships between attitudes, social norms, intentions, and behaviour.

---

5   Quoted from Pieters (1988, 172).

However, some scholars argue that most environmentally sensitive behaviour is not completely voluntarily (Pieters 1988; Stern and Oskamp 1987; Thøgersen 1999). They assert that it is therefore incorrect to assume that intention is the sole determinant of behaviour. At the other extreme, however, one finds the economists Frey and Foppa (1986). They claim that human behaviour is primarily determined by constraints that limit the set of possible actions. Thus, no or very limited choice is left to the individual. A growing number of scholars, however, seem most comfortable in the middle ground between these two extremes (Ölander and Thøgersen 1995). They assert that most behaviour contains volitional elements to a greater or lesser extent.

During the 1980s, several attempts were made to develop an attitude model covering behaviour that is not completely voluntary. According to Thøgersen (1999), the most successful attempt was Ajzen's *Theory of Planned Behaviour*. 'Perceived behaviour control' was introduced into the theoretical model, in order to account for the determinants that are not completely under volitional control. However, there can be a world of difference between perceived and actual control. Thøgersen (ibid.) emphasises that a theory that aims at explaining or predicting behaviour must include a component that reflects opportunities and restrictions as they *actually* are, not only as they are perceived by the individual. A person's actual control regarding certain behaviour may be constrained by both individual abilities and his surroundings. Thøgersen (ibid.), due to substantially different practical implications of these two types of constraints, distinguishes between personal abilities and opportunities to perform the behaviour. The MAOB model (Motivation-Ability-Opportunity-Behaviour), developed by Ölander and Thøgersen (1995), reflects Thøgersen's view.

This chapter pays special attention to the influence of motivational factors and opportunity and ability determinants on household consumption. Motivational factors include attitudes, personal norms and social norms. Opportunity and ability determinants consist of two groups of factors: (i) land use characteristics (the design of the house and location of the residential area), and (ii) socioeconomic and sociodemographic conditions. As demonstrated in chapter 7, a number of studies have shown that two groups of factor (determinants), the design and location of a dwelling, and the socioeconomic and sociodemographic characteristics of the people that live in it, influence household consumption. Both groups are included in the empirical investigations and are described in detail in the section on methodology. Habit is not included as a specific factor in the empirical investigations, but the importance of habit is discussed at the end of the second section.

Figure 6.1 illustrates hypothetically causal relations between motivational factors, opportunities, abilities, and behaviour, and household energy consumption.

A Quantitative Study of 'Green' Attitudes: The SusHomes Project

Methodology

The sampling of respondents was limited to eight residential areas within the Greater Oslo Region. In contrast to analyses based on surveys of entire cities and whole metropolitan regions, this approach allows for better control of key contextual factors, such as local density, access to public transport, and sociodemographic characteristics. This approach also enables a more detailed discussion of the possible effects of attitudes on household consumption when different contexts are considered. The eight areas include areas that consist of single-family houses on the urban fringe and areas that are characterised by multifamily housing in the city centre.

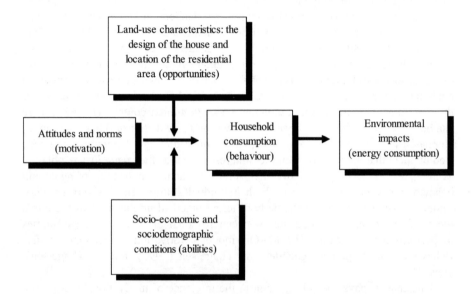

Figure 6.1   Causal relations between motivational factors, opportunities, abilities, and household consumption and energy consumption

Questionnaires were sent during March and April 2003, to 2,500 randomly selected individuals above the age of 17. An average of 120 respondents per area answered the questionnaires, a response rate of 40 per cent. The questions concerned the individual's and the household's consumption of energy and transport, as well as family structure, income and housing facilities.

Both bivariate correlation analyses and multiple regression analyses were applied. However, bivariate correlation analysis yields a number which gives an immediate picture of how closely two variables correlate. Even though a correlation might establish that two variables actually move together, no claim can be made that this necessarily indicates cause and effect (Wonnacott and Wonnacott 1990). Furthermore, the correlation might be spurious. To establish whether there is a cause-and-effect relationship between variables, the effects of confounding variables (other determinants) must be allowed for. This is done by multiple regression analyses.

Thus, in this study, the bivariate correlation analyses deal with the 'is' questions, while multiple regression analyses deal with the 'when' questions. When dealing with the 'how' questions, a synthesis of the empirical analyses and other knowledge on this field are applied.

The Dependent Variables

Household consumption   Household consumption includes consumption of energy for housing, everyday travel and long-distance leisure-time travel by plane and car. All data are taken from the questionnaire. Energy for heating and operating the house includes electricity, paraffin, fuel oil, wood, and energy sources used in remote heating systems. The questionnaire asked respondents to make a best estimate of their yearly energy consumption. Furthermore, respondents were asked to estimate the distance travelled daily by car, bus, tram and train in the preceding week (Monday to Sunday) for all reasons except business – work, shopping, school, and leisure. Their estimates were used to measure everyday travel. Only the responses of those respondents who reported their travels as being representative of their travels during a typical week in their lives are included in the analyses. Finally, the questionnaire asked respondents to state the number of long-distance leisure-time trips by plane and car they took during the previous 12 months to different destination categories.[6] An average travel distance, that is the distance between Oslo Airport and the most visited destination within each destination category, is estimated for each destination category.

Environmental impacts   All household consumption data are converted into appropriate units of measure and stated as yearly energy consumption per household member. Energy consumption correlates with a large number of environmental issues – for example, emissions of greenhouse gases, substances that cause health problems and damage to buildings, and emissions that cause acidification – and is therefore a good indicator of environmental impacts. Dividing the household's total annual energy consumption by the number of household members gives the annual energy consumption per household member for heating and operating the house. Energy consumed weekly for everyday travel is calculated by multiplying the typical distance travelled weekly for private purposes, by all modes of transport (car, bus, tram, and train), by a corresponding specific energy coefficient.[7] Annual energy consumption for everyday travel is calculated by multiplying energy consumed weekly by 47 weeks.[8] Annual energy consumption for long-distance leisure-time travel by car and plane is calculated by multiplying the kilometres travelled by each mode annually, by a corresponding specific energy coefficient. Separate energy coefficients have been used for travel by car, domestic travel by plane, and international travel by plane, respectively.[9]

---

6   Long-distance leisure-time travel by car is defined as travel of more than 100 km one way. Destination categories for travel by car are: Three regions of Norway, the Nordic Countries, Northern Europe, and Southern Europe. Destination categories for travel by plane are: Three regions of Norway, the Nordic Countries, Europe and countries outside Europe.

7   Different coefficients are used for travel undertaken Monday to Friday and on the weekend, respectively. All coefficients used are found in Holden and Norland (2004).

8   Excluding five weeks for holiday each year.

9   Coefficients used are found in Holden and Norland (2004).

The Independent Variables

Land use characteristics   Data regarding land use characteristics is divided into two groups. Data in the first group is related to physical-structural characteristics of the house, including type of housing,[10] size, age, and access to a private garden. Data are taken from the questionnaire. The second group of data is related to physical-structural characteristics of the residential areas, including location (distance from the house to the city centre and nearest sub-centre), housing density (number of houses per decare (1000 square meters)), local land mix (the percentage of developed area that is used for housing within a residential area). Data are taken from national and local data sources and maps.

Socioeconomic and sociodemographic factors of the household   Variables in this group include the respondent's sex, age, education, occupation, and income as well as the household's income, car ownership, and access to a private holiday house. Data are taken from the questionnaire.

Attitudes   Attitudes are measured at different levels which reflect whether an attitude is directed towards a higher level of generality (household consumption as a behaviour category) or whether it is directed towards specific acts within a category (for example, everyday travel). At the same time, attitude levels reflect to what extent social and personal norms are internalised by an individual. Four attitude levels are identified.

At the highest level of generality of attitudes and internalisation of social and personal norms, membership in NEHG has been used as a measurement of attitude.[11] Since its launch in October 1991, the NEHG has developed into the major green consumer's network in Norway. Over 100,000 people have joined the movement and committed themselves to changing their everyday behaviour and consumption habits. The NEHG's activities aim to achieve important environmental goals, including reduced use of natural resources, reduced use of environmentally harmful substances, reduced energy consumption and reduced production of waste. To achieve these goals, the NEHG focuses on two major types of change: (i) a general reduction in the level of consumption and (ii) changes in consumption patterns towards more environmentally friendly alternatives, regarding both products and services. Thus, members of the NEHG are assumed to have highly positive attitudes towards environmental issues both in general and related to specific consumption practices. They are, through their commitment to the organisation's goals, assumed to have internalised the social norms of both the organisation and the other members. Furthermore, personal norms related to a moral obligation to act in an environmentally

---

10 Types of housing include: single-family house, row house and multifamily house.

11 The NEHG approaches environmental activism along the lines of a military home guard in the sense that members were thought of as 'environmental soldiers' who did their national service within their local communities. They were 'armed' (through their environmental awareness and environmentally friendly behaviour) to defend the environment against damage.

responsible way are held to be important. The sample includes 133 responses by NEHG members who are spread throughout the eight residential areas.

At the second attitude level respondents were asked whether they were registered members in an environmental organisation other than the NEHG. In this study, it is assumed that members of an environmental organisation other than the NEHG also have highly positive attitudes towards environmental issues both in general and related to specific consumption practices. Moreover, personal norms related to a moral obligation to act in an environmentally responsible way are held to be important. However, they are assumed *not* to have internalised the social norms of both the organisation and the other members to the same extent as members of the NEHG have.

The third and fourth attitude levels are analysed using a Likert Scale whereby attitudes are measured according to whether a respondent expresses agreement or disagreement with statements (scale items) on household consumption. A weakness of the Likert Scale approach, however, is that the statements could be difficult to characterize as solely positive or negative in relation to the overall attitude under consideration (Hellevik 1991). In our case the given values are based on our own evaluations. Therefore the correlations based on the index have to be interpreted with some caution. Despite this, we find the index useful due to its simple and illustrative presentation of the respondents' attitudes. To measure correlation between attitudes and behaviour, two attitude measurements were established. Six statements that relate to different aspects of household consumption are used to measure *general* attitudes. Only statements that specifically concern the household consumption category in question are included when measuring *specific* attitudes. This approach makes it possible to investigate the relationship between household consumption and both general and specific attitudes.

Throughout this chapter, respondents who are members of the NEHG or other environmental organisation are called 'green' household members. Also, individuals with a high score on the index-based attitudes are called 'green,' whereas non-members and individuals with a low score on the index-based attitudes are called 'ordinary' people.

Is There a Relationship Between Attitudes and Household Consumption?

Figure 6.2 shows how household consumption varies between green and ordinary respondents. Among the four groups, the difference in average yearly energy consumption per household member is not large. For example, the high-energy group consumes only five per cent more energy than does the low-energy group. Members of an environmental organisation (NEHG or other) have *higher* energy consumption than non-members. This is certainly surprising, given the NEHG's commitment to the goal of 'a general reduction in the level of consumption.'

Figure 6.2 does not show the measurement of the two index-based attitude levels. Nor does it show whether the differences indicated in the figure are statistically significant. Therefore, bivariate correlation analyses have been carried out to investigate the relation between household consumption and the four attitude levels. The bivariate analyses will further elaborate on the question: *Is* there a relationship between attitudes (measured at various levels) and household consumption? The results are shown in table 6.1.

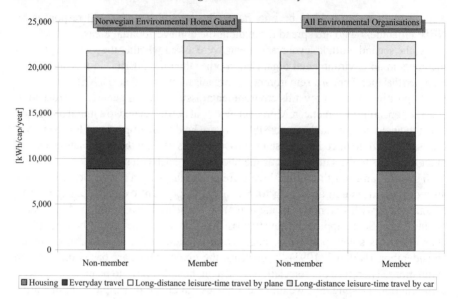

Figure 6.2   Annual per capita energy consumption of members versus non-members of the Norwegian Environmental Home Guard, and of members versus non-members of all environmental organisations (N=445)

Three conclusions can be made from the bivariate analyses in table 6.1. First, there are only small differences between the total household consumption of green individuals and that of ordinary individuals. To the extent that there are differences, they do not favour the green individuals. Namely, the results confirm that green individuals use more energy than ordinary ones. Second, a high score in the measurement of an index-based attitude is a better indicator than membership in an environmental organisation that one consumes little energy. Third, although green individuals are more environmentally responsible in their everyday lives than ordinary ones, they nevertheless cast aside their environmental concerns when travelling for leisure.

However, as already emphasized, the bivariate correlation analyses yield a number that gives an immediate picture of how closely two variables move together. To further investigate the relationship between attitudes, other determinants and household consumption, multiple regressions are needed.

When is There a Relationship between Attitudes and Household Consumption?

The multiple regression analyses reveal the extent to which the identified correlations between attitudes and consumption are spurious. Four regressions have been run for each household consumption category to measure the influence of each of the four attitude levels. Annual energy consumption per household member is the dependent variable. In this chapter, 'significant' refers to 'statistically significant at the 5 per cent significance level.' The analyses show that a number of other determinants

Table 6.1 **Pearson's correlation coefficients: energy consumption and attitude levels**

Attitude level	Energy consumption (i)				
	Housing	Everyday travel	Leisure travel by plane	Leisure travel by car	Household consumption
	N=528-546	N=679-702	N=815-850	N=777-810	N=413-422
The NEHG (ii)	-,010	-,033	,069*	,037	,057
Env. org. (iii)	,000	-,078*	,090**	,017	,026
General attitude (iv)	-,106*	-,164**	,039	-,038	-,025
Specific attitude (v)	-,015	-,287**	-,005	-,009	-

*/**correlation is significant at the 0.05 / 0.01 level (2-tailed). Energy consumption levels that exceed extreme values (SPSS 1998, 41) are omitted from the analyses.
(i) kWh/ household member/year.
(ii) NEHG = Norwegian Environmental Home Guard. Non-member of NEHG=0; Member of NEHG = 1.
(iii) Non-member of an Environmental Organisation = 0; Member of an Environmental Organisation =1.
(iv) General attitude towards household consumption: Ranges from very negative attitude (low score) to very positive attitude (high score).
(v) Specific attitude towards the specific consumption category in question: Ranges from very negative attitude (low score) to very positive attitude (high score).

have significant effect on household consumption. The significance levels of land-use characteristics, and of socioeconomic and sociodemographic conditions, can be found in Holden and Norland (2004).

The answer to the 'when' question seems to be 'never'. Significant relationships between attitudes and consumption were few. Even so, some interesting relationships between attitudes and consumption do appear.

First, specific attitudes directed towards specific acts are by far the best predictors of sustainable household consumption. The literature gives theoretical grounds for believing that specific attitudes are negatively correlated to the specific consumption in question (Moisander and Uusitalo 1994; Thøgersen 1999). The negative regression coefficient and the (admittedly weaker than one would like) statistical evidence confirm this belief. General attitudes are *not*, as suggested in the literature, negatively correlated to specific household consumption. Thus, the analyses confirm that it is a mistake to use general attitudes to explain or predict specific acts.

Second, membership in either NEHG or other environmental organisations does not seem to be a good predictor of sustainable household consumption. Rather, our material suggests the opposite; that is, members of environmental organisations have higher total household consumption and specific consumption (except energy for housing) than non-members. The relationship between ones membership in an environmental organisation and ones energy consumption for travel by plane is particularly strong. Thus, the multivariate regression analyses give further support to the idea that supposedly green individuals cast aside their green concerns when travelling for leisure. At least this seems to be the case when they are travelling by plane.

Third, the two points above imply that index-based attitudes are better predictors of sustainable consumption than membership in an environmental organisation. This is particularly the case when the attitude is directed towards a specific act. In other words, in trying to change people's consumption patterns it would be more effective to increase the greenness of their attitudes towards specific consumption than it would be to try to change their consumption patterns by encouraging them to join an environmental organisation.

Fourth, total household energy consumption is not significantly affected by attitudes. However, it should be noted that the regression coefficients are positive, which implies that green households have the highest total energy consumption.

The Relationship between 'Green' Attitudes and Sustainable Household Consumption

So far the 'is' and 'when' questions have been answered. Based on these answers I present three theses in chapter 8 (theses 8–10) that suggest how attitudes can guide sustainable household consumption in general and sustainable mobility in particular. The three theses – concerned with the importance of specific attitudes, the difference between everyday and leisure-time travel and the ambiguous role of membership in environmental organisations – are based on the results from figure 6.2, table 6.1 and the multivariate regression analyses. In addition to the three theses, three variables and processes are presented here that moderate the relationship between attitude and behaviour – and thus possibly increase consistency between attitudes and sustainable household consumption.

Habit   Discrepancies between what individuals intend to do and what they actually do may be attributable to 'the force of habit' (Fishbein and Ajzen 1975, 371). Heating the house, taking a shower, using electrical appliances, and driving to and from work are repeated actions. According to Ronis et al. (1989), most repeated actions are in fact habitual. Thus, to promote sustainable household consumption, understanding habits is important.[12] Repeated behaviour is characterized by at least two stages:

---

12 However, in previous research on the attitude-behaviour relationship, habit has been treated differently. In the original Reasoned Action Theory, it is argued that most behaviour is voluntary, and therefore can be predicted from intention. Thus, neither habit nor prior behaviour is included in the theoretical model (Fishbein and Ajzen 1975). Others have argued that habits do indeed have an important role to play in explaining a particular behaviour. Habits have been conceptualised as: (i) independent (other) determinants of behaviour (Ronis et al.

initiation and persistence (ibid.). The factors that determine persistence may be different from those that determine the initiation of the behaviour. Thus, reasons for performing repeated behaviour are likely to differ from and at the same time be more complex than reasons for performing non-repeated behaviour. According to Ronis et al. (ibid.), the repetition of behaviour is often determined by habits rather than attitudes and beliefs. On the other hand, attitudes and beliefs are important in the initiation of such behaviour. Thus, unsustainable household consumption patterns may be largely determined by habits rather than by attitudinal variables. Furthermore, even though attitudes are important when initiating a habit, attitudes and behaviour can easily diverge after the behaviour becomes habitual (ibid.). When behaviour becomes habitual, it is relatively autonomous and therefore, independent of attitudes and beliefs. Thus, attitude change can occur without a corresponding change in behaviour, leading to attitude-behaviour inconsistency. If a person has developed a car-dependent habit prior to experiencing a new and more positive attitude towards environmental issues, his new attitude might not influence his travel habit.

Attempts to eliminate bad (and unsustainable) habits often combine two approaches (ibid.). The indirect approach involves changing one's lifestyle to avoid situations associated with the habitual behaviour. A person who moves into a flat near a public transport node in a densely developed area, and at the same time sells his car, has chosen an effective indirect strategy for reducing energy consumption for housing and transport. This approach is not always enough, however, so it is also necessary for the individual to take the direct approach, that is, to suppress the behaviour in the contexts strongly associated with it. A number of studies have shown that energy consumption in similar types of housing can vary by a factor of up to five (Næss 1997).

Attitude accessibility, direct experience and attitude strength   Attitude accessibility (Pieters 1988), direct experience (Ajzen 1996) and attitude strength (Petty and Krosnick 1995) are three variables that moderate the relationship between attitudes and behaviour. Furthermore, these three variables interact and therefore influence each other. Direct experience makes attitudes stronger and consequently makes them more accessible when an act is performed (ibid.). This process, that is the interaction between moderating variables, leads to greater attitude-behaviour consistency.

An example from empirical investigations of everyday travel patterns shows how this process works. People living in densely developed areas have more direct experiences, *and* more intense ones, in two ways: First, they are exposed to higher pollution levels due to heavy traffic which generates high emissions. This gives them a direct experience with environmental issues. In less densely developed areas, people are not exposed to this problem to the same extent. Furthermore, in densely developed areas, people have more direct experiences with the use of sustainable modes of transport. Short distances between home, work and private and public services give people increased opportunities to walk or cycle. At the same time they have better access to the public transport system. Thus, the direct experiences of

---

1989), (ii) variables moderating the relationship between intention and behaviour (Bagozzi 1982), and (iii) contributing in both these respects (Triandis 1977).

traffic pollution and better access to sustainable modes of transport lead to increased attitude strength (Holden and Norland 2004) and possibly better attitude accessibility. Finally, this process results in higher attitude-behaviour consistency.

Facilitation   The arguments so far rest on the assumption that actions are completely voluntary. However, actions are certainly not completely voluntary. Based on the findings of a large research programme about environmentally friendly behaviour in Denmark, Thøgersen (1999) demonstrates the importance of facilitation when attitudinal factors have been controlled for. Facilitation is important for a number of environmentally sensitive behaviours, including recycling, choosing packaging and buying organic food. Thus, Thøgersen concludes that 'there is more point to investing scarce campaign resources in reducing barriers that restrict peoples' opportunities or abilities to follow their attitudes' than in improving the attitudes' (ibid., 41).

The empirical evidence in this study shows that facilitation is also important for household consumption. Facilitation through the physical planning system, by controlling land use, contributes to lower energy consumption for housing and everyday transport. The key is densification. Thus, multifamily houses in densely developed residential areas are favourable in this respect. Proximity to a city centre or large sub-centre with good access to private and public services must be encouraged. A well-developed public transport system completes the picture. However, there remains a problem regarding leisure travel. How can one facilitate for sustainable leisure travel? Physical planning does not seem to be the answer. Empirical evidence suggests that densification might have the opposite effect on leisure travel to that which it has on everyday travel (Holden and Norland 2005). Furthermore, positive attitudes towards environmental issues do not seem to affect people's energy consumption for leisure travel. Household income, on the other hand, influences the amount of people's leisure travel most (ibid.). Thus, facilitating sustainable leisure travel must include the application of economic measures.

A Qualitative Study of Consumption Mechanisms: One Plain and Two Purl

The main conclusion from the quantitative analyses is that an ambiguous relation exists between positive environmental attitudes and energy consumption for transport; the green respondents hardly behave in a more environmentally friendly way than other people. However, these analyses do not explain the reason for this disappointing result. In fact, the statistical analyses do not provide an understanding or explanation of the underlying mechanisms that lead to this pattern, or perhaps lack of pattern. Why do the green respondents travel by plane more than other people? Why are they apparently unable to do much to limit everyday energy consumption for transport? It should be mentioned, however, that the green respondents seem to have some success in achieving an environmentally friendly level of consumption in some other areas. To understand this and find credible explanations, it is necessary to turn away from the questionnaires and talk to people directly.

I will therefore turn my attention to a series of in-depth interviews conducted in 1999 with households in Greater Oslo and Førde (Holden 2001). The objective was to find explanations by developing an understanding of what was happening in individual households. The questions discussed in this section are as follow: Which are the consumption categories where we find that positive environmental attitudes are to a large degree translated into environmentally friendly behaviour? Which are the consumption categories where we find that positive environmental attitudes are only to a limited degree translated into environmentally friendly behaviour? Which mechanisms can be used to explain the relationship or lack of relationship between attitudes and behaviour?

On the Track of Mechanisms and the Conditions That Trigger Them

According to the Norwegian sociologist Willy Martinussen (1999), it has become more and more common to make sociological explanations by finding the mechanisms that result in particular events or create and maintain a social pattern. In this chapter I consider the actions that make up household consumption as a process – a complex process that takes place in the form of negotiations between the members of the household within the framework of their everyday lives. The process includes several mechanisms, which I shall identify here.

In his book, *Nuts and Bolts for the Social Sciences*, Jon Elster (1989) discusses the concept of mechanisms in detail and argues that it is key to explaining complex social phenomena. To explain an event (e_2), which may be either a physical or a mental action, it is necessary to explain why it took place. This is generally done by finding an earlier event (e_1) that caused the event that is to be explained, and a causal mechanism (m) that links the two events. Thus, it is not sufficient to find a statistical correlation between two events such as a positive environmental attitude and a lack of environmentally friendly behaviour. A statistical correlation is not an explanation, regardless of how many control variables are included in the analysis. There must also be a mechanism linking the two events.

Elster gives an example of this. A person has changed his mind about a job he previously considered to be very attractive (e_1), but has now lost interest in (e_2). The explanation for this has two elements. Firstly, before changing his opinion, the person learned that he was not in the running for the job. The second element of the explanation requires identification of the mechanism that caused the person to change his mind. In this case, it is a mechanism called cognitive dissonance, which persuades us to give up ambitions that appear to be impossible to achieve. In the case discussed here, it is necessary to find mechanisms that link positive environmental attitudes (e_1) and consumption behaviour (e_2).

Moreover, Elster points out that several mechanisms exist at the same time in each of us, and that it is impossible to know in advance when a particular mechanism will operate. 'As far as I know, we have no theories that tell us when one or the other of these mechanisms will operate. When one of them does operate, we recognize it immediately, and so we can explain the behaviour it generates. But we cannot reliably predict when it will operate' (ibid., 9). This is also a crucial point according to Andrew Sayer in *Method in Social Science* (Sayer 1992). Like Elster, Sayer states that finding an explanation does not mean finding statistical correlations between two events, but rather means describing the mechanisms that link them. He agrees that it is not possible to say when a particular mechanism will be activated. The specific conditions pertaining determine whether this will happen. 'Whether a causal power or liability [Sayer uses the three terms "causal power," "liability" and "mechanism" as synonyms] is actually activated or suffered on any occasion depends on conditions whose presence and configuration are contingent' (ibid., 107).

Thus, it is of crucial importance to identify both the relevant mechanisms and the conditions that activate each of them when attempting to explain the complex and somewhat unclear relationship between positive environmental attitudes (which in principle involve an intention to act in an environmentally friendly way) and actual consumption.

In my efforts to reveal the mechanisms and the conditions under which they operate, I have taken inspiration from grounded theory. This method was originally developed by the two sociologists Barney Glaser and Anshelm Strauss (1967) and is generally very influential in qualitative research. Briefly, the method involves approaching the observations, the empirical material, as much as possible without preconceived ideas, using concepts to categorise the data and finally, finding relationships between the categories and the concepts. In this study, categories and concepts need to be linked to mechanisms and conditions, respectively. In the final analysis, the aim of grounded theory is to develop a theory about a phenomenon. However, it is not necessary to set high ambitions – the method is also useful for systematising and analysing a large body of written material. I realise, of course, that it is almost impossible to look at data without having any preconceived ideas. We all carry the baggage of our ideas around with us, as the Danish writer Carsten Jensen (1998) puts it. Nevertheless, I have tried to travel as lightly as possible when carrying out my analyses. They provide support for the claim that there are at least three mechanisms that influence whether households are able to behave in an environmentally friendly way: a desire to project an environmentally friendly image, a sense of powerlessness, and a desire to indulge oneself (Holden 2001).

A Desire to Project an Environmentally Friendly Image: 'Who do I want to be?'

In the modern world, it is often argued that people are no longer searching for their identity, but rather deciding who they want to be. This is often connected with the general trend towards individualisation that is sweeping across the whole (Western) world. Individualisation and opportunities for people to shape their own lives are often linked to the lifestyle concept; attitudes are an important element of a lifestyle, which is why lifestyle is relevant to the questions discussed in this chapter. Several authors argue that lifestyle forms a more important basis for who we want to be and our consumption patterns than do the more frequently invoked concepts of tradition, social class and Bourdieu's 'habitus.' The Danish sociologist Bente Halkier (1999) writes that lifestyle, more than any other concept, has replaced more traditional sociological concepts. Similarly, the Norwegian social anthropologist Marianne Gullestad (1989) states that individuals no longer merely follow social traditions and cultural rules; rather they are more concerned with making individual lifestyle choices.

Anthony Giddens (1991) uses the term 'life politics.' Giddens argues that 'in modern social life, the notion of lifestyle takes on a particular significance' and that lifestyle choices are becoming more and more important to the development of self-identity and in people's everyday activities. According to Giddens, life politics is a politics of lifestyle. It is a politics for realisation of the self that gives individuals the opportunity to shape their own lives, to break away from tradition and to avoid a feeling of powerlessness. Giddens believes that life politics is necessary to enable people to answer the question 'How should I live?'

But what do my informants have to say about this? Do they choose their own lives? Are they aware of what kind of lifestyle they have, and are their lifestyle choices deliberate? And not least, are lifestyle and attitude important for their consumption behaviour? For the moment, I would just like to say that the answer to these questions is, 'Yes.' There is a mechanism at work in my informants that can trigger environmentally friendly behaviour and that influences certain aspects of their consumption behaviour.

A Sense of Powerlessness: 'It won't work anyway.'

Many of my informants defended their environmentally unfriendly behaviour by saying that they had no choice. Circumstances made certain types of behaviour almost inevitable. A large proportion of the respondents expressed a sense of powerlessness. They felt that they could not behave in the way that they ought to, as environmentally responsible people. There may be various underlying reasons for a sense of powerlessness, and they may be complex. However, there were two areas where it was particularly strong. The first and easiest to identify was transport, and particularly transport by car. And this does not mean only travel to work, as is often thought. The sense of powerlessness is just as strong when it comes to short everyday leisure trips. In the second, it is more difficult to define and is ascribed to the inherent pressure to consume which is characteristic of the consumer society.

The first example of powerlessness can be explained by the concept used by the Norwegian sociologist Dag Østerberg (1990), which can be expressed as powerlessness transmitted by people's material environment. Østerberg points out that all human activity – which he calls a 'project' – takes place in an environment. This environment – which he calls the 'situation' – limits what it is possible to do. Østerberg generally uses the terms 'environment', and 'situation', to mean physical structures (although a person's abilities, preferences and skills also help to determine the limits to what a person can do). The physical surroundings are the framework for all human 'projects.' Gullestad (1989) stresses the idea of 'everyday powerlessness,' meaning situations where there is a collision between social structures, including physical structures, and people's everyday lives.

The second form of powerlessness can be explained by sociologist Zygmunt Bauman's description of the consumer society (Bauman 2000) which, Bauman argues, needs to engage its members as consumers. Consumption, playing the role of a good consumer, is the norm. Bauman claims that the way today's society shapes its members is primarily dictated by their duty to play their roles as consumers.

Østerberg, Gullestad and Bauman all use the concept of powerlessness to describe more than just a feeling of being forced into driving a car or consuming more goods. There are underlying mechanisms or social processes that trigger the feeling of being trapped in a particular pattern of behaviour.

A Desire to Indulge Oneself: 'I'm not a fanatic, after all.'

Finally, everyone has a domain where they relax, where they do not submit to their own convictions and attitudes. Furthermore, they do not feel powerless in this domain. Thus, they do not feel that they *have to* do something (in order to project a particular image) or that they have no other choice (a sense of powerlessness). Rather, when the act in this domain they do so because they *want* to.

The green respondents are not at all proud of this type of behaviour. There is no question of projecting an image, rather the reverse. They do not wish to be identified with this type of consumption, and would rather it remain a well-kept secret. Every time this type of behaviour was mentioned in interviews, the 'confessions' were followed by slightly embarrassed laughter. Or they were uttered as quietly as possible. Often, people spoke so indistinctly that I could not hear what they said on the tapes. Moreover, they often used phrases like 'a little bit of pleasure,' 'a bit of luxury now and then,' and, 'it is something I really wanted to do.' Clearly, they were neither projecting an image nor expressing a sense of powerlessness. Rather, they were confessing to deliberately taking more than they felt was their due.

Is this a form of hedonism? Is it a necessary counterweight to the strict norms involved in projecting a green image and to the depressing sense of powerlessness? In *The Unmanageable Consumer*, Yiannis Gabriel and Tim Lang (1995) argue that hedonism is one aspect of modern consumption. A hedonist continually seeks pleasure. Gabriel and Lang refer to Colin Campbell (1987), who distinguished between traditional and modern hedonism: 'Traditional hedonism is a hedonism of a multitude of pleasures, a hedonism of sensations attached to the senses – taste, smell, touch, sight and hearing. Modern hedonism, on the other hand, seeks pleasure not in sensation but in the emotion accompanying all kinds of experiences.'[13] This gives a basis for discussing two main categories of hedonism which can be considered as examples of unrestrained consumption. The first category includes food, clothes and not least, luxurious goods for the home. The second category is holiday travel. My respondents were perfectly aware of how politically incorrect it was to fly to the tropics or drive all the way through Germany. Their actions exemplified both the traditional and modern forms of hedonism.

Hero, Victim and Villain: Three Theses on Green Attitudes and Behaviour

It appears that all three mechanisms described above are to some extent hard-wired into all of us. A person is not a 'hero' (projecting an environmentally friendly image), a 'victim' (with a sense of powerlessness) *or* a 'villain' (indulging himself). On the contrary, the same person plays all three roles. All three mechanisms are at work

---

13 Quoted from Gabriel and Lang (1995).

in all of us, but in different areas. In my view, this is a very important point, and is highly pertinent to the question of how far we can hope to influence consumers. It appears that on the whole, the three mechanisms operate in different areas of private consumption. They affect decisions concerning environmentally friendly behaviour relating to different categories of consumption.

Everyday transport and energy consumption in the home are forms of 'invisible consumption'. The dominant mechanism is the sense of powerlessness. People have to run their homes and get to and from work, shops and regular leisure activities. I have deliberately linked everyday leisure activities to this mechanism. We are not as free as we might think during our everyday leisure activities.

In contrast to invisible consumption, the category 'other consumption' is highly visible. In fact, it is supposed to be visible because it is used to project a person's image as a green consumer. This category has to do with the kind of clothes people wear, the kind of food they eat, and so on.[14]

The third mechanism, in particular, influences long-distance leisure-time travel. Many respondents indicated that in some situations, they had a desire to indulge themselves, to free themselves from the constraints involved in environmentally friendly behaviour. An alternative or supplementary explanation for the high level of travel activity among the green respondents could be as follows: People with a high level of environmental awareness are also concerned about global environmental issues, because environmental and development problems are increasingly global in character, and are linked to conditions in developing countries. Environmental publications frequently include articles on problems and conflicts in distant parts of the world. People, including greens, who are aware of these issues may well wish to see and experience such places for themselves. However, I cannot claim to have found any evidence for this explanation in the interviews.

Thus, my analyses suggest that the sense of powerlessness is related to running a home and everyday use of transport, and that the desire to indulge oneself dominates during leisure hours when, consequently, 'other consumption' becomes the primary way one projects an environmentally friendly image. My analysis of the interviews indicates that these are the *typical* relationships. This is not an average result based on statistical calculations, but rather a (theoretical) system that I have constructed – a consumer system in which attitudes, mechanisms and consumption categories are linked together. The mechanisms in this system are abstractions, each representing one aspect of the consumer.

My qualitative study gives a basis for constructing the following three theses that form central elements of the system:[15]

---

14 Food is a rather more complicated category of consumption than I have been able to indicate here. What we eat is obviously not only an expression of the image we would like to project. We have a genuine need to eat. However, my starting point here is the mechanisms that affect whether we make 'green' choices – in this case, whether we make environmentally friendly choices when buying food; I do not discuss, however, which types of food are environmentally friendly. In this context, projecting an environmentally friendly image is important.

15 Another very interesting characteristic of these mechanisms is that they appear to be linked. Each influences the strength of the others (Holden 2001). In my view, we need to learn more about this.

- The sense of powerlessness means that positive attitudes to conservation and environmental issues are not to any great extent translated into low energy consumption in the home or for everyday transport.
- The desire to indulge oneself means that positive attitudes to conservation and environmental issues are not to any great extent translated into low energy consumption for long-distance leisure-time travel.
- The desire to project an environmentally friendly image does not have much influence in areas such as energy consumption in the home, everyday transport and leisure travel. It does appear to help in translating positive environmental attitudes into environmentally friendly consumption in some other areas, but these have little or no impact on the environment.

The empirical basis for these theses is derived from both the quantitative and the qualitative studies. In the quantitative analyses, I found few encouraging relations between people's attitudes and their behaviour relating to energy consumption in the home, everyday transport and leisure-time travel. I believe that two of the three mechanisms I have identified through the qualitative interview-based study – that is the sense of powerlessness and the desire to indulge oneself – provide possible explanations for this discouraging relations. The qualitative study suggests that, in areas of consumption other than energy consumption in the home and transport, there is a link between attitudes and behaviour, and that this results from a third mechanism, the desire to project an environmentally friendly image. However, I had no opportunity to supplement the empirical material with quantitative data on 'other consumption', and therefore could not establish this link.

Summary

This chapter assesses the role of green attitudes in achieving sustainable household consumption in general and sustainable mobility in particular. In addition to an introduction to attitude theory, the results from one quantitative and one qualitative study are presented. The quantitative study shows that although significant relationships between attitudes and consumption were few, some interesting relationships between attitudes and consumption nevertheless did appear. First, specific attitudes directed towards specific acts are by far the best predictors of sustainable household consumption. Thus the study suggests that it is a mistake to use general attitudes to explain or predict specific acts. Second, membership in either NEHG or other environmental organisations does not seem to be a good predictor of sustainable household consumption. Rather, our material suggests the opposite. Third, the two points above imply that index-based attitudes are better predictors of sustainable household consumption than is membership in an environmental organisation. This is particularly the case when the attitude is directed towards a specific act. In other words, in trying to change people's consumption patterns it would be more effective to increase the greenness of their attitudes towards specific consumption than it would be to try to change their consumption patterns by encouraging them to join an environmental organisation. Fourth, total household energy consumption is not significantly affected by attitudes.

The qualitative study reveals three mechanisms that explain the relationship or lack of relationship between green attitudes and behaviour. Three theses form central elements in this explanation. First, the sense of powerlessness means that positive attitudes towards conservation and environmental issues are not to any great extent translated into low energy consumption in the home or for everyday transport. Second, the desire to indulge oneself means that positive attitudes towards conservation and environmental issues are not to any great extent translated into low energy consumption for long-distance leisure-time travel. Third, the desire to project an environmentally friendly image does not have much influence in areas such as energy consumption in the home, everyday transport and leisure travel. It does appear to help in translating positive environmental attitudes into environmentally friendly consumption in some other areas, but these have little or no impact on the environment.

Chapter 7

The Role of Land-Use Planning

We shape our dwellings and afterwards our dwellings shape us. (Winston Churchill)

This chapter assesses the role of public land-use planning in achieving sustainable mobility. Under examination is the hypothesis that suggests land-use structures must change to increase accessibility for low-mobility groups and moreover to reduce energy consumption for passenger transport.

The study of this hypothesis raises three questions: Does planning matter?[1], What is sustainable urban form? and How can sustainable urban form be achieved? The first two questions relate to the planning *product*, that is, the outcome of planning, whereas the third question relates to the planning *process*, that is, how planning is carried out. This chapter mainly concerns the planning product.

Whether planning matters is a fundamental question. Does the result of land-use planning, for example the way we locate and design our residential areas, influence people's travel behaviour? Within planning research it is commonly assumed that it does. It is believed that land-use planning renders possible more sustainable consumption patterns in general and sustainable mobility in particular. This view has received increased attention since 1987 when 'the sustainable development imperative [...] revived a forgotten, or discredited idea: that planning ought to be done, or can be done, on a big scale' (Breheny 1996, 13). According to Breheny (ibid.) the use of the planning system seems to be a common solution for achieving major environmental improvements, and particularly for achieving sustainable development.

However, there are, and have been for decades, critical voices concerning the role of planning in these matters. According to Boarnet and Crane (2001), this whole issue must be treated as a *hypothesis* rather than a fact, and therefore, the relationship between travel patterns and the built environment should be regarded as a subject for research. This chapter presents such research and gives empirical evidence to support the idea that planning in fact does influence travel behaviour.

Also, scholars disagree about which urban form is sustainable. There are two opposing theories: the compact city and the dispersed city theories. Each is claimed to be the superior urban form by its proponents. The empirical evidence supports the compact city theory as far as everyday sustainable mobility is concerned, that is, travel for production and reproduction (see chapter 3). However, there remains an important question regarding the relation between urban form and leisure-time mobility. Little attention has been paid to the possible relationship between

---

1   In this chapter, 'planning' is understood as land-use planning.

long-distance leisure-time travel by car and plane, and the design and location of residential areas within the city.

Therefore, this chapter will also discuss the so-called 'compensatory mechanism' hypothesis.

This hypothesis suggests that people who live in densely populated urban areas (in flats in inner cities) and who have limited need for everyday transport, tend to undertake longer travel in their leisure time to compensate for their having limited access to green outdoor areas. If such compensatory effects indeed apply, they could have major consequences for physical planning practices. Why strive for urban planning practices that reduce the need for everyday transport if it results in more extensive travel during holidays and leisure time? The empirical evidence in this chapter suggests that extreme forms of the compact city might increase in people's needs or wishes to travel for leisure. Thus, moderate forms of compact cities in terms of the size and density of cities (or sub-centres within cities), as supported by decentralised concentration, seem preferable.

The main concern in this book is travel behaviour. However, as was the case in chapter 6, travel behaviour is set in a broad household consumption perspective. Therefore, we have studied the relationships between land-use planning and four distinct consumption categories: (i) energy consumption for housing (heating and operating the home); (ii) energy consumption for everyday travel; (iii) energy consumption for long-distance leisure-time travel by plane; and (iv) energy consumption for long-distance leisure-time travel by car. Throughout this chapter we will refer to these four consumption categories as 'household consumption.'

The chapter has three sections. The first reviews the literature on sustainable urban form. The second presents further results from the SusHomes Project discussed in chapter 6. The SusHomes Project included two studies based on one large household survey in Greater Oslo: one study where attitude theory was used to study the relation between green attitudes and household consumption – presented in chapter 6 – and one study (Holden and Norland 2005) – presented here – where planning theory was used to study the relation between land-use planning and household consumption. The third section presents the results from a research project, entitled *Housing as a Basis for Sustainable Consumption,* carried out by at the Western Norway Research Institute (WNRI) and the Norwegian Institute for Urban and Regional Research (1997–2001). A central part of the project was a household survey in the Norwegian towns of Greater Oslo and Førde, were data on household consumption from 537 households were collected and analysed by way of the ecological footprint (Holden 2004).

Sustainable Urban Form

According to Breheny (1996), until the 1960s planning was an important instrument for realising visionary ideas. Planning had long provided credible answers about how we should form our built environment and subsequently our society. However, beginning in the 1960s 'the public lost confidence in planners, and planners lost confidence in themselves' (ibid., 13). But this did not last long. Following the

Brundtland Commission Report of 1987, *Our Common Future* (WCED 1987), a new optimism about planning emerged. Since then, a debate about the role of planning in promoting sustainable development has been going on. The crucial question is, according to Breheny, as follows: Which urban forms will most effectively deliver the greatest environmental protection? In other words, what is sustainable urban form?

Regarding sustainable urban form, three important questions arise: First, is there actually a connection between urban form and sustainable development? Second, for those who insist that such a connection exists, what is sustainable urban form? And finally, how is a sustainable urban form to be achieved?

Does Planning Matter?

Even though planning seems to have regained much of its legitimacy, there has been a lot of scepticism about and even rejection of the very idea that planning has an important role in promoting sustainable development. Most profoundly, the dispute has been about energy consumption and urban form: Does changing urban forms tend to reduce the frequency and length of journeys, and hence energy consumption? This is illustrated by the debate in the late 1980s between the Australian researchers Newman and Kenworthy and the Americans Gordon and Richardson, in the *Journal of the American Planning Association* (Breheny 1992a). Newman and Kenworthy (1989) provided an analysis of the relationship between levels of petroleum consumption and various features of a number of US and other world cities. They concluded that substantial fuel savings were possible by transforming low-density cities into more compact structures. Gordon and Richardson (1989) savaged this analysis, rejecting both the logic and the arguments used by Newman and Kenworthy.

To this day the disagreement persists, with Gordon and Richardson being joined by a number of other critics. The critiques have many different forms, including:

- Claims that engine technology, taxes on gasoline and driving, and tolls are more effective measures for reducing energy consumption than urban planning (Gordon and Richardson 1989; Boarnet and Crane 2001).
- The assertion that socioeconomic and attitudinal characteristics of people are far more important determinants of travel behaviour than urban form. Critics taking this position assert that the importance of form is highly overestimated in empirical studies (Stead et al. 2000).
- Doubts about the assumption that proximity to everyday services and ones workplace will contribute to reducing travel in a highly mobile society (Owens 1992; Simmonds and Coombe 2000).
- Assertions that the relationship between non-work travel, especially long-distance leisure-time travel, and urban form has been neglected (Titheridge et al. 2000).
- The assertion that travel preferences rather than urban form influence travel behaviour; that is, that people live in city centres because they prefer to travel less, not that they travel less because they live in city centres (the 'self-

selection bias') (Boarnet and Crane 2001).

*   That planning decisions are seen as difficult and expensive ways to influence travel behaviour. Market pressures for decentralization out of cities are always likely to be stronger influences on city development (Banister 2005).

Even though these critiques should not be taken lightly, there seems to be overwhelming support in the literature for the idea that planning *does* matter in determining the level of energy consumption in urban areas. This view is based on both theory and empirical studies.[2] Thus planning, in our opinion, is an important instrument for promoting sustainable development.

What is Sustainable Urban Form?

Even among the supporters of planning, there is a lively debate about which urban form and land-use characteristics actually promote a more sustainable society. There are two dominant and contradictory theories about sustainable urban form: the compact city and the dispersed city.

The main principle in the compact city theory is high-density development close to or within the city core with a high mixture of housing, workplaces and shops. This implies densely and concentrated housing development, which favours semi-detached and multifamily housing. Under this theory, development of residential housing areas on (or beyond) the urban fringe, and single-family housing in particular, are banned. Furthermore, central, high-density development supports a number of other attributes that are favourable to sustainable energy consumption: low energy consumption for housing and everyday travel, efficient remote heating systems, proximity to a variety of workplaces and public and private services, as well as a highly developed public transport system.

The supporters of the compact city theory (for example, Jacobs 1961; Newman and Kenworthy 1989; CEC 1990; Elkin et al. 1991; Sherlock 1991; Enwicht 1992; McLaren 1992) believe that the compact city has environmental and energy advantages, as well as social benefits. The list of advantages is remarkably long, including a better environment, affordable public transport, the potential for improving the social mix, and a higher quality of life (Frey 1999). However, the main justification for the compact city is that it results in the least energy-intensive activity pattern, thereby helping us cope with the issues of global warming. The supporters of the dispersed city suggest the green city, that is, a more open type of urban structure, where buildings, fields and other green areas form a sort of mosaic (Næss 1997). The list of arguments against the compact city theory is even longer than the list in support of it, and includes: that it rejects suburban and semi-rural living, neglects rural communities, affords less green and open space, increases congestion and segregation, reduces environmental quality, and lessens the power for making local decisions (Frey 1999).

---

2   For example, Banister (1992), Næss (1997, 2000, 2006), Newman and Kenworthy (1999), Holden (2001, 2004), Høyer and Holden (2003), Frey (1999), Newton (2000), Buxton (2000) and Masnavi (2000).

However, until fairly recently an international consensus favouring the compact city as a sustainable development approach has dominated the debate (Williams et al. 2000a). Although there has always been considerable scepticism, the concept of the compact city has been so dominant that it:

seems inconceivable that anyone would oppose the current tide of opinion towards promoting greater sustainable development and the compact city in particular (Smyth 1996, 103).

In this context, it is not surprising that the 'move towards the compact city is now entrenched in policy throughout Europe' (Jenks et al. 1996, 275). Also in Norway, resistance against the dominance of the compact city has been modest (Skjeggedal et al. 2003). The disagreements between the compact city and dispersed city discourses can to a large extent be summarised as a debate about two issues: Which form affords the greatest energy efficiency, and which aspects of sustainable development are more important?

The relationship between urban form and energy efficiency – especially energy consumption for travel – is at the core of the sustainable urban form debate. During the last two decades there have been a multitude of empirical studies supporting the relative energy efficiency of the two urban forms. Boarnet and Crane worked through this literature and came to a rather surprising conclusion: 'Very little is known regarding how the built environment influences travel' (Boarnet and Crane 2001, 4). Although these authors were referring to the USA, we find the same scepticism in Europe. Williams et al. (2000a, 355) conclude that 'a great deal still needs to be learnt about the complexity of different forms and their impacts.' This includes the relationship between urban compactness and travel patterns. A possible relationship between the built form and long-distance leisure-time travel by car and plane is part of this new knowledge that must be learnt.

The possible impacts of urban forms are not limited to travel behaviour. The built form also influences social conditions, economic issues, environmental quality, and ecology within the city (ibid.). All these aspects are also important parts of the sustainable development concept, and therefore can be used as criteria for a discussion about sustainable urban form. It should come as no surprise that a study that has minimizing energy consumption as an overall goal, could easily reach different conclusions than a study that aims at using urban form to 'reduce the number of people exposed to fine particles' or to 'promote social equity.' Ultimately it will be necessary to balance these impacts because sustainable urban form is essentially about values (Buxton 2000).

The dispute between the two camps has led to the development of a number of middle positions, which try to combine the best aspects of both the compact and dispersed city forms while at the same time trying to avoid the disadvantages of each. Among such alternative middle positions are the urban village (Newman and Kenworthy 1999; Thompson-Fawcett 2000), New Urbanism[3], the sustainable urban matrix (Hasic 2000), transit-oriented development (Boarnet and Crane 2001),

---

3   www.newurbanism.org.

smart growth (Stoel 1999), and decentralised concentration (Breheny 1996; Høyer and Holden 2003; Holden 2004). These alternatives all try to combine the energy efficiency gained from a compact urban form with the broad quality of life aspects gained from the dispersed city. Still, whether a specific urban form will be more energy efficient than others is an empirical question. Therefore, this was the research question of our empirical study in the Greater Oslo Region.

Land-use Characteristics and Household Consumption

While the compact-versus-dispersed debate represents the big picture, specific land-use characteristics constitute the basic principles that ultimately give the city its form and lead to the impacts mentioned above. Regarding energy consumption in houses, Næss (1997) points to two land-use characteristics that, in addition to local climate conditions, influence energy consumption for heating and operating homes: type of housing and grouping of the houses.[4] Even though climate conditions and grouping of houses do influence energy consumption, these factors to a large extent depend on local conditions and therefore will not be discussed further here.

Regarding the relationship between type of housing and energy consumption, both theoretical and empirical studies show that single-family housing is less efficient than multifamily housing (Owens 1992; Djupskås and Nesbakken 1995; Næss 1997; Holden 2001), while the efficiency of semi-detached houses falls in between. However, the differences in energy consumption between the three types of houses have decreased since 1980. While the energy consumption per capita in single-family housing is almost twice the energy consumption in multifamily housing in the overall housing stock, single-family housing built during the past two decades uses only 20 per cent more energy per capita than multifamily housing (Holden 2001; Aall et al. 2003). If this trend continues, it will become an important factor in the debate about multifamily housing (compact city) versus single-family housing (dispersed city).

When it comes to land-use characteristics that influence energy consumption for everyday transport, Næss (1997) concludes that the following characteristics are favourable for reducing per capita energy consumption: high population density for the city as a whole; high density within each residential area; centralised settlement within cities and towns (that is, higher density in the inner part than on the fringe); centralised workplace location; low parking capacity at workplaces; decentralised concentration at the regional level; and, a high population for each city.[5] Based on empirical evidence, Næss (1997) claims that these characteristics are favourable in cities as different as Paris, London, New York, Melbourne, San Francisco, Copenhagen and Frederikshavn (Denmark). Furthermore, he claims that those

---

4   In addition to these factors, energy consumption is influenced by architectural and technical solutions (such as heat recovery, ventilation and energy control systems) which are, however, outside the scope of this study.

5   Næss regards the first five characteristics as the most important and significant factors that have strong support in both theory and other empirical investigations. The importance of the last two factors is more uncertain.

studies rejecting the influence of urban structural factors in general, and the prospect of the compact city in particular, all have three flaws in common (Næss 2006):

First, the conclusions of such studies stem from model simulations where the results might simply reflect that the assumption of the model does not capture the actual influence of urban structure on travel behaviour. Second, the apparent lack of any relationship between urban form and transport is due to the absence from theoretical considerations of variables that could be expected to exert the strongest influence on each other. For example, some studies have focused on trip frequency, some on travel time, and some on both, while travel distance and modal split represent the most important variables regarding energy consumption. Finally, in some studies, conclusions are made about an absent or insignificant relationship between urban structure and travel, based on a comparison of travel survey data from cities of different sizes. However, according to Næss, the number of inhabitants is hardly a good indicator for testing whether urban structure affects travel behaviour.

As an antithesis to Næss' (and others') compact city theory, there is a school of thought amongst environmentalists that:

> The most sustainable way to live would be to return to rural areas and local self-sufficiency, to reduce the importing of goods and services from far-off lands, and to commune more closely with nature (Jenks et al. 1996, 170).

This theory challenges the compact city on nearly all land-use characteristics, thus promoting dispersed, low-density cities (Orrskog and Snickars 1992; Rådberg 1995; Troy 1996).

Long-distance Leisure-time Travel: Compensatory Travel?

Although housing location influences the distances to various facilities, and the spatial location of most of these facilities suggests that average travel distances will be shortest for inner-city residents, this pattern might be counteracted by certain compensatory mechanisms (Vilhelmson 1990; Næss 1997; Holden 2001, 2004; Næss 2006). For example, high accessibility to services might create an increased demand for transport. Opting for a wider range of jobs, shops and leisure activities, might establish the need for more everyday travel.

An important question that arises from looking at the wider issue of energy consumption and greenhouse gas emissions is whether, for certain income levels, reduced local everyday travel will be compensated for by increased long-distance leisure-time travel. Is it so – for certain income levels – that the sum of 'environmental vices' is constant, and that households managing on a small everyday amount of transportation, create even heavier environmental strain through, for instance, weekend trips to a cottage or long-distance holiday trips by plane? In the professional debate, some (for example, Kennedy 1995) have claimed that people living in high-density, inner-city areas will, to a larger extent than their counterparts living in low-density areas, travel out of town on weekends, for instance to a cottage, to compensate for the lack of access to a private garden. In addition to this 'hypothesis of compensation' others, including the Swedish mobility researcher

Vilhelmson (1990), have launched a 'hypothesis of opportunity,' which asserts that the time and money people save due to short-distance daily travel, will probably be used for long-distance leisure-time travel. In order to get more knowledge about the possible existence of compensatory travel and also the connections between such travel and land-use characteristics, we have included energy consumed for long-distance leisure-time travel by plane and car as a consumption category.

Three Challenges for the Compact City: The SusHomes Project

As in other countries, the perspectives of the compact city discourse are being adopted in Norwegian environmental urban policies for sustainable development (MoE 2002; Skjeggedal et al. 2003). Also in the City of Oslo, arguments supporting new inner city development projects are increasingly based on this approach to sustainable urban form. However, the results of the SusHomes Project raise three challenges to the compact city discourse, and therefore call for a more nuanced debate on sustainable urban form.

In particular, the SusHomes Project raised the following questions: Do land-use characteristics influence energy consumption for housing and everyday transport, and if so, how? Is it possible to identify a correlation between land-use characteristics and the residents' long-distance leisure-time travel? How important is the influence of land-use characteristics compared to the influence of individuals' socioeconomic positions and environmental attitudes? What do the answers to these questions imply for urban sustainable development policies and strategies?

Methodology

The SusHomes Project conducted surveys in eight residential areas in the Greater Oslo Region, and used bivariate and multiple regression analyses. Our purpose in using multiple regressions is to learn more about the relationship between several independent variables, and a dependent variable. In general, multiple regression analysis allows the researcher to ask (and hopefully answer) the question, What is the best predictor of ...? Correlations identified by initial bivariate analysis might not represent real explanatory relationships, since most phenomena result from multiple causes. Multiple regression analysis therefore enables us to integrate the variation in several variables into the same analysis, and isolate the effects of single independent variables. Unimportant variables can then be left out of the overall interpretation of the results.

Figure 7.1 illustrates the possible causal relationships between the physical and non-physical characteristics of households and the houses in which they live, and their consumption behaviour studied in this project.

Concerning research design, as our units of analysis we have chosen households in a limited number of residential areas within a city region. In contrast to studies that base their analysis on surveys of cities and city regions as a whole, this approach allows us to better control for key contextual factors such as local density, access to public transport, and sociodemographic characteristics, and thereby also the

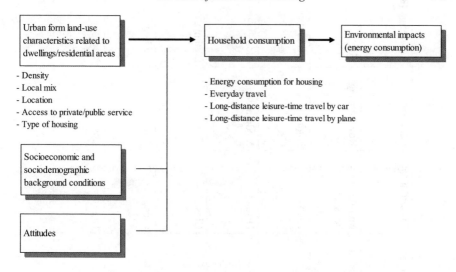

Figure 7.1 Causal relations between characteristics of households and their houses, household consumption and environmental impacts

respondents' representation within each area. Eventually, this enables us to discuss in detail the possible effects of different housing models, locations and transport systems on household consumption in an urban region.

The selection of residential areas is based on a set of criteria representing key land-use characteristics, and on specific aspects expected to represent possible causal factors effecting consumption at the household level: i) type of housing (single-family, row or multifamily housing)[6]; ii) housing density (number of housing units per area unit); iii) location relative to the city centre; iv) access to public transport (distance to tram or subway station); v) distance to local sub-centre; and vi) local mix (to what extent the area is homogenous with respect to type of housing and/or mix of housing, business and services). The first three factors are of course to some extent interlinked – a residential area's density is often linked to its location relative to the city centre, while density is a reflection of the type of housing.

The Research Area

The Greater Oslo Region in this study includes the City of Oslo and the Municipality of Bærum, which represent the geographical area within a radius of approximately 15 km from Oslo's centre. About 608,000 people[7] live in this area of about 615 square km, two-thirds of which comprises protected natural areas outside the urban zone. This urban zone represents the most densely populated urban area in Norway; it is part of the much larger Capital Region with more than 1 million people.

---

6   'Row housing' includes semi-detached houses. 'Multifamily housing' includes all kinds of blocks of flats.

7   A total of 507,000 in the City of Oslo and 101,000 in Bærum Municipality.

Table 7.1   Key characteristics of the eight residential areas

Criteria	Bjorndal (1)	Grünerløkka (2)	Holmlia (3)	Hovseter (4)	Rykkinn (5)	Sandvika (6)	Silkestrå (7)	Vålerenga (8)
Type of housing	Single-family/row housing	Multifamily housing	Multifamily/row housing	Multifamily housing	Row housing	Multifamily housing	Row housing	Mix
Relative housing density	Low	High	High	High	Low	High	High	Medium
Relative location from city centre	Distant	Close	Distant	Medium	Distant	Distant	Medium	Close
Relative distance to tram/subway	Distant	Close	Close	Close	Distant	Close	Close	Distant
Relative location from local sub-centre	Distant	Close	Close	Medium	Close	Close	Close	Medium
Local mix	Low	High	Low	Medium	Low	High	Low	Medium

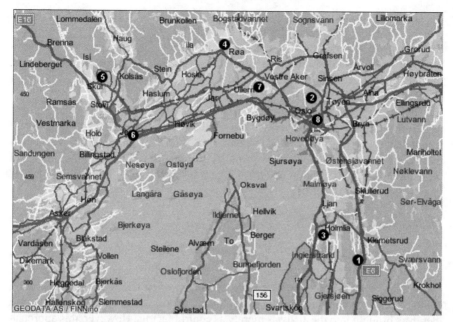

Figure 7.2   Map of the Greater Oslo Region, including the eight residential areas of the study (Scale: 1:400,000)

Note: See table 7.1 for numbering.

The location and characteristics of the residential areas within the region must be understood in light of shifting planning and urban development paradigms and trends. While the city centre and nearby areas are dominated by brick multifamily houses mostly from the period 1870–1930 (for example, Grünerløkka), the surroundings include single-family housing areas from the interwar years and since (such as Rykkinn and Bjørndal), densely developed bedroom communities from the 1950s to the 1970s on the urban fringe (such as Holmlia and Hovseter) and more recent urban development including all sorts of housing within the existing urban zone (for example, Silkestrå). All in all, 59 per cent of the population in this region live in multifamily houses, 22 per cent in row houses and 19 per cent in single-family houses.[8]

Concerning local mobility in the region, about 250,000 cars pass daily into the toll zone of the core urban area; the Oslo Public Transport Company (Oslo Sporveier) registers about 435,000 passengers each day. (The public transport system includes trams, subways and buses.) This reflects the fact that the city centre of Oslo is an important working area in this region and that about 124,000 commute from the surrounding municipalities. On the other hand, about 54 per cent of the 310,000 households of the region have one or more cars. Survey data from the City of Oslo show also that 48.7 per cent of the city population commute daily by car, while 30.5 per cent commute by public transport and the remaining 20.8 per cent cycle or walk (ECIP 2003).

---

8   Data are from the Population and Housing Census 2001 (Statistics Norway) (http://www.ssb.no/english/subjects/02/01 /fobhushold_en/).

The eight residential areas in this study represent different reflections of the six criteria presented above, as illustrated in table 7.1. The areas also represent key features of the general housing situation in the region. The map (figure 7.2) shows the location of the areas within the Greater Oslo Region; six of the areas lie within the City of Oslo, while the remaining two are located in the Municipality of Bærum (Rykkinn and Sandvika).

The survey was conducted in March–April 2003; questionnaires were sent to 2,500 randomly sampled individuals above the age of 17. We averaged 120 respondents per area, a 40 per cent response rate. While the questionnaire was sent to individuals within households, they responded on questions regarding their own and the household's consumption of energy and transport, as well as family structure, income and housing facilities.

Multiple Regression Analysis

The multiple regressions give us insight into the relationship between the different physical housing situations (representing different land-use characteristics) and the households' consumption of energy and transport, when taking into consideration demographic, socioeconomic and attitudinal factors. These three factors are therefore brought into the analysis merely as control factors. However, this approach is not sufficient for identifying causal mechanisms regarding the variables and the consumption patterns. Another critical aspect of the multiple regression approach is the impossibility of including two significant and correlating independent variables within the same analysis. It is therefore difficult to point to the most important factor. The findings of this study should therefore be further explored using more qualitative methods.

The results presented in this chapter are based on a multiple regression analysis of the material as a whole. The starting point of the analysis is that possible explanatory variables must be searched for at three levels: 1) the residential area; 2) the household level; and 3) the individual level. The dependent variables of the analysis are:

- Consumption data (consumption of energy for housing, everyday travel and long-distance leisure-time travel by plane and car), from the questionnaire.

The independent variables (the possible explanatory factors for the registered consumption data) are:

- Land-use characteristics: a) physical-structural characteristics of the house (type of housing, size, access to private garden, etc.), from the questionnaire; and b) physical-structural characteristics of the residential areas (location, density, local mix, access to public transport, etc.), from national and local data, and map sources.
- Socioeconomic and sociodemographic factors of the household (family structure, education, income, car ownership, etc.), from the questionnaire
- Registered attitudes and preferences of the individuals (that we assume might influence their consumption), from the questionnaire.

The respondents' attitudes and preferences, in this case meaning 'their attitudes towards the environmental consequences of the increasing private consumption in Norwegian households,' are brought into the analysis in two ways: by way of a Likert scale (see chapter 6), based on the respondents' expression of agreement or disagreement with statements (scale items) on consumption of energy for housing and transport; and by the respondents' registered membership in one or more environmental organisations.

Energy Consumption in Residential Areas

Figure 7.3 shows the results from bivariate analysis of empirical data on consumption of energy for housing and transport in eight residential areas. The data indicates that there are substantial differences in the average energy consumption per capita between the eight residential areas. Residents living in Bjørndal and Rykkinn use the most energy, while residents of Sandvika and Hovseter use the least. The difference is approximately 25 per cent, while the remaining four areas fall in between these extremes.

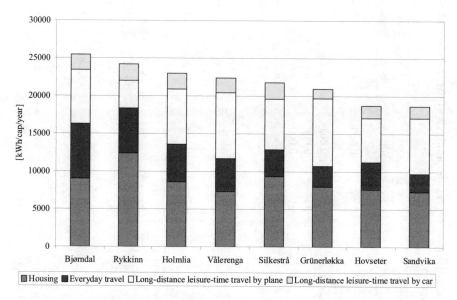

Figure 7.3   Annual per capita energy consumption in eight residential areas in Greater Oslo Region (N=445)

Taking a closer look at the areas, we find interesting aspects for further analysis. Bjørndal and Rykkinn are both dominated by single-family and row housing, and are low-density and distant from the city centre. Even though the total energy consumed in each area is fairly equal, the residents seem to use energy differently. Residents in Rykkinn use substantially more energy for housing, while residents in Bjørndal use more energy for travel. The average resident in Sandvika and Hovseter, which are

Table 7.2   Results from a multivariate regression analysis of the influence of various independent variables on annual per capita energy consumption

Independent variables	Housing[i] B[ix]	Housing[i] Significance[x]	Everyday travel[ii] B[ix]	Everyday travel[ii] Significance[x]	Leisure travel by plane[iii] B[ix]	Leisure travel by plane[iii] Significance[x]	Leisure travel by car[iv] B[ix]	Leisure travel by car[iv] Significance[x]
Land use characteristics								
Single-family house SFH (SFH=0; otherwise=1)	-4,783	0.000	n.i.	-	n.i.	-	n.i.	-
Row house RH (RH=0; otherwise=1)	-2,306	0.003	n.i.	-	n.i.	-	n.i.	-
Size of house (m²)	33	0.000	n.i.	-	n.i.	-	n.i.	-
Age of house (years)	31	0.000	n.i.	-	n.i.	-	n.i.	-
Access to garden (yes=0, no=1)	n.i.	-	n.i.	-	802	0.032	213	0.044
Housing density in residential area (housing/daa)	-193	0.035	22	0.684	102	0.074	-13	0.423
Local mix [v]	n.i.	-	5	0.585	n.i.	-	n.i.	-
Distance from residence to the city centre (km)	n.i.	-	108	0.001	n.i.	-	n.i.	-
Distance from residence to local sub-centre (km)	n.i.	-	233	0.037	n.i.	-	n.i.	-
Socio-economic and -demographic factors								
Sex (male=0, female=1)	n.i.	-	-845	0.002	309	0.374	n.i.	-
Age (years)	-1 [xi]	0.968	-12	0.285	-49	0.000	-11 [xi]	0.002
Education (up to upper secondary school =0, higher education=1)	n.i.	-	-103	0.725	575	0.134	n.i.	-
Occupancy (have employment /student=0, other=1)	n.i.	-	-1,050	0.019	n.i.	-	n.i.	-
Number of household members	-2,944	0.000	n.i.	-	n.i.	-	20	0.662
Personal annual income (1000 NOK)	n.i.	-	2	0.034	6	0.000	n.i.	-
Household annual income (1000 NOK)	-1	0.278	n.i.	-	n.i.	-	1	0.000

	(1)		(2)		(3)		(4)	
	coef.	p	coef.	p	coef.	p	coef.	p
Car ownership (yes=0, no=1)	n.i.		- 1,727	0.000	- 547	0.204	- 697	0.000
Discount ticket[(vi)] (yes=0, no=1)	n.i.		662	0.016	n.i.		n.i.	
Access to holiday house (yes=0, no=1)	n.i.		n.i.		140	0.690	- 415	0.000
Attitudinal factors								
Environmental attitude [(vii)]	- 205	0.778	- 9	0.778	n.i.		n.i.	
Membership in environmental NGO (yes=0, no=1)	n.i.		- 80	0.856	- 1,272	0.030	- 55	0.717
Constant [(viii)]	17,103	0.000	2,730	0.019	4,354	0.000	1,712	0.000
Adjusted R^2	0.425		0.231		0.095		0.168	
F (significance)	44.630 (0.000)		16.034 (0.000)		10.040 (0.000)		19.737 (0.000)	
N	591		650		778		743	

n.i. = Not included as an independent variable for the given consumption category (either because of problems with high multicolinearity or lack of theoretical foundation)

(i) Energy consumption for housing. Respondents that have stated an annual energy consumption of firewood exceeding 43,000 kWh have been left out.

(ii) Energy consumption during the week of the survey multiplied by 47 weeks (excl. holidays). Respondents that have experienced an 'unusual travel pattern' during the week of the survey have been left out. Extremes (>= 14,735 kWh per capita/year) are also left out.

(iii) Extremes (>= 20,846 kWh per capita/year) are left out.

(iv) Extremes (>=5,999 kWh/capita/year) are left out.

(v) Percentage of developed area for housing within a residential area

(vi) Special discount public transport tickets for multiple rides, e.g. flexi-cards, daily, weekly, monthly, and annual passes

(vii) Likert scale. Higher values indicated a positive attitude towards environmental issues.

(viii Represent the basis alternative when all independent variables are given the value 'zero.' However, in our analysis giving the value 'zero' is meaningless for a number of independent variables, e.g. age of household members, size of house, or distance between the residence and the city centre. The figure's constant is here reported, but cannot be given any reasonable interpretation.

(ix) Nonstandardised regression coefficient

(x) Two-sided p-value

(xi) Average age of the adults in the household.

densely populated areas dominated by multifamily housing, consumes less energy for *both* housing and transport than the average resident in Bjørndal and Rykkinn. However, Sandvika and Hovseter differ from each other in their respective distances to local sub-centre and city centre.

Vålerenga, Silkestrå and Grünerløkka are residential areas that are located either close to or a moderate distance from the city centre. Like Hovseter and Sandvika, they are mostly dominated by high-density, multifamily housing, with proximity to a large variety of public and private services. However, in spite of their proximity to the city centre they have substantially higher energy consumption. As can be seen from figure 7.3 this is mainly the result of higher energy consumption for long-distance leisure-time travel by plane (from now on, 'travel by plane'). This is especially the case for Grünerløkka, which has both the shortest distance to the city centre and the highest energy consumption for travel by plane.

Holmlia is a residential area that is dominated by multifamily housing but also has a considerable number of row houses. This housing mix is reflected by the relatively high energy consumption for housing. Holmlia is far from the city centre, which might be one cause for its residents' higher level of energy consumption for everyday travel compared to the energy consumption of residents of other densely populated areas closer to the city centre.

The above findings indicate the existence of a connection between land-use characteristics and the consumption of energy for housing and transport. However, this initial analysis does not take into account the possible differences in socioeconomic and sociodemographic conditions between the residential areas. The variation in energy consumption between areas could easily be the result of differences in income level, the household structure or the employment rate. Initially, we expect these non-physical characteristics to contribute to the identified differences in energy consumption. To study the isolated effects of both physical and non-physical characteristics (including attitudinal factors), we have conducted a multivariate regression analysis for each of the four consumption categories.

The Influence of Land-use Characteristics

The results of the multivariate regression analyses are shown in table 7.2. For each consumption category we have included a number of land-use characteristics, socioeconomic and sociodemographic contextual factors, as well as attitudinal factors. In this chapter, we emphasise the statistical correlations between land-use characteristics and household consumption. This is not to say that the other two independent variables are unimportant, but they are here brought in as controls to single out the specific effects caused by the physical-structural conditions.

Regarding energy consumption for housing, four land-use characteristics have significant and isolated effects: First, the type of housing is important. Controlled for other factors, there are significant differences in energy consumption between single-family housing, row houses and multifamily housing. While single-family housing represents the least energy-efficient alternative, multifamily housing is the most energy-efficient. Of second and third importance, respectively, are the size and age of the housing. The larger the house, the more energy is used per household member.

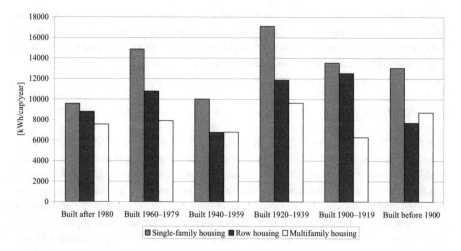

Figure 7.4   Annual per capita energy consumption for housing as a function of housing type and the age of the house (N=907)

Similarly, residents of older houses use more energy than residents of newer ones. Finally, density matters. In densely developed areas, residents use less energy than do residents in areas with lower density housing. This is mainly the result of using more energy-efficient supply systems – for example, remote heating systems based on heat pumps – in these densely developed areas.

We find that two significant land-use characteristics, both related to distance, affect energy consumption for everyday travel: First, it seems that the distance to the city centre is important. The longer the distance, the more energy is used for transport. This result is in line with other studies (for example, Næss 1996; Næss 2006). Second, the distance to the local sub-centre correlates with the extent of everyday travel. Thus, proximity to a centre – with corresponding accessibility to private and public services – is favourable regarding energy consumption. However, neither density nor local mix has significant effect on energy consumption for everyday travel. Density and distance are, however, strongly correlated, but it can be difficult to separate their respective effects. Therefore, high density and high local mix must be combined with proximity to a centre offering everyday services to bring about a reduction in energy consumption for everyday travel.

In the leisure-time sphere we find a very different picture. Two factors have significant effects on energy consumption for travel by plane: housing density and access to a private garden. Higher density housing corresponds to higher energy consumption for travel by plane. Furthermore, access to a private garden seems to reduce residents' desire to travel by plane in their leisure time. Access to a private garden also influences energy consumption for long-distance leisure-time travel by car. Residents having regular access to a private garden spend less of their leisure time travelling by car, and consequently use less energy for this purpose.

It is important to recognise that the above relationships between density, access to a private garden and travel by plane or car are statistical correlations. They do not necessarily imply causation. More in-depth knowledge about the residents' motives and leisure-time preferences is needed to understand these relationships; it can only be obtained by in-depth interviews.

The Challenges

The results from the above analysis of energy consumption for housing and everyday travel strongly support the compact city theory. Low energy consumption correlates with high-density housing located a short distance from a centre, and offering a range of private and public services. There remains, however, a question about size. Previous studies indicate that *large* compact cities might counteract the advantages of compactness (Næss 1997; Holden 2004). Relatively small and compact cities in a region, or compact villages within a larger city might be favourable compromises. Three aspects of our analysis challenge the compact city theory and support the need to nuance the existing debate on sustainable urban form. We will elaborate on these aspects in the following sections. (These challenges are further elaborated on in chapter 8.)

Challenge No 1: Density and Long-distance Leisure-time Travel by Plane

As we have shown above, high-density housing in residential areas corresponds to higher energy consumption for travel by plane. Thus, residents living in high-density areas use far more energy than do others for travel by plane. At the same time they use less energy than do others for everyday travel. Residents in Grünerløkka and Vålerenga fit this picture well. These are the most densely developed areas in our study, situated close to the city centre. Compared to the residents of the other areas, the residents here use far more energy for travel by plane in their leisure time. At the same time they do not use much energy for everyday transport. In Rykkinn we find the opposite situation, with low-density housing located far from the city centre. The travel behaviour of Rykkinn residents is characterized by high energy consumption for everyday travel and an almost negligible (compared to residents of the high-density residential areas) energy consumption for travel by plane. Thus, this identified pattern might possibly support the 'compensatory mechanism hypothesis' discussed above.

But there could be other possible explanations for this pattern. The residents in Grünerløkka and Vålerenga might simply use for leisure travel the money they save by using little energy in everyday travel. However, high living expenses characterize these two residential areas (especially Grünerløkka) and the savings might also be used for such expenses. Another possible explanation might be that travel by plane is an integral part of the urban lifestyle of these residents. As already stressed, a more thorough, qualitative-oriented analysis is needed to understand the correlation between travel by plane and living in areas of high-density housing.

Challenge No 2: Access to a Private Garden and Leisure-time Travel

The second challenge for the compact city theory is the apparent reduction in leisure-time travel when residents have access to a private garden. When relevant socioeconomic and attitudinal factors are controlled for, residents having access to a private garden use on average 1,000 fewer kWh annually for long-distance leisure-time travel by car and plane than do residents without such access.

This might not come as a surprise. It is reasonable to expect that they spend time in their gardens, both for relaxation and necessary gardening, and therefore travel less. However, the causal mechanism is not evident – such residents might travel less *because* they want to spend time in their gardens, and not because they have access to such an environment. This is an interesting issue for a qualitative follow-up study.

The important point is that access to a private recreation area seems to relate to a reduction in leisure-time travel. The above finding holds even for residents living in flats. In other words, access to a private garden reduces travel by residents of *all* types of housing. This underlines the importance of available nearby recreation facilities, even in areas of high-density housing. Whether such facilities need to be private, or whether collectively shared gardens create the same correlations, are both interesting questions for further investigation.

Challenge No 3: The Reduced Effect of Housing Type

The annual energy consumption for housing differs substantially with the type of housing. In our empirical material, the per capita average energy consumption for single-family housing, row houses and multifamily housing is approximately 12,000, 9,000 and 8,000 kWh, respectively. Thus, residents in single-family housing use about 50 per cent more energy than residents in multifamily housing.

However, concerning housing built after 1980, the picture changes. The difference in per capita energy consumption between the three types of housing is reduced, as can be seen in figure 7.4. The difference in energy consumption between single-family housing and multifamily housing is reduced by 50 per cent. This pattern is confirmed in a similar study in the Greater Oslo Region (Aall et al. 2003). Thus, there has been a significant reduction in the energy consumption per capita in single-family housing built after 1980 compared to the energy consumption in housing built earlier. In our study this is reflected in the difference in energy consumption between Rykkinn and Bjørndal. In Bjørndal, 99 per cent of housing was built after 1980, while the majority of housing in Rykkinn was built in the period 1960–1979. Residents of Rykkinn consume per capita approximately 3,000 more kWh annually for housing than do residents of Bjørndal.

We do not find a corresponding reduction in energy consumption for residents of row houses and multifamily housing. Energy consumption per square meter in row houses has been reduced by almost 30 kWh annually over the last decades. In the same period, energy consumption per square meter in multifamily housing has increased.

Three factors explain this pattern: First, there has been, through public information campaigns, increased focus on the reduction of energy consumption in single-family housing. Households in single-family housing have caught up with more energy efficient households living in multifamily housing by investing in energy-saving equipment. Second, recent public regulations on energy consumption in new buildings (for example, standards for insulation) have reduced energy consumption for heating relative to the overall energy consumption for housing. While in older housing energy consumption for heating accounts for approximately 60–70 per cent of total energy consumption, in new housing it is 50 per cent, and even less in 'low-energy housing.' This implies that the importance of housing type is reduced. Finally, household size matters. We found that in single-family housing built after 1980, family size is larger than family size in older single-family housing. This also contributes to lower energy consumption per household member, which can be seen in figure 7.4.

At the same time, family size in multifamily housing of all ages is about the same. This tendency cannot necessarily be regarded as a tribute to single-family housing; rather it is a possible consequence of complex sociodemographic tendencies in our society. Even so, it explains some of the apparent harmonization in energy consumption across all types of housing. Still, our material shows that living in multifamily housing *is* more favourable than living in single-family housing as far as energy consumption is concerned, as clearly indicated in the multivariate regression analysis in table 7.2. Our point is merely that the difference in energy consumption between the two types of housing has been reduced in the last decades. This phenomenon might present a challenge to promoters of the compact city.

Theoretical Perspectives and Policy Implications

Above all, the SusHomes Project supports the hypothesis that there *is* a connection between land-use characteristics and household consumption of energy and transport. This connection indicates that planning does matter. However, there remains a lack of knowledge regarding the importance of location preference. As Boarnet and Crane (2001) emphasize, perhaps residents of densely developed areas near or in the city centre consume less energy for everyday travel because they choose to live where they do precisely because less travel is required. However, the 'self-selection bias' does not seem to change the assumption that urban form matters. Indeed, people who prefer to live in a way that encourages walking and bicycling in everyday life, and discourages use of a car, *are* very good examples of the importance of urban form. Their *reasons* for living where they live, therefore, are not an important issue in this matter.

Regarding the question of what constitutes a sustainable urban form, our empirical material points in several directions. Our analysis of energy consumption for housing and everyday travel supports the idea of the compact city. There are, however, a number of challenges that have to be considered. The most important one is related to the residents' travel by plane.

Based on the analysis of total energy consumption for housing and transport and the different land-use characteristics of the eight residential areas, we can divide the areas into three categories:

- High-energy-consumption residential areas: Here we find Rykkinn and Bjørndal – residential areas that are dominated by low-density and single-family housing located at the urban fringe. Additionally, these areas are located far from both a local sub-centre and a tram/subway/railway station.
- Medium-energy-consumption residential areas: Grünerløkka, Vålerenga and Silkestrå are in this category. High-density and mainly multifamily housing characterise these areas, which are located relatively close to the city centre with proximity to workplaces, public transport systems and private and public services. Residents use, however, a large amount of energy for travel by plane.
- Low-energy-consumption residential areas: The residents with the lowest energy consumption for housing and transport reside in Sandvika and Hovseter. These areas are dominated by high-density, multifamily housing. They are located close to local sub-centres that to a varying extent have proximity to workplaces, public transport systems and private and public services.

As the categorisation shows, decentralised concentration within cities having more than 500,000 inhabitants could lead to lower energy consumption in households – a conclusion that seems to be enjoying widespread support (Breheny 1992a; Banister 1992; Owens 1992; Newman and Kenworthy 2000; Buxton 2000; Masnavi 2000; Holden 2001, 2004; Høyer and Holden 2001).

What if a policy that encourages decentralised concentration were to be integrated within the Greater Oslo Region? Land use of the kind that characterises Sandvika and Hovseter would be encouraged, whereas that which characterises Rykkinn and Bjørndal would be discouraged. Furthermore, the protected natural areas outside the urban zone would be preserved. New housing would, therefore, be located near or within the existing urban zone. The development of very high-density areas would, however, be avoided. Presumably, such a policy should be applied to other large cities as well.

The soundness of the decentralised concentration concept is that it maximises advantages offered by while at the same time it minimises disadvantages caused by versions of the compact city. It offers on the one hand the advantages of compaction. Data show that increased densities lead to low energy consumption for both housing and everyday travel. On the other hand, decentralised concentration avoids the disadvantages caused by extreme densities, as typically can be found in the large, monolithic compact city. Data show that extreme densities statistically correlate with high energy consumption for long-distance leisure-time travel.

However, the rationale for residents to undertake leisure-time travel is a subtle issue. Whether high energy consumption for long-distance leisure-time travel is due to the physical characteristics of the large, monolithic city, or instead to the preferences of its residents remains a question for further research.

Ecological Footprints and Sustainable Urban Form

What are the overall physical characteristics of a living situation that has the smallest negative impact on the environment? The term 'living situation' is used here to express the physical design and location of a house. Impacts on the environment are measured in terms of ecological footprints. The following land-use characteristics are included: town size and national settlement pattern; location of houses within a town, municipality or built-up area; residential area; and type of housing.

These four characteristics can be linked to overriding housing planning principles. The questions of a town's size and national settlement patterns are closely related to the question of centralization versus decentralization at a national level. The location of housing refers to the distance from the house to the centre of town and relates to urban sprawl, whereas 'residential areas' refers to housing density. Obviously, housing density is not the only measure of density. In a broad discussion about density, additional criteria for measuring density should therefore be included in the assessment, for example, population density and development density. Finally, the question of housing type deals with the ongoing debate about single-family houses as a separate form of living, compared to more dense and concentrated forms of living. Indeed, these four land-use characteristics are closely interrelated. They influence each other and, in the overall scheme of residential planning, it can be difficult to consider them as clearly separate aspects.

Methodology

The empirical research plan consisted of a household survey and ecological footprint calculations.

Survey

The survey consisted of a questionnaire sent by post to households in Greater Oslo and in the western Norway community, Førde (figure 7.5). Greater Oslo, which comprises the capital Oslo and the surrounding district, with a population totalling approximately 1 million, represents consumption patterns and volumes in a large urban context. Førde, on the other hand, with only around 12,000 inhabitants, gives a corresponding picture for rural conditions. The team carried out a stratified probability sample to ensure an adequate number of respondents from different housing types (single-family houses, semi-detached houses and multifamily residential buildings) and housing (central/suburban, sparsely/densely developed) within each of the study areas. The distinction between urban and rural areas was ensured by the selection of these two study areas. The surveys were carried out between October and November 1998.

The questionnaire primarily focused on surveying household consumption and other consumption (mainly consumption in connection with holidays and leisure activities) based on physical and structural conditions concerning the location of the house, as well as attitudes to individual, more general environmental problems. The survey consisted of two separate forms: one completed by the entire household as

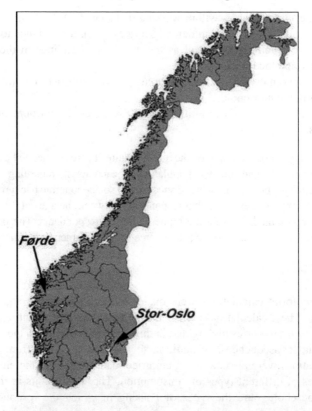

Figure 7.5   Survey areas: Førde and Greater Oslo (Stor-Oslo)

a group, and the other completed by each household member over 18 years of age. Data was collected on the following conditions:

- Consumer behaviour: information was collected on a broad range of household consumption regarding conditions (directly or indirectly) connected to the house.[9] Consumption was also studied in connection with holidays and recreation activities.
- Characteristics of the each house: such as housing type, size (m² floor area), construction type (wood, brick, concrete) and the total size of the plot (m²).
- The physical and structural properties of the surroundings: data was collected

---

9   The study includes 'material housing consumption', defined as consumption required for operating and maintaining a housing unit. This concerns furniture and other fittings, technical equipment and electrical appliances, equipment for maintaining and operating indoor and outdoor areas, etc. Individually, these products do not represent major consumption, but together they represent extremely high consumption levels. We must emphasize here that, as far as the material housing consumption category is concerned, we have concentrated only on the type of consumption that relates to running a house or an apartment. Material consumption, with respect to new construction and demolition work, has not been included.

on, inter alia, services within walking distance (500–1,000 m) of the house (shops, public offices, commercial services, etc.), the distance to the nearest service of each type, as well as the density of buildings in the immediate vicinity and local community.

- Socioeconomic and sociodemographic background data on the individuals living in the households.
- Environmental attitudes: attitudes towards general, environmental political issues.

A total of 537 households completed the questionnaire. There seemed to be a reasonable ratio between the sample and the population of each town, regarding the physical characteristics of the houses and a broad spectrum of socioeconomic background factors. It should, however, be mentioned that respondents between the ages of 30 and 60 were slightly overrepresented, as were the higher-educated respondents. The percentage of female respondents was close to the actual percentage of women living in these areas.

Ecological Footprints

Ecological footprint calculations were made to link consumption and sustainable development. These calculations indicated which overall living situations – based on the consumption categories highlighted in this chapter – resulted in the least serious environmental consequences. In addition to the data obtained from the survey, these calculations were also based on empirical data relating to the environmental consequences of different types of consumption. The focal points in these studies were the households and the types of housing in which the respondents lived. The characteristics of the individuals concerned were also included, to provide a supplementary or alternative perspective.

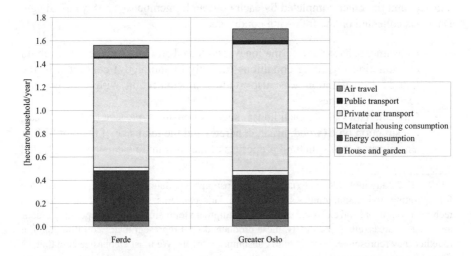

Figure 7.6   Annual ecological footprint per household in Førde and Greater Oslo (N=253)

Results

This section presents the results of the footprint calculations, which were based on data taken from the surveys; the results are presented according to the four land-use characteristics mentioned in the introduction.[10]

Size

Figure 7.6 shows the average ecological footprint per household and per household member. Once again, note that the ecological footprints calculated include only 'household consumption' (as defined above) and not the household's total consumption (food, clothing, etc.). Let us look more closely at what these figures mean, starting with the dimension of urban size. Although it is interesting to compare the two survey areas, caution is recommended for several reasons. Greater Oslo and Førde are two areas that are so different (in size, extent, and perhaps also culture) that a direct comparison must be treated carefully.

Nevertheless, it is interesting to note that the average ecological footprints per household for the two areas are 1.56 ha/year (Førde) and 1.70 ha/year (Greater Oslo). Per household member, these figures are 0.76 ha/year and 0.83 ha/year, respectively. This shows that the inhabitants of the small rural town of Førde have an ecological footprint that is 10 per cent less than that of their urban counterparts in Greater Oslo.

What causes this? Mainly differences in travel patterns.[11] Regarding daily journeys, the Greater Oslo results are favourable. Per household member, the residents of the capital travel 60 km per week, while the corresponding figure for Førde's residents is 98 km. This is mainly because car density is greater in Førde, where 92 per cent of households have access to a car, compared with 85 per cent in Greater Oslo. However, if we look at the total distance travelled by car throughout the year, and if we now include the long-distance holiday and leisure-time journeys, this picture is reversed. Despite having lower access to cars, households in Greater Oslo have the greatest mobility. In fact, household members in Greater Oslo travel an average of 1,500 kilometres more per year and travel further on privately booked flights. This implies that average household members in Greater Oslo use 14 per cent more energy yearly on total passenger transport (for all reasons and by all modes) than their rural counterparts in Førde.

---

10 The specific survey data from each of the four consumption categories will not be given here. The data that are briefly mentioned in the text are presented fully elsewhere (Holden 2001, 2004; Høyer and Holden 2001).

11 The average ecological footprint per household member for energy consumption in the home and material housing consumption were both about equal for Førde and Greater Oslo. The differing circumstances point us in different directions but, in total, the two come out fairly equal (Holden 2001).

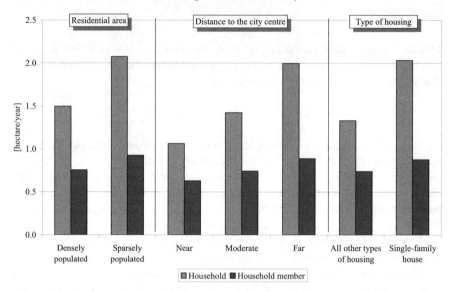

Figure 7.7   Annual ecological footprint per household and household member in Førde and Greater Oslo combined according to residential area, distance to the city centre and type of housing (N=253)

High Density, Less Urban Sprawl and Less Single-family Housing

Figure 7.7 shows the ecological footprint per household member according to residential area, distance to the city centre and types of housing. There can be no doubt that high density, moderate distances between houses and the city centre, and concentrated forms of housing are the most favourable for reducing a household's ecological footprint. There are many reasons why dense and concentrated housing turns out positively, from an environmental point of view: First, sparsely populated areas have a much higher percentage of single-family (detached) houses. People living in single-family houses have a significantly higher energy consumption as well as material housing consumption than people in all other types of housing. Second, the houses are generally larger in sparsely populated areas, which again influences consumption patterns significantly. Finally, the percentage of households with access to a private car is higher in sparsely populated areas. Car access is the most important factor influencing a household's energy consumption for transport.

Everything that has been said about densely versus sparsely populated areas also applies to distances to the city centre. Households living near the city centre tend to live in multifamily residential buildings or smaller houses and have less access to a private car than those living near, or on, the urban fringe. One interesting point should be made, however. On average, household income levels are generally higher for those living in densely populated areas and near the city centre than for those living in sparsely populated outlying areas. However, despite this additional income, people living in the city centre have a smaller ecological footprint. When it comes to types of housing, the single-family (detached) house is a poor alternative, at least regarding the ecological footprint. On average, the ecological footprint per household member in a single-family house is almost 20 per cent bigger than that of household members living in more concentrated types of housing, that is, semi-detached or terraced houses and multifamily residential buildings (blocks of flats).

The Significance of Non-physical Factors

The question that occurs is: Are differences in people's physical living situations, like city size, density, distance and housing type, the only differences that matter in passenger transport patterns? Is it not possible that passenger transport patterns are really due to other differences such as social class, income, and the composition of the household? Or at least due to a combination of these factors? Yes, of course conditions such as income and household composition matter. But even when such conditions are controlled for using multivariate regression techniques, the physical/ structural dimensions remain central to the household's ecological footprint. It should be emphasized, however, that we did not find unambiguous significant relations between all land-use characteristics and footprint size. Further investigations are therefore needed to verify the connections between the living situations and the ecological footprints of the inhabitants.

Which non-physical factors play a role? The analyses show three predominant factors with significant influence on the ecological footprint per household member: First and most important is the number of people living in the house. There is an economy of scale present where the footprint can be shared among more people. The second factor is car occupancy. Households with access to a private car have a significantly bigger footprint than those without. The third factor is income. The fact that the number of people living in the household, car occupancy and income are important for the size of the ecological footprint comes as no surprise to us. Interestingly, however, the land-use characteristics also have a strong influence on the household's footprint.

Summary

The SusHomes Project supports the hypothesis that there is a connection between land-use characteristics and household consumption of energy and transport. Findings from the survey also lend great support to the compact city as a sustainable urban form. However, three distinct findings indicate that decentralised concentration could lead to even lower energy consumption in households: while the extent of everyday travel decreases in densely populated areas, the central urban areas represent the highest level of leisure-time travel by plane; the access to a private garden limits the extent of leisure travel; and, the difference in energy consumption for housing between single-family and multifamily housing is reduced in housing built after 1980, indicating that the established conclusions concerning which housing is most energy-efficient should be questioned.

The calculations of ecological footprint show that decentralized concentration could lead to smaller ecological footprints of households – a conclusion that seems to be enjoying widespread support. This could be integrated into policies that encourage the development of smaller compact towns and cities, or into policies that encourage decentralized concentration within existing cities.

PART III
The Theses and EU
Policy Implications

Chapter 8

Fourteen Theses of Sustainable Mobility

The empirical studies in chapters 4–7 and supplementary data are synthesized into fourteen theses of sustainable mobility. These theses, which are related to the extra prima characteristics of sustainable mobility, are described in relation to the roles of the following: new conventional and alternative technologies, public transport, green attitudes, and land-use planning.

Most of the theses are related to various ways of halving per capita energy consumption for transport, that is, the first extra prima characteristic, which is considered as the *main* aim of EU policy on sustainable mobility. Some theses are related to ensuring access to appropriate transport, that is, the second extra prima characteristic, and equitable distribution in space and time of the positive and negative impacts of transport activities, that is, the third extra prima characteristics. The relevance of the theses is not limited to EU policy; many of them apply to developed non-European countries and moreover, to developing countries. However, due to differences in socioeconomic and cultural contexts, care should be taken when applying them to non-European countries – particularly the theses that relate to the role of green attitudes.

Some of the fourteen theses are well known within the sustainable mobility literature but nevertheless can and should be backed by fresh empirical evidence. Others are not so well known, and some are even new, bringing new perspectives to the discussion of sustainable mobility, particularly the five theses that pertain to leisure-time travel. Some of the theses are supplemented by sub-theses to give them further strength. Taken together, the theses, well-known and new ones alike, constitute the basis for a theory of sustainable mobility.

The Role of Conventional Technology

I argue in this book that the *main* aim of EU policy on sustainable mobility is halving per capita energy consumption for transport. Although the EU has not acknowledged this aim, it has pursued energy reductions in the area of conventional technology through its work with the European Automobile Industry (ACEA[1]), including a July 1998 agreement to reduce the average CO_2 emissions of new cars sold in

---

1 ACEA: Association des Constructeurs Européens d'Automobiles (European Automobile Manufacturers Association). In 2002, ACEA had an 86.4 per cent market share in the EU-15. The ACEA's market shares of petrol and diesel vehicles were 56.3 per cent and 43.6 per cent, respectively. Between 1995 and 2002, their market share of petrol cars sank by 17.1 per cent and their market share of diesel cars rose by 19.6 per cent. The total number of new cars registered in the market increased by 13.8 per cent between 1995 and 2002.

2008 by 25 per cent (compared to 1995). Subsequently, ACEA reported that for the period 1995–2002 they cut average fuel consumption per vehicle for new petrol and diesel cars by 13.2 per cent; it fell from 7.6 l/100km to 6.6 l/100km, nearly meeting the intermediate target (CEC 2004). Over the same period, however, *total* fuel consumption by European cars rose by 8.1 per cent (EC 2003).

Therefore, despite the 1998 EU-ACEA agreement and impressive results through 2002, energy-efficiency technology in new petrol and diesel cars did not reduce *total* energy consumption. Figure 8.1 powerfully illustrates that the gains from this technology have been negated by other processes, a fact often referred to as 'the rebound effect.'

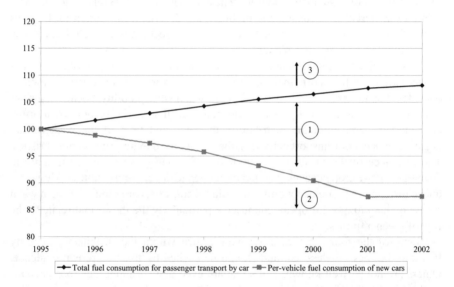

Figure 8.1   Total fuel consumption for passenger transport by car, and per-vehicle fuel consumption of new cars sold in the EU-15, 1995–2002 (1995=100)

Sources: European Commission (EC 2003; CEC 2004). Data for total fuel consumption for passenger transport by car (including motorcycles, which account for 3.7 per cent of total passenger kilometres).

Three factors contributed to this rebound effect: Two of them, an increase in total mileage travelled for passenger transport and an increase in sales of larger vehicles, increased *total* fuel consumption. For example, total mileage travelled for passenger transport increased by 13 per cent in the period 1995–2002. Furthermore, sales of larger vehicles with greater comfort features and more powerful engines also increased. The effect of larger vehicles on fuel consumption has been particularly strong since 2001, essentially negating the fuel savings from greater engine efficiency. However, the *full dimensions* of the increase in total fuel consumption were not completely clear due to the third factor, a flaw in the data which is caused by the certified measuring techniques. There is a gap, often called 'shortfall,' of up to 25 per cent between the fuel consumption levels indicated by official certification tests and actual on-road fuel consumption. Therefore, *actual* total fuel consumption for passenger transport by car increased even more than shown in figure 8.1.

These three factors are illustrated in figure 8.1. Growth in total mileage for passenger transport by car prevented engine-efficiency improvements from reducing total fuel consumption (1). The increased sales of larger vehicles with greater comfort features and more powerful engines prevented per-vehicle fuel consumption from falling as much as it could have (2). Finally, flawed data obscured the fact that the actual total fuel consumption for passenger transport by car is higher than indicated by the figure (3). The first three theses are concerned with the factors that contribute to the rebound effect.

Increases in the sales of larger vehicles and in the growth of total mileage travelled for passenger transport by car are expected to continue (OECD 2004). The gap between fuel consumption as measured by present certification tests and actual on-road consumption will continue to grow (OECD 2005). Therefore, unless measures are taken to address both issues, a reduction in total fuel consumption for passenger transport by car is not likely to happen. The rebound effect applies to not only passenger transport by car; a very similar pattern is found for passenger transport by plane. The International Air Transport Association (IATA) reports that today's world fleet of aircraft is about 70 per cent more fuel-efficient per passenger kilometre than the 1960s fleet. In the period 1990–2000, according to IATA, the fleet's fuel efficiency improved by 17 per cent. In the same period, however, *total* fuel consumption for passenger transport by plane rose by 58 per cent (EC 2003), mainly due to a dramatic increase in total annual mileage travelled by plane.[2]

Thesis 1: Growth in passenger transport mileage counteracts reductions in fuel consumption from increased engine efficiency.

The fact that growth in transport volumes counteracts reductions in per capita fuel consumption from increased engine efficiency is acknowledged by a number of scholars (for example, Banister et al. 2000; Banister 2005; Høyer 2000; OECD 2004). Figure 8.2 shows total annual mileage for passenger transport by car and plane, and total annual mileage for passenger transport by all means (including train, boat, etc.) in the EU-15 in the period 1970–2002. Total annual mileage for passenger transport by car increased from 1,562 billion passenger kilometres in 1970 to 3,882 billion passenger kilometres in 2002, a 149 per cent increase (EC 2004). Total annual mileage for travel by all means of motorized transport increased from 2,118 to 4,927 billion passenger kilometres in the same 32-year period, a 133 per cent increase. Thus, passenger transport by car makes up a larger share of total motorized transport than previously.

There are no indications that the total annual mileage for passenger transport by car will decrease. Instead, it is expected to increase by 16 per cent in OECD countries 2000–2010 and by 32 per cent 2000–2020 (OECD 2004). In the EU-15,

---

2   The increase is based on domestic flights and intra-EU flights. If, however extra-EU flights were included, the increase in fuel consumption would be even larger.

the total annual mileage for passenger transport by car is estimated to increase 38 per cent by 2030 (EC 2003). To compensate for this increase it would be necessary to improve the fuel efficiency of the whole European fleet by the same magnitude – which would represent a real challenge. This suggests that vehicle fuel-saving technology alone cannot be relied on to reduce fuel consumption for passenger transport by car in the next decades (OECD 2004).

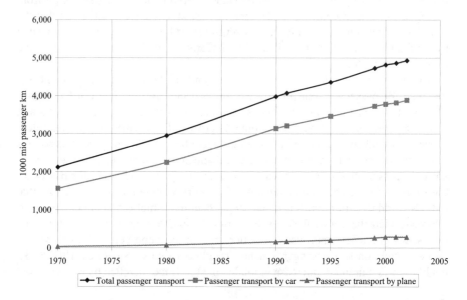

Figure 8.2   Passenger transport in the EU-15: total mileage, passenger transport by car and plane, 1970–2002

Source: EC 2004. Passenger transport by plane includes domestic and intra-EU-15 flights.

Total annual mileage for passenger transport by plane increased from 33 billion passenger kilometres in 1970 to 280 billion passenger kilometres in 2002, a staggering 748 per cent increase (EC 2004). Between 1995 and 2002, the increase was 39 per cent, compared to 12 per cent for passenger transport by car and 13 per cent for passenger transport by all means. Thus, the increase in total mileage travelled for passenger transport by plane mainly characterises the increase in individual mobility during the last decade. The figures for air travel in the EU-15 in figure 8.2 are greatly underestimated because they include only domestic and intra EU-15 flights. Of the total passengers transported by air in the EU-25 in 2004, 24 per cent were carried on domestic flights, 42 per cent on intra-EU flights and 34 per cent on extra-EU flights. The 34 per cent carried on extra-EU flights, which tend to be much longer distance than domestic and intra-EU flights, adds a substantial mileage to the mileage shown in figure 8.2. (Extra-EU flights are included in the scenario analyses in chapter 9.)

The total kilometres travelled on domestic and intra-EU flights is expected to reach 850 billion passenger kilometres by 2030 (EC 2003). In addition, a large increase in passenger kilometres travelled in extra-EU flights is expected in the same period (Åkerman 2005). Even though the potential for fuel-saving in aviation by using conventional technology is considerable, as much as a 30–40 per cent reduction seems realistic by 2050, this reduction will still offset only a minor part of the projected increase in mileage for passenger transport by plane (ibid.). Thus, fuel consumption for passenger transport by plane will increase rapidly if the growth is not curbed or if more radical technological solutions are not found.

Thesis 2: Heavier, more powerful vehicles with energy-demanding auxiliaries are less fuel-efficient, which counteracts reductions in energy consumption from increased engine efficiency.

Heavier, more powerful vehicles with energy-demanding auxiliaries are less fuel-efficient, which counteracts reductions in energy consumption from increased engine efficiency. The average per-vehicle fuel consumption of new European passenger cars improved significantly during the 1970s and early 1980s. However, this trend towards improved fuel efficiency has slowed in recent years, due to the increased popularity of heavier, more powerful cars (OECD 2004). The average per-vehicle fuel consumption of new US passenger cars[3] shows an even less promising pattern: substantial decreases in fuel consumption until the mid 1980s and then, because of heavier and more powerful vehicles, increases in fuel consumption thereafter (ibid.). For example, because they were heavier and more powerful, model year 2001 US passenger vehicles had about the same average fuel consumption as model year 1981 vehicles. Had they had the same average weight and performance as the 1981 models, they would have had more than a 25 per cent reduction in fuel consumption (Hellman and Heavenrich 2001).

Per-vehicle fuel consumption in the EU-15 fell less than expected because of increases in individual model's weight and performance (power). For example, the Volkswagen Golf's weight increased from 800 kg in the 1970s (Golf I model) to more than 1,100 kg in 2000 (Golf IV model). Similar trends can be found in Japanese and US vehicles. Added weight has increased fuel consumption, and individual model's greater performance (power, acceleration and top-speed characteristics) has also increased fuel consumption. Between 1995 and 2002, the average engine power in a Volkswagen Golf increased from 55kW to 80kW. Increased engine power usually leads to increased fuel consumption. The weight and performance of the Volkswagen Golf are shown in figure 8.3, which shows how weight, performance and fuel consumption are interrelated. Between 1975 and 1985, vehicle weight and performance increased only slightly. However, *despite* this increase and *thanks* to simultaneous major improvements in engine fuel efficiency, there was a significant reduction in fuel consumption during the same period. The same pattern was repeated between 1985 and 1995, although a slightly larger increase in vehicle weight and performance cut into the reduction in fuel consumption made possible by other technology; so, the reduction in fuel consumption was less than in the

---

3   Referring to new light vehicles, which include sport utility vehicles (SUVs). SUVs represent around 50 per cent of the US light-vehicle market.

previous 10-year period. After 1997, however, there has been no reduction in fuel consumption, due to large increases in both vehicle weight and performance which have counteracted reductions from fuel saving technologies.

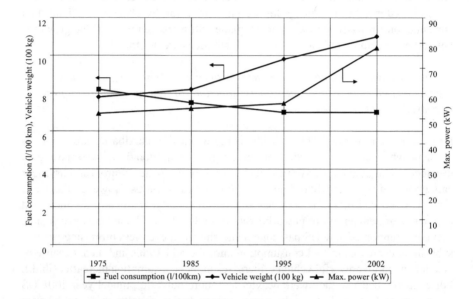

Figure 8.3   Volkswagen Golf: Fuel consumption, vehicle weight and max. power, 1975–2002

Source: Volkswagen.

Not only did cars become heavier and more laden with high-performance, fuel-guzzling features – such cars, especially SUVs, took an increased market share in the EU-15. This increase in the sales of heavier, more powerful, and therefore less fuel-efficient vehicles, is a second reason for the smaller than expected reduction in per-vehicle fuel consumption in the EU-15. Worse, despite overall weakness in the West European car market, sales of SUVs there increased 11.6 per cent to a record 947,200 units in 2005 (Schmidt 2006). Sadly, this represented a record market share for SUVs for the second year running – 6.5 per cent which was up from 5.8 per cent in 2004. The European car fleet is increasingly becoming heavier and therefore less fuel efficient.

Over all, the average physical characteristics of the EU-15 passenger vehicle fleet increased between 1995 and 2002 (CEC 2000; CEC 2004). Average vehicle weight increased by 10.3 per cent, from 1,101 kg to 1,214 kg. Average vehicle weight increased for both gasoline and diesel cars. Average engine capacity increased by 5.4 per cent, from 1,654 cm^3 to 1,744 cm^3. Average engine power increased by 23.8 per cent, from 63 kW to 78 kW.

If the weight and performance of new cars continue to increase, per-vehicle fuel consumption of new cars (which decreased 1995–2002) will increase. While the

EU-15 fleet's physical characteristics increased between 1995 and 2002, figure 8.1 shows that average per-vehicle fuel consumption of new cars actually decreased in the same period (CEC 2004). According to ACEA this indicates that the reduction in fuel consumption due to increased engine efficiency compensated for the increase in fuel consumption due to increased vehicle weight and performance. For two reasons, however, it is uncertain whether this compensation effect will continue to contribute to reductions in per-vehicle fuel consumption for new cars: First, about one-third of the ACEA-reported 1995–2002 reduction in per-vehicle fuel consumption results from increased sales of diesel vehicles, which are more fuel-efficient than petrol vehicles. The market share of diesel vehicles in the EU-15 increased by 20 per cent in the 7-year period. Obviously, at some point this trend towards more diesel vehicles will cease contributing to a reduction in the fleet's total fuel consumption. Second, the full effect of increased SUV sales in the European market, which have been particularly strong since 2002, is not reflected in the latest EU-ACEA report. The report gives, however, an indication of the effects of increased sales of heavier and more powerful vehicles: Figure 8.1 shows that the fuel consumption for new cars remained unchanged between 2001 and 2002. Thus, unless sales of small and fuel-efficient vehicles are greater than sales of SUVs, there is every reason to believe that the 1995–2002 reduction in per-vehicle fuel consumption of new cars will be neither matched nor improved on in the future.

Thesis 3: There is a significant gap between fuel consumption measured by official certification tests and actual on-road fuel consumption.

A gap, often referred to as 'shortfall', is widely known to exist between per-vehicle fuel consumption as measured in official certification tests and actual on-road fuel consumption (OECD 2005). Furthermore, in recent years it has been speculated that this gap is growing. Consequently, there are two major concerns: first that consumers will regard fuel consumption figures as unreliable, and second that fuel consumption reduction goals might not actually be achieved despite official certification tests suggesting that they have been.

In an extensive review of shortfall data, the OECD found few recent assessments of shortfalls in OECD countries and therefore called for new empirical studies. Meanwhile, available studies report that on-road fuel consumption is 20–30 per cent higher than fuel consumption measured by certification tests.

There are six main reasons for shortfalls (OECD 2004; OECD 2005): First, ambient conditions during real-world driving differ substantially from ambient conditions during certification tests. The tests are usually conducted at 20–25°C, whereas actual temperatures in most populated areas range from –30°C to +40°C. The tests are also conducted under zero wind and precipitation conditions. However, temperature significantly influences fuel consumption, especially when the engine is started cold; during the first kilometre after a 'cold' start at 20°C, fuel consumption is up to three times higher than it is when a fully warmed-up engine is tested. However, even when the engine is fully warmed up, low ambient temperatures increase fuel consumption significantly.

Second, the certification test conditions differ from real-world traffic conditions. Many observers have commented that the 'typical' travel mix used for US and EU fuel certification testing is incorrect. Due to increased congestion in the suburbs and on highways, real-world traffic conditions include more so-called 'urban driving' than the certification tests do. Fuel consumption is typically 30–40 per cent higher in urban (slow, stop-and-go) driving than in (uncongested) highway driving.

Third, during certification tests all power-consuming accessories are turned off. However, when these accessories are turned on, vehicle fuel consumption increases dramatically – from 20 per cent to up to 100 per cent (in smaller vehicles). Modern cars are increasingly equipped with accessories like air conditioners, auxiliary heaters, and a wide variety of electronics which enhance comfort and safety. In today's cars these draw about 1kW; in cars to be built in the next decade they are expected to draw up to 12 kW.

Fourth, the certification tests are not neutral with respect to type or technology; for example, all regenerative braking possibilities in electric and hybrid vehicles, even where available, are not taken into account. This is another way in which the certification test conditions differ from real-world traffic conditions. Furthermore, the tests are not neutral with respect to vehicle size; the tests unfairly disadvantage small, very fuel-efficient cars.

Fifth, studies show that several factors, for example, low tyre pressure and bad quality oil, could increase shortfall by 10–20 per cent. Engine-related maintenance, in contrast, does not have much impact on shortfall because modern engines are designed to need less maintenance. However, modern engines have customized control chips instead of old-style electronic engine-management systems. These customized control chips are designed to maximise performance in terms of power output in on-road conditions regardless of the effect on fuel consumption. Anecdotal evidence suggests that such chips may contribute significantly to the growing shortfall.

Sixth, driving styles introduce large variations in fuel consumption because driver behaviour is complex and influenced by numerous parameters. The parameters most effecting fuel consumption are gear selection, acceleration and deceleration patterns, high-speed driving, and prolonged idling. Many consumers choose to accelerate rapidly and to drive fast despite knowing that these reduce fuel efficiency and therefore cost them money. Behavioural changes could reduce fuel consumption significantly; studies conducted in Europe and the US suggest that driver training could reduce fuel consumption 5–20 per cent.

As mentioned above, the shortfall is problematic for two reasons: First, certified test data are a basis for consumer information. However, many consumers neither understand the limitations of the official certification tests nor realise that official test conditions are *not* representative of real-world driving conditions. If they were to have accurate information about real-world fuel consumption, consumers might be motivated to buy smaller, less powerful cars. Second, as long as official tests are performed with all auxiliary systems switched off, manufactures will be encouraged to develop vehicles which perform best in terms of the official test conditions rather than in terms of real-world driving conditions. If the tests were to reflect real-world driving conditions, manufacturers would have an incentive to develop an optimal engine-calibration strategy for low fuel consumption that would take the additional loads from auxiliary systems into account.

The Role of Alternative Technology

Due to the rebound effects presented in the previous section, the new conventional technology approach has its limitations regarding the goal of halving per capita energy consumption for transport. Therefore, the alternative technology approach has been suggested as a way around these limitations. However, the rebound effects, and hence the limitations, apply just as much to the alternative technology approach. Thus, continuous increases in passenger transport mileage and in sales of larger and more powerful vehicles would also counteract the benefits derived from the alternative technology approach. Furthermore, flaws in official certification tests measuring fuel consumption apply regardless of the technology tested.

Moreover, alternative technology introduces two *new* rebound effects: the geographic transfer of energy consumption and the thematic transfer of environmental impacts. Before presenting two theses which describe these two new rebound effects I want to briefly discuss the terms 'energy chain', 'new, conventional technology', and 'alternative technology'. (These terms are defined in detail in chapter 4.)

An energy chain links three parts, an energy source, a fuel and a vehicle's drive system, all of which are important in determining total energy consumption. Whereas the new conventional technology approach seeks incremental improvements in various parts of *existing* conventional energy chains, the alternative technology approach seeks to implement fundamentally *new* technology into one or more of the parts composing energy chains, for example, a new energy source, a new fuel, or a new vehicle drive system. Hence, in this sense such energy chains could be called alternative energy chains; however, the difference between conventional and alternative energy chains is not so sharp in all cases because a specific alternative energy chain could include elements from both conventional and alternative technologies. An energy chain made up of alternative technology in all three parts is called a *pure alternative* energy chain, for example, hydropower-based (alternative energy source), hydrogen-fuelled (alternative fuel), fuel-cell vehicles (alternative drive system). An energy chain made up of conventional technology in some parts and alternative technology in other parts is called a *hybrid alternative* energy chain, for example, biomass-based (alternative energy source), diesel-fuelled (conventional fuel), ICE vehicles (conventional drive system).

Therefore, an assessment of the role of alternative technology must include an evaluation of all energy chains that contain fundamental technology changes in *one or more* of their parts. Thus, both pure alternative energy chains and hybrid alternative energy chains are included when assessing below the role of alternative technology. In most literature in this area, the terms 'alternative fuels' and 'alternative energy chains' essentially mean the same thing; hence, these terms are used interchangeably below.

Thesis 4: The use of alternative fuels merely transfers energy consumption geographically (that is, from the vehicle to the production site and the distribution process); it does not reduce total energy consumption.

The well-to-wheel analysis presented in chapter 4 powerfully illustrates this geographic transfer effect: Fuel-cell vehicles are more energy efficient than vehicles with conventional internal combustion engines (ICEs), which means that they consume less energy per kilometre driven. Figure 8.4 shows that whereas vehicles with conventional diesel-fuelled ICEs consume 1.64 MJ/km, the fuel-cell vehicles consume 1.22–1.45 MJ/km (data from chapter 4). However, the hydrogen to power the fuel cell generally requires more energy to produce and distribute from its energy sources than is required to produce and distribute petrol and diesel from their energy source, raw oil. Thus, the well-to-wheel (WTW) energy consumption of the fuel-cell energy chains is higher than the WTW energy consumption of the conventional ICE energy chains.

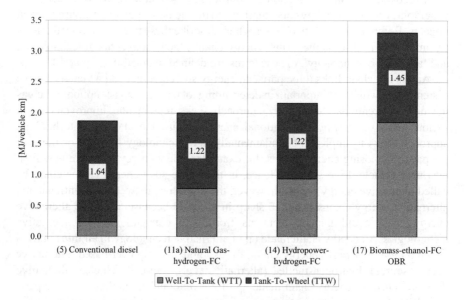

Figure 8.4   Well-to-wheel energy consumption in 2010 (passenger car under mixed driving conditions)

More specifically, figure 8.4 shows that compared to the WTW energy consumption of the energy chain with the conventional ICE diesel vehicle (energy chain 5): the WTW energy consumption of energy chain 11a is 7 per cent higher; the WTW energy consumption of energy chain 14 is 16 per cent higher; and finally the WTW energy consumption of energy chain 17, in which hydrogen is reformed from ethanol on the vehicle, is 77 per cent higher. Thus, these three alternative energy chains do not reduce total energy consumption.

Moreover, the analysis in chapter 4 shows that, compared to the WTW energy consumption of the energy chain with the conventional ICE diesel vehicle (energy chain 5), *all but two* energy chains have equal or higher WTW energy consumption. However the respective WTW energy consumptions of these two energy chains are based, in one case, on a very optimistic assumption of the efficiency of the fuel cell (energy chain 11b), and in the other case, on a pure electric vehicle (energy chain 13).[4] The optimistic assumption regarding a very highly efficient fuel cell remains to be verified. Furthermore, the pure electric car has considerably reduced performance compared to present conventional vehicles.

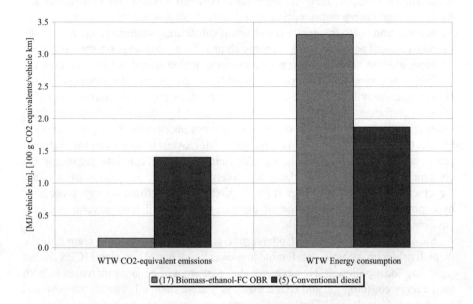

Figure 8.5　Well-to-wheel energy consumption and CO_2-equivalent emissions in 2010 (passenger car under mixed conditions)

Thus, the great amount of energy required to produce and distribute alternative fuels counteracts the benefits derived from the fuel efficiency of vehicles using them. Hence, due to this 'geographical rebound effect', the use of alternative fuels merely *transfers* energy consumption *geographically*, that is, from the vehicle to the production site and the distribution process; it does not reduce total energy consumption.

4　Energy chain 14 starts with hydropower. However, electric vehicles are more likely to be powered by natural gas–based or coal-based electricity. In both these cases, the WTW energy consumption will be greater than the WTW energy consumption of the conventional ICE energy chains (Bang and Holden 1991).

Thesis 5: There are always trade-offs involved in the use of alterative fuels because their use merely changes environmental impacts thematically, rather than reducing the total overall environmental impacts.

This thematic trade-off is illustrated in figure 8.5. Based on the WTW analyses in chapter 4, the figure shows the environmental trade-off from substituting raw oil–based conventional ICE diesel vehicles (energy chain 5) with biomass-based ethanol fuel-cell vehicles (energy chain 17). On the one hand, the substitution reduces GHG emissions substantially. On the other hand, it increases total energy consumption substantially. Thus, the thematic trade-off is between reduced GHG emissions and increased total energy consumption.

Similar trade-offs frequently occur when substituting alternative energy chains for conventional petrol and diesel energy chains. Three examples are shown below:

First, electric vehicles have zero emissions, which would seem to make them preferable to conventional petrol and diesel ICE vehicles regarding local pollution. However, there will be large increases in both total energy consumption and CO_2 emissions if these electric vehicles are powered by electricity produced from fossil energy sources like raw oil or coal (but not necessarily if they are powered by electricity produced from natural gas). Moreover, if these electric vehicles are powered by hydropower-based electricity, land-use conflicts regarding the construction of hydropower dams are likely. Therefore, regardless of whether the electricity needed to power them is produced from fossil energy sources or hydropower, the implementation of electric vehicles will have several negative environmental impacts.

Second, fuel-cell vehicles also have zero emissions, which would seem to make them, like electric vehicles, preferable to conventional petrol and diesel ICE vehicles regarding local pollution. However, as above, there will be large increases in both total energy consumption and CO_2 emissions if these fuel-cell vehicles are powered by coal-based hydrogen. Furthermore, producing hydrogen by the electrolysis of water, which requires substantial amounts of electricity, would further increase total energy consumption. If such electricity were from nuclear-power plants, which is the most likely long-term scenario for widespread use of hydrogen, a trade-off would have to be made between the advantages of zero local pollution and the potential risks from storing large quantities of radioactive nuclear waste. Therefore, the implementation of hydrogen-fuelled fuel-cell vehicles, although eliminating local pollution, would have, as above, several negative environmental impacts.

Third, the use of biomass-based fuels instead of raw oil–based fuels would substantially reduce GHG emissions. However, growing biomass feedstock would cause land-use conflicts, for example loss of biodiversity. Therefore, the implementation of an alternative fuel would once again have negative environmental impacts.

Is there any alternative energy chain that offers significant promise without significant trade-offs? As indicated by the ecological footprint analyses in chapter 4, the natural gas–based energy chains, mainly because they emit less NO_x and SO_2, have smaller ecological footprints than the conventional energy chains. However, they have virtually the same WTW energy consumption. Surely, one must expect more of an alternative energy chain than *marginal* reductions in WTW energy consumption and the ecological footprint.

Thus, the use of alternative fuels generally reduces the environmental impact in one impact category – for example it reduces total CO_2 emissions thereby reducing greenhouse gas emissions – but this lone positive impact is counteracted by increased negative environmental impacts in other impact categories, such as increased total energy consumption and environmentally harmful land use. Hence, the use of alternative fuels merely *changes* environmental impacts *thematically*. Consequently, due to this 'thematic rebound effect,' it is not very likely that the use of alternative fuels will reduce overall total environmental impacts.

The Role of Public Transport

Continuous growth of passenger transport by car and plane counteracts efforts at halving energy consumption for passenger transport through the use of new conventional and alternative technologies. Furthermore, such growth also counteracts efforts at halving energy consumption through the expansion of public transport because, in practice, expanded public transport cannot take up more than a small part of such growth. Therefore, unless policies to dampen such growth are applied *along with* policies to expand public transport, the expansion of public transport will not lead to reduced energy consumption for passenger transport.

Nevertheless, an effective, well-functioning and affordable public transport system is a prerequisite for ensuring access for low-mobility groups of people to their basic transport needs. Moreover, in cities facing major congestion problems, a good public transport system offers better mobility for everyone. Thus, public transport is an important part of a sustainable mobility strategy; however, the realisation of its inherent energy-reduction potential relies on the simultaneous implementation of policies to reduce growth in passenger transport by car and plane.

There are, furthermore, indirect links between improving a public transport system and reducing energy consumption for passenger transport by car and plane (IEA 2002a). First, a better public transport system could have mode-switching impacts: increased access to bus, tram, or light rail in cities could attract routine car travellers; and new inter-city high-speed rail connections could attract routine air travellers. Second, over time, a better public transport system could affect people's choices of living and working locations; for example, a high-speed bus or rail service, with stops every one-half kilometre, could spur housing and business development close to those stops. Research shows that high accessibility to public transport influences people's transport mode choices and subsequently their energy consumption for transport. Third, improved public transport technology could also have mode-switching impacts; for example, due to their new features, a modern low-floor bus or an automatically guided rail system may attract new groups of travellers.

Although these indirect links between improved public transport and people's *potentially* increased use of it are interesting, they will not be treated further here. The theses below focus on the direct links between increased use of public transport and total energy consumption for passenger transport, and on the *direct* links between improved public transport and improved accessibility to transport for low-mobility people.

Thesis 6: Without strategies for reducing the total mileage for passenger transport by car and plane, the role of public transport as a means of reducing total energy consumption will be modest.

The relations between passenger transport volume, proportion of public transport and total energy consumption for passenger transport are shown in table 8.1. The table shows how energy consumption develops in the three 2016 scenarios of the Greater Oslo study presented in chapter 5: the private car scenario, the public transport scenario, and the sustainability scenario.

Table 8.1   Scenarios for total passenger transport, proportion of public transport and total energy consumption for passenger transport in Greater Oslo

Scenario	Total passenger transport[i] [Mill pkm]	Public transport[ii] [Mill pkm]	Public transport, proportion of total [%]	Energy consumption [% of 1996]
1996 Base case	4,446	807	18.2	100%
2016 Private car scenario	5,324	807	15.2	92%
2016 Public transport scenario	5,324	1,389	26.1	81%
2016 Sustainability scenario	4,049	1,389	34.3	44%

(i) Includes travel by non-motorised transport, but not aviation.
(ii) Includes travel by bus, train, tram and metro.

The private car scenario assumes that total transport volume increases at present rates and that public transport volume remains unchanged at the 1996 level. The public transport scenario also assumes that total transport volume increases at present rates, but that there is simultaneously a strong increase in public transport volume. The sustainability scenario assumes that total transport volume decreases and that the public transport volume increases at the same rate as in the public transport scenario. All three scenarios assume that new, improved technologies will be implemented in all means of transport.

Three conclusions can be drawn from table 8.1. First, the private car scenario shows that the reduction in energy consumption due to use of more energy-efficient technologies in *all means* of public and private transport is almost negated by the increase in energy consumption due to transport growth (as already stated in thesis

1). Thus, only a modest 8 per cent reduction in total energy consumption can be expected over a 20-year period. Second, compared to the private car scenario, the public transport scenario shows that the additional reduction in energy consumption due to increased use of public transport is a mere 11 per cent because, even in the public transport scenario, a significant part of the transport growth is taken up by cars. Third, only when an increase in use of public transport is combined with a reduction in total passenger transport volume, as assumed in the sustainability scenario, can a large reduction in energy consumption be achieved.

The conclusions from the scenario analyses for Greater Oslo find support in two other studies. A study of a 2030 *national* public transport scenario in Norway – including an increase in long-distance railway travel at the expense of plane travel – shows an 11 per cent reduction in total energy consumption (Aall et al. 1997). A study of a 2030 *Nordic* public transport scenario (Norway, Sweden, Denmark, Finland and Island) shows a stabilisation of total energy consumption in the Nordic countries (Jahn Hansen et al. 2000).

The conclusions from the Norwegian and Nordic studies also find support in a recent study by the International Energy Agency (IEA 2002a). Two 2020 scenarios were developed for New Delhi; in one, transport by bus as a proportion of the total passenger transport volume declines (the reference scenario) and in the other, it increases (the aggressive bus scenario). The same forecast for growth in passenger transport volume was used in both scenarios. The New Delhi scenarios are comparable to the scenarios developed in the Greater Oslo study, and the conclusions from the IEA study are similar to the conclusions of the Greater Oslo study. First, the IEA study shows a strong increase in energy consumption when total passenger volume increases and the proportion of transport by bus decreases. Second, the study shows that in the aggressive bus scenario, when both total passenger volume and the proportion of transport by bus increase, the energy consumption still increases, although at a much lower level than in the reference scenario. This is because the reduction in energy consumption derived from the increased proportion of transport by bus is negated by the increase in energy consumption due to the increase in total passenger volume. Finally, the study concludes that unless policies aimed at increasing the proportion of transport by bus are implemented simultaneously with policies aimed at reducing the growth in passenger transport by car and plane, as in the Greater Oslo sustainability scenario, sustainable mobility will not be achieved.

True, a small reduction in, or even a stabilisation of, present level of energy consumption would be steps in the right direction. However, it is far from achieving the 50 per cent reduction in per capita energy consumption which is necessary to comply with the first extra prima characteristics of sustainable mobility. Such a reduction is only possible when policies increasing public transport are implemented simultaneously with policies reducing growth in passenger transport by car and plane.

The conclusions of the empirical studies referred to above are relevant for assessing energy consumption and public transport scenarios in EU cities and countries.[5] Based on the Millennium Cities Database for Sustainable Transport,

---

5   The means by which an increase in public transport could be achieved would, however, be different city-by-city.

Kenworthy and Laube (2002a) report that in 1995, public transport in 35 Western European cities averaged 19 per cent of total motorized passenger transport volume. Increasing this to the 26.1 per cent of the Greater Oslo public transport scenario would bring the average proportion of public transport in the EU-15 cities near to Vienna's 31.6 per cent, which is the highest in the EU-15 at present. *On a country level*, the 2016 Greater Oslo pubic transport scenario is relevant too. In 2002, the average proportion of public transport in the EU-15 (including non-urban areas) was 16.6 per cent (15.5 when travel by plane is included) (EC 2004). Increasing this to the 26.1 per cent of the Greater Oslo public transport scenario would bring the average proportion of public transport in the EU-15 up to Austria's 25.9 per cent, presently the highest proportion of public transport in the EU-15.

Without doubt, increasing public transport proportions in European cities to Vienna's level and in European countries to Austria's level represents a major challenge for the EU's public transport sectors. Yet, without simultaneous policies to decrease growth in passenger transport by car and plane, increased public transport would hardly affect the cities' and countries' total energy consumption for passenger transport.

Thesis 7: An affordable and well-functioning public transport system must ensure accessibility for low-mobility groups of people to their basic needs so as to prevent their social exclusion.

Being mobile – having access to public transport to meet basic needs and prevent social exclusion – is a basic necessity of people living in modern societies. However, mobility, unlike movement, is a contextualized phenomenon which can be interpreted in various ways. Jones (1987) interprets mobility in terms of individual action, potential action and freedom of action. As individual action, mobility is expressed in observed movement and travel. As potential action, mobility is expressed in journeys people would like to take, but are unable to take because of various limitations. As freedom of action, mobility is never expressed in action, but it gives one options from which to select and the knowledge that one could do something. All three interpretations influence individual mobility.

Although average individual mobility has increased dramatically during the last century, particularly in the developed countries, it has not increased for all groups of people. Whereas concepts like 'time-space compression' and 'social fluidification,' both of which nourish and express increased mobility, have come to be accepted as given characteristics of the present times, these concepts remain grossly under-examined in terms of their social distribution (Uteng 2006). Research has demonstrated that access to mobility is distributed extremely unevenly in societies.

People having low mobility – expressed as individual action, potential action and as freedom of action – have inadequate access to appropriate means of private and public transport to meet their basic human needs, like travel to work and to vital private and public services. Consequently, they face social exclusion. A very simple, basic definition of social exclusion is presented by Hine and Mitchell (2001, 12): 'Social exclusion is a process which causes individuals or groups, who are geographically resident in a society, not to participate in the normal activities in that society.' In treating social exclusion as a 'process', this definition emphasizes not only income-based indicators of poverty, but also access to transport. Uteng (2006) uses 'transport-related exclusion' to refer to social exclusion resulting from a lack of access to transport.

In a workshop on transport and social exclusion at the 10th International Conference on Travel Behaviour Research, three interpretations of social exclusion were outlined (Lyons and Kenyon 2003). The first interpretation refers to social exclusion as 'experiencing public service failure.' This interpretation recognizes that the system or societal structure gives rise to the social exclusion suffered by an individual or a group. The second interpretation refers to social exclusion as 'the discrepancy between what you can do and what you want to do.' This is a helpful interpretation which reflects the perspective of the affected individual and suggests the beginnings of a means to measure in absolute and relative terms the extent of the exclusion experienced. The third interpretation refers to social exclusion as 'a spectrum of deprivation.' This interpretation asserts that social exclusion does not have a binary state (that is, an individual A is either excluded or included); instead, it asserts, an individual's social exclusion can only be measured on a multi-dimensional scale of deprivation. Therefore, social policy determines the point on that scale beyond which the deprivation is considered unacceptable. In all three interpretations, access to well-functioning and affordable public transport would prevent social exclusion, whereas lack of such access would give rise to transport-related social exclusion.

Studies have identified several categories of people who face transport-related social exclusion (Litman 2003; Uteng 2006). The extent of the transport-related social exclusion is not the same for all these categories; furthermore, it can be assumed that the more the following factors apply to an individual or a group, the greater the degree of social exclusion they are likely to experience:

- Lack of an automobile (Households lacking an automobile are sometimes called zero-vehicle households.).
- Lack of a driver's license.
- Low income.
- Unemployment or underemployment.
- Dependence on social assistance and other programs to help disadvantaged groups.
- Recent immigration from a developing country (Such immigrants tend to face language barriers and social isolation, to experience poverty and unemployment, to have low rates of vehicle ownership, and to lack a driver's license.).
- Residence in outlying and very remote areas.

Public transport is likely to be the primary mode of transport for the individuals and groups most affected by these factors. Furthermore, their transport-related exclusion is likely to be increased if there are inadequacies in the public transport system such as expensive tickets, limited frequency and availability, and a lack of punctuality.

A recent survey of the mobility patterns of first-generation non-Western immigrants in Norway gives some insight into transport-related social exclusion (Uteng 2006).[6] These immigrants experience many forms of social exclusion. Moreover, even though this group differs from other Norwegian low-mobility groups in terms of cultural background, their socioeconomic backgrounds are quite similar. Thus, the results from the study are relevant for all low-mobility groups.

The survey reveals that only 40 per cent of the immigrants live in a household which owns or has use of a car, compared to 85 per cent of the Norwegian population as a whole. Thus, the immigrants depend to a much greater extent than others on public transport for their daily mobility needs. While only 9 per cent of the Norwegian population use public transport for their daily mobility, 73 per cent of the immigrants depend on it for their daily mobility.

Lack of access to a car and thus dependency on public transport are closely linked to transport-related social exclusion. First, employment opportunities in the Norwegian labour market, especially for those who live outside the large cities, are greater for candidates who own or have use of a car. About 55 per cent agreed that having a driver's licence would make it easier for them to get a job; some were denied jobs solely because they lacked a driver's licence. Second, a large number of the employed respondents work irregular hours when the availability of public transport is severely limited. Likewise, the availability of public transport on weekends and holidays is severely limited. Third, the above-mentioned limitations also apply to non-work and leisure-time travel. Shopping, taking children to child care and school, and visiting friends and family (which typically takes place outside public transport peak hours) are cumbersome for those who are dependent on public transport. Fourth, a comparison of the respondents' and the Norwegian population's disposable incomes, reveals that a fairly significant number of respondents are struggling financially. Thus, the expense of public transport is a hardship faced by a majority of the respondents.

The results from the survey of the mobility patterns of first-generation non-Western immigrants can be generalised to other low-mobility groups. All categories of Norwegians facing transport-related social exclusion would experience mobility problems due to these limitations of public transport. Moreover, the results can to a large extent be generalised into a European context. The EU White Paper on Transport (CEC 2001) gives much attention to achieving increased accessibility to public transport for low-mobility groups. Clearly, the goal of increased accessibility to public transport for these groups is based on an understanding that at present they face transport-related social exclusion. Consequently, an affordable and well-functioning public transport system is necessary to ensure accessibility for low-mobility groups and thus to achieve sustainable mobility.

---

6   The questionnaires were sent to 125 randomly selected individuals living in three Norwegian cities – including a large city, a medium-sized city and a rural town – which reflect the living situation for Norwegian households as a whole. Thus, even though the sample is small, the results are representative of the mobility patterns of the larger population of first-generation non-Western immigrants in Norway.

The Role of Green Attitudes

Having green attitudes – positive attitudes towards conservation and environmental issues – is often seen as a prerequisite for reducing individuals' energy consumption for transport. However, the relation between individuals' green attitudes and their transport behaviour is ambiguous. Furthermore, the relation is a *contingent* one, that is, it is *situational* in nature. Thus, assessing the role (indeed the efficacy) of green attitudes in bringing about low-energy transport behaviour must take individuals' situations into account.

Situations wherein green attitudes lead to low-energy transport behaviour involve, according to attitude theory, attitude-behaviour consistency. On the other hand, situations wherein green attitudes do *not* lead to low-energy transport behaviour involve attitude-behaviour *in*consistency. The three theses presented in this section regarding the role of green attitudes are all concerned with situations that lead to either consistent or inconsistent behaviour.

The three theses describe the *direct* relations between green attitudes and low-energy transport behaviour. Alas, as the theses will show, these relations are not very encouraging for those who rely on green attitudes alone to bring about low-energy transport behaviour.

There are, however, potentially important *indirect* relations between green attitudes and transport behaviour. On the one hand, people with green attitudes (sometimes referred to as 'greens' or 'green people' below) might not take the bus as often as they wish they did, or they might be far too keen on driving their cars even if they know they should not. On the other hand, greens accept restrictions designed to reduce car traffic, and support increased investment in public transport infrastructure – which could lead to reductions in energy consumption for transport. Thus, in essence, greens willingly make long-term sacrifices to reduce their own energy consumption for transport as well as that of others.

Ultimately, however, it remains to be seen whether greens are willing to 'walk the walk' or merely 'talk the talk,' to *truly* sacrifice to achieve significant reductions in energy consumption for transport or merely to *talk* about sacrifice. In any event, in democracies, any low-energy transport measure must be supported by a majority. Therefore, greens must eventually be successful in persuading their fellow citizens to adopt their green attitudes on sustainable transport. Moreover, greens must get busy putting together a majority of voters who agree with them on low-energy transport measures.

Thesis 8: The correlation between specific attitudes towards everyday travel and everyday travel behaviour is significant, whereas the correlation between general environmental attitudes and everyday travel behaviour is insignificant.

Acceptance by public officials of the existence of this (as described above) *contingent* relation between green attitudes and actual everyday travel behaviour will have profound consequences on how these officials will formulate public information and awareness campaigns designed to promote sustainable mobility. Such campaigns will only be effective if they are *targeted* at specific behaviour – for example, informing the public of specific transport mode-switches designed to reduce energy consumption – rather than at lecturing the public about the general desirability of sustainable mobility.

Figure 8.6 illustrates this point by showing the bivariate relation between, on the one hand, yearly energy consumption for everyday travel, and specific green transport and general environmental attitudes on the other. Both specific and general attitude strength show a negative correlation with energy consumption for everyday travel. The correlation is, however, stronger for specific attitudes than for general attitudes. This result is supported by the multivariate analyses, which show that specific attitudes have a significant influence on energy consumption for every travel, whereas general attitudes do not.[7] Thus, specific attitudes are far better predictors of sustainable everyday travel behaviour than are general attitudes. This result is in line with previous research (Moisander and Uusitalo 1994).

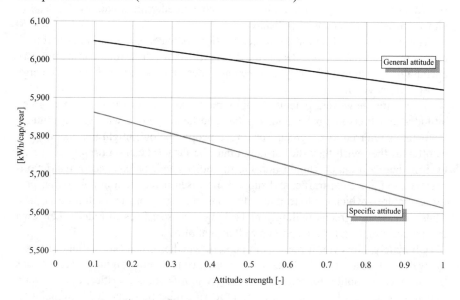

Figure 8.6   Relation between respondent's attitude strength and their annual energy consumption for everyday travel; attitude strength is normalised and measured as general attitudes and specific attitudes, respectively (N=680/694)

The consistency between specific attitudes and behaviour is particularly strong for everyday travel. Regarding energy consumption for leisure-time travel, however, specific attitudes show a weaker correlation to behaviour than is the case for

---

7   Independent variables in the model are sex, age, education, household occupancy, distance from residence to the city centre, distance from residence to a local sub-centre, car ownership, possession of a driver's licence and personal annual income (Holden and Norland 2004).

everyday travel. This is not surprising. Leisure-time travel represents *collective* behaviour which means a continuous bargaining process between the members of the household (Kirchler 1988). This is especially true for decisions related to energy consumption for leisure-time travel (ibid.). Thus, a green individual's commitment to environmentally responsible behaviour in such matters might not be translated into corresponding behaviour if the not-so-green members of the same household overrule the green individual. On the other hand, one's decision on an everyday–travel pattern is, to a greater extent, an individual decision. In the study, *individual* attitudes have been measured. Therefore, greater consistency between attitudes and behaviour was found in this particular area. To understand a household's bargaining processes and the correspondence between 'household attitude' and leisure-time travel, however, further research is needed.

Thesis 9: People with green attitudes cast aside those attitudes in their leisure-time travel behaviour.

Figure 8.7 shows that a green attitude is a better predictor of sustainable *everyday* mobility than of sustainable *leisure-time* mobility. For most green individuals, environmental problems related to their leisure-time activities do not seem to be of great concern. This conclusion holds true for all attitude levels in the analyses which are used as measurements of a green individual's behavioural consistency: general attitudes, specific attitudes and membership in environmental organisations (NEHG or other). The multivariate regression analyses of variables that influence energy consumption for everyday travel and leisure-time travel by plane strengthen this pattern. First, as mentioned in relation to thesis 8, general and specific attitudes correlate negatively with energy consumption for everyday travel (that is, an increase in attitude strength leads to a reduction in energy consumption), although only specific attitudes have a *significant* impact. Second, membership in an environmental organisation correlates positively (and significantly) with energy consumption for long-distance leisure-time travel by plane (that is, being a member leads to an increase in energy consumption).[8] General and specific attitudes also correlate positively with energy consumption for leisure-time travel by plane, although not significantly.

At a glance, this seems to be a paradox. One would expect that positive environmental attitudes would lead to reduced energy consumption for everyday travel. But it might come as a surprise that greens – holding positive environmental attitudes about *everyday* transport (and in general) – travel during their leisure time such that their overall consumption of energy for transport is essentially equal to that of people that do not hold such positive environmental attitudes. There is a plausible explanation for this, however. By way of in-depth interviews of Norwegian households, relationships between attitudes and household consumption were studied (Holden 2001). The study confirms that statistical analyses do not provide an understanding of or explanation for the underlying mechanisms that connect

---

8   Independent variables in the model: sex, age, education, housing density in residential area, car ownership, access to private garden, access to holiday home and personal annual income (Holden and Norland 2004).

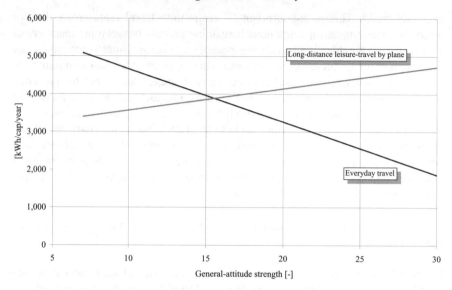

Figure 8.7   Relation between general environmental attitudes, everyday travel and long-distance leisure-time travel by plane (N=616)

environmental attitudes and travel behaviour. Rather, the explanation can be found in the following three sub-theses concerning the relation between environmental attitudes, everyday transport behaviour and long-distance leisure-time travel behaviour:

- *Sub-thesis 9.1*: The sense of powerlessness means that positive attitudes towards conservation and environmental issues are not to any great extent translated into low energy consumption in the home or in everyday transport.
- *Sub-thesis 9.2*: The desire to indulge oneself means that positive attitudes towards conservation and environmental issues are not to any great extent translated into low energy consumption for long-distance leisure-time travel.
- *Sub-thesis 9.3*: The desire to project an environmentally friendly image does not much influence one's behaviour in areas such as energy consumption in the home, everyday transport and leisure-time travel. Although this desire does appear to help in translating positive environmental attitudes into environmentally friendly consumption in some other areas, such consumption has little or no positive environmental impact.

These three sub-theses provide support for the claim that there are *at least* three mechanisms that influence whether individuals are able to behave in an environmentally friendly way: a desire to project an environmentally friendly image, a sense of powerlessness, and a desire to indulge oneself. It appears that all three mechanisms are to some extent hardwired into all of us. A person is not a 'hero' (projecting an environmentally friendly image), a 'victim' (having a sense of powerlessness) *or* a 'villain' (indulging himself). On the contrary, a person is all three. Furthermore, all three mechanisms are at work in all of us, but in different areas. It appears that on the whole, the three mechanisms operate in different areas of private consumption. They have an effect on decisions concerning environmentally friendly behaviour relating to different categories of consumption. While green individuals strive to act in an environmentally responsible manner in their everyday lives, they seem to have a conflicting need to cast aside their environmental concerns when travelling for leisure. Many respondents indicated that in some situations they have a desire to indulge themselves, to free themselves from the constraints involved in environmentally friendly behaviour. Moreover, they seem to feel that they do their fair share for the environment in their non-leisure time, and that they therefore should not have to continue behaving environmentally responsibly during their leisure time.

Thesis 10: Membership in an environmental organisation does not ensure sustainable travel behaviour by members.

Figure 8.8 indicates that being a member in an environmental organisation does not ensure sustainable mobility. Although many people join environmental organisations with the intent of promoting more sustainable household consumption patterns – and moreover living according to such patterns – they simply do not accomplish the latter. How can this be explained? The key is found by looking at the variables that *moderate* the attitude-behaviour relationship.[9] On one hand, there are variables that positively moderate attitude-behaviour consistency. On the other, unfortunately one might say, there are variables that negatively moderate attitude-behaviour consistency.

According to Pieters (1988), involvement moderates the relationship between attitudes and behaviour. Attitudes formed under high involvement predict subsequent behaviour better than attitudes formed under low involvement. 'Involvement' generally refers to the personal relevance of an object, issue or situation. Environmental issues are likely to be important to people who are registered members of an environmental organisation. Furthermore, members are supposed to be in a state of high self-awareness related to the environmental consequences of their behaviour. According to self-awareness theory, it is difficult for one to psychologically dissociate one's attitudes and attitude-relevant behaviour when one is in a state of self-awareness (ibid.). Conditions that lead to self-awareness (for example, being a member of an environmental organisation), lead to greater awareness of inconsistencies between attitudes and behaviour, and thus increase attitude-behaviour consistency. Thus, members are: (i) involved, and at the same time (ii) in a state of self-awareness. These two variables should, therefore, result in sustainable consumption. And they probably would, were it not for the fact that other variables counteract the influence of involvement and self-awareness.

---

9   In this line of research 'other determinants' are often not included (Pieters 1988). Therefore, it is difficult to extend the conclusions of this line of research to that dealing with the other determinants. Furthermore, it is hard to draw conclusions about the relative utility of the 'moderating variable' approach to the 'other determinants' approach.

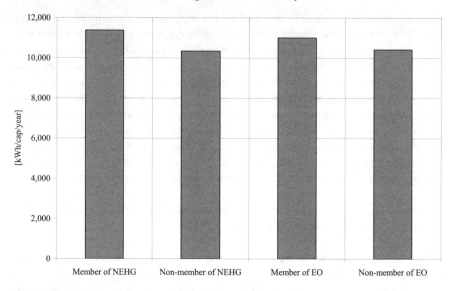

NEHG = the Norwegian Environmental Home Guard

EO = Environmental Organisation

**Figure 8.8   Annual per capita energy consumption for everyday and
leisure-time travel of members versus non-members of NEHG
and of members versus non-members of all environmental
organisations (N=638)**

In addition to the desire to indulge oneself (sub-thesis 9.2), one such moderating
variable has already been touched upon: Members of environmental organisations
might easily feel that they have done their fair share. They buy organic food, recycle
their garbage, and compost their organic waste in the garden, and therefore they feel
that they have done enough. Another variable is self-monitoring. The tendency to
engage in self-presentation (that is, presenting oneself as green by referring to one's
membership in an environmental organisation) is called 'self-monitoring'. Individuals
that self-monitor to a high degree are particularly sensitive to the opinions of others.
They are concerned about form more than about substance. Thus, self-monitoring
individuals can be expected to show low attitude-behaviour consistency.[10]

Ölander and Thøgersen (1995) present a third variable that explains why members
of environmental organisations do not behave as environmentally responsibly as might
be expected. Within the household energy consumption category, there are several
actions that can be taken. To a greater or lesser degree, all these actions contribute
to sustainable household consumption. One can chose the action(s) most appropriate

---

10 There is, however, no evidence in the empirical material studied to support the idea
that members are high in self-monitoring. Further research is needed in this field.

to one's circumstances: take the bus, walk, cycle, or buy an energy-efficient car. However, it is possible that being a member of an environmental organisation is considered to be an environmentally friendly act in itself. This perspective suggests that rather than being considered merely as an expression of an attitude, membership is considered to be an environmentally friendly action in and of itself, and moreover, perhaps one which relieves members, to a greater or lesser degree, of the duty to take truly meaningful actions in their everyday lives.

Taken together, the moderating variables presented above weaken the attitude-behaviour consistency of members of environmental organisations. Thus, in order to achieve sustainable consumption, it is more effective to directly increase specific environmentally friendly attitudes towards specific consumption, than it is to persuade individuals to join environmental organisations. Further research is needed, however, to understand why people join environmental organisations. Why do they become members? What are their motives? Do they consider membership as an environmentally friendly *action* in and of itself? Does membership represent a way to transfer responsibility for acting environmentally responsibly from the individual to the environmental organisation?

The Role of Land-use Planning

Land-use planning plays a key role in achieving sustainable mobility. It contains the *potential* both to reduce energy consumption for transport and to increase accessibility for low-mobility groups to public transport. For example, dense and mixed development of cities, or of sub-centres within cities, make it easier for people to move about and get to places they need to go because such development reduces distances between people and services and functions fundamental to their existence. Furthermore, such development also lays the foundation for a better public transport system. In both cases, one would expect that the following would result: reduced energy consumption for passenger transport and increased accessibility for low-mobility groups to public transport.

Yet a number of scholars question whether this potential is in fact realized. More specifically, they have doubts as to whether land-use planning really does matter. Furthermore, assuming that it does, they are not in agreement as to which urban form would best facilitate sustainable mobility. These doubts have been thoroughly discussed in chapter 7. My view in this matter is that planning does indeed matter and that a certain type of urban form – decentralised concentration – offers the best possibility for achieving sustainable mobility. The theses presented in this section support this view.

However, the doubts expressed by other scholars should not be taken lightly. They raise fundamental questions regarding the relation between the built environment and human behaviour. Truly, this relation is not a simple matter of a one-way cause and effect but rather a mutual relation whereby the built environment and human behaviour mutually influence and transform one another: We form the built environment and subsequently the built environment forms us. Moreover, the relation between the built environment and human behaviour has a time dimension.

Closing off a street to cars or restricting parking forces us to change travel behaviour immediately, whereas changing urban form, which inevitably takes decades, changes travel behaviour gradually. The relationship between the built environment and human travel behaviour, and its time dimension are shown in figure 8.9.

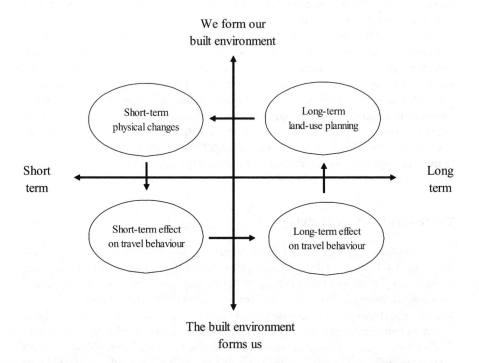

Figure 8.9   The relation between the built environment and travel behaviour, and its time dimension

The arrows in the figure show that long-term land-use planning is a *catalyst* for changes in the formation of deep-rooted travel behaviour patterns. Thus, long-term land-use planning is the key to developing long-term travel behaviour that complies with sustainable mobility requirements. Alas, from a sustainability perspective, land-use planning in most European countries has during the last decades been dominated by decentralisation, and also separation of residential and commercial development. This planning practice has spurred short-term development on cities' fringes, which eventually has led to increased urban sprawl. This development has caused increased dependence on the car. Indeed, urban sprawl would probably not have been possible without the car. In any event, increased travel distances due to urban sprawl and the separation of residential and commercial locations have manifested themselves in overwhelmingly car-dependent travel behaviour. Finally, this car dependence has put pressure on long-term land-use planning to comply with people's needs and wants. To summarize, people must travel greater distances due to urban sprawl and residential areas that are far from commercial areas. Furthermore, due to the lack of a suitably extensive and well-functioning public transport network, dependence on the car has increased. Therefore, we seem to be stuck in a self-perpetuating cycle of land-use planning that increases dependence on the car. To break this cycle and dependence on the car requires significant changes in the principles of long-term land-use planning. Gradually, these land-use planning changes will lead to a built environment that will in turn make sustainable mobility possible.

The relation between long-term land-use planning and sustainable mobility illustrates another important point. It took several decades to develop a car-dependent society. Therefore, there is every reason to believe that developing a less car-dependent society could also take decades. Consequently, important as long-term land-use planning is, it must be supplemented with measures that reduce energy consumption for transport in the short term. The theses presented in this section suggest the principles that long-term land-use planning should be based on to achieve sustainable mobility in the long term.

Thesis 11: People living in high-density residential areas consume less energy for everyday travel than people living in low-density residential areas, but they consume more energy for leisure-time travel by plane than those people.

The relations between everyday travel and travel by plane, and housing density (as revealed by data from the Greater Oslo study) is shown in figure 8.10. The figure illustrates that, compared to the residents in low-density areas, the residents in high-density areas consume far less energy for everyday transport and far more energy for leisure-time travel by plane.

Moreover, the multivariate regression analysis shows that the negative relation between housing density and energy consumption for everyday travel and the positive relation between housing density and energy consumption for leisure-time travel by plane are significant even when relevant socioeconomic and attitudinal factors are controlled for (table 7.2).[11] Thus, the multivariate regression analysis resoundingly confirms that increased housing density affects people's everyday travel and leisure-time travel by plane in opposite ways.

The identified pattern in figure 8.10 seems to lend some support for the 'compensatory hypothesis' discussed in chapter 7. This hypothesis suggests that people who live in densely populated urban areas (in flats in inner cities), and who have limited need for everyday transport, tend to travel more by plane in their leisure time than do residents of low-density housing areas. Perhaps they do so, in part, to compensate for the scarcity of nearby green recreational areas in the high-density urban areas where they live. However, many of those who travel long distances by

---

11 Housing density and distance from residence to the city centre correlate strongly and are thus problematic to include in a single model. When distance is removed from the model, housing density correlates significantly with energy consumption for everyday travel. The p-value between housing density and energy consumption for leisure-time travel by plane is 0.074.

plane during their leisure time probably go to even more densely populated cities having even less green recreational areas than Oslo. Therefore, this compensatory hypothesis is of dubious validity.

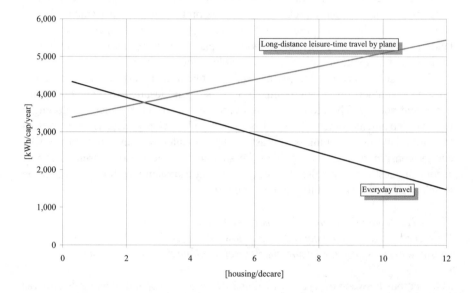

Figure 8.10   Relation between housing density in residential areas, everyday travel and long-distance leisure-time travel by plane (N=703/840)

Are there other explanations for this leisure-time travel pattern amongst residents of densely populated residential areas? For example, do they spend for leisure-time travel the money they save by economizing on everyday travel? Perhaps, but they might actually be spending the bulk of such savings on necessities. Concerning the cost of such necessities (food, housing, etc.), the residents of the two high-density residential areas have a very high cost of living – indeed, one of the highest in Greater Oslo. Further research is needed to determine precisely how much they save by economizing on daily travel and how much they spend on long-distance leisure-time travel, and then to compare the two. Or is leisure-time travel by plane rather an integral part of the urban, cosmopolitan lifestyle of these residents? In other words, do such residents, a large portion of whom are students and academics, just happen to have a lifestyle which is uniquely characterized by both a preference for inner-city living and an increased propensity for long-distance leisure-time travel by plane? Do their lack of ready access to green areas and their savings due to economizing on everyday travel therefore have little or nothing to do with their leisure-time travel by plane?

Three Danish studies of residents' leisure-time travel patterns in Copenhagen (Næss 2006), Aalborg (Nielsen 2002) and Frederikshavn (Næss and Jensen 2004),[12]

---

12 Copenhagen Metropolitan Area has 1.8 million inhabitants; Aalborg has 160,000; and Frederikshavn has 26,000 in the contiguous urban area and 35,000 in the municipality.

respectively, give some support to the urban, cosmopolitan-lifestyle explanation. The Copenhagen and Aalborg studies showed that – controlled for socioeconomic and attitudinal variables – the frequency of flights is higher amongst residents of high-density areas close to the city centres than it is amongst residents of low-density areas on the cities' fringes. However, this difference in flight frequencies between inner-city residents and those residing on the fringes was not found in the study on Frederikshavn, which is a smaller Danish town. Thus, the three Danish studies give some support to the urban, cosmopolitan-lifestyle explanation because increased flight frequencies among inner-city dwellers were found in large cities like Copenhagen and Aalborg, but not in the smaller town of Frederikshavn in which the urban, cosmopolitan lifestyle is hardly widespread, not even in its central parts. Moreover, the Greater Oslo study also gives some support to the urban, cosmopolitan-lifestyle explanation because Greater Oslo is large enough to develop lifestyles like those found in Copenhagen and Aalborg. However, a more thorough, qualitative-oriented analysis is needed to understand the correlation between leisure-time travel by plane and residence in densely populated urban areas. Also, it remains to be seen whether this form of compensatory travel exists in other European cities.

Thesis 12: People having regular access to a private garden consume less energy for long-distance leisure-time travel by car and plane than people without such access.

The Greater Oslo study suggests that people with access to a private garden consume less energy annually for long-distance leisure-time travel by car and plane than do people without such access (figure 8.11). Moreover, multivariate regression analysis shows that the difference in energy consumption is significant when relevant socioeconomic and attitudinal factors are controlled for (table 7.2). Thus, such analysis clearly confirms that access to a private garden is related to a reduction in energy consumption for leisure-time travel.

The findings from the Greater Oslo study are supported by the findings in other studies. Kennedy (1995), Tillberg (1998) and Schlich and Axhausen (2002) all claim that people living in high-density, inner-city areas, to a larger extent than their counterparts living in low-density areas, will travel out of town on weekends to compensate for their lack of access to a private garden and green recreational areas. Furthermore, their claims are supported by empirical evidence from studies of cities in Austria, Sweden and Switzerland.

Their reasoning and findings have much in common with the 'escape hypothesis' which is used in studies of leisure-time travel and, according to which, people who are dissatisfied with their dwelling and its surroundings will spend a large portion of their leisure time elsewhere (Kaiser 1993, quoted from Ness 2006). The escape hypothesis implies that residents of densely populated urban areas are, so to speak, 'forced' for psychological reasons to make leisure trips to compensate for deficiencies in their residential environments. Among people living in suburban areas, however, the need for trips out into the green countryside are not that important, because a large portion of these residents have a private garden and other nearby green, open areas.

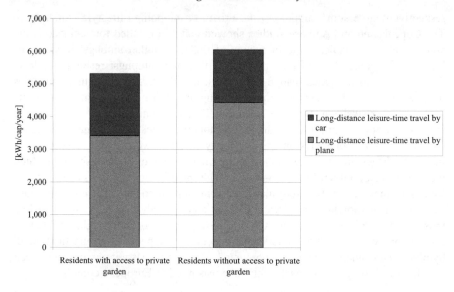

Figure 8.11   Annual per capita energy consumption for long-distance leisure-time travel by car and plane with and without access to a private garden (N=771)

It is reasonable to assume that people with access to a private garden spend time in their gardens for both relaxation and necessary gardening. However, the causal mechanism is not evident – such residents might have a garden not because they want to travel less, but rather they might have a garden simply because they want to spend time in such an environment. The important point is that access to a private recreation area seems to relate to a reduction in leisure-time travel. As shown in chapter 7, the above finding holds even for residents living in flats. In other words, access to a private garden or common green area reduces travel by residents of *all* types of housing. This underlines the importance of having nearby green recreation facilities, especially in areas of high-density housing. Whether only private gardens create such correlations, or whether common gardens and green recreation areas create the same correlations, is an interesting question for further investigation.

Thesis 13: People living in medium-density residential areas consume less energy for transport than people living in high- or low-density residential areas.

As shown in thesis 11, the housing density of an area, which strongly correlates with its proximity to the city centre, seems to affect people's energy consumption for everyday travel differently than it does their energy consumption for leisure-time travel. While high-density living reduces energy consumption for everyday travel, the opposite applies to energy consumption for leisure-time travel. High-density living correlates with increased energy consumption for travel by plane. Living close to the city centre, residents of densely populated areas consume far less energy for everyday travel than people living in more remote areas, whereas they consume far more energy for travel by plane.

This is not to say that living in high density conditions *causes* travel by plane. In other words, I do not suggest that living in a densely populated residential area triggers an immediate need to buy a plane ticket. Rather, the relation revealed by the empirical material indicates that high energy consumption by residents of these areas for travel by plane is a possible long-term indirect effect of high-density living. Therefore, there seems to be a *limit for densification*, that is, the potential for densification to reduce energy consumption for transport is limited as illustrated in figure 8.12.

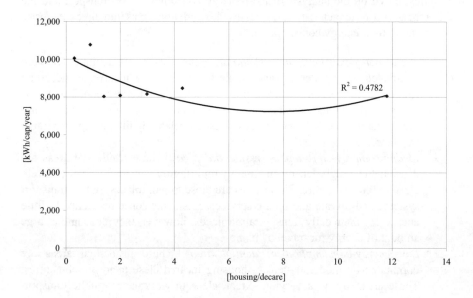

Figure 8.12   Annual per capita energy consumption for all travel as a function of housing density (N=559)

Figure 8.12 shows the total energy consumption per capita for both everyday and leisure-time travel as a function of housing density in the eight residential areas. When housing density exceeds a certain level, residents increase their compensatory travel which in turn causes their energy consumption for transport to increase. Other studies support this finding: Tillberg (2001) found that residents of Gävleborg County, Sweden, living in high-density areas close to the city centre travel longer distances for leisure purposes than residents living in low-density areas in the same county. The same tendency was found in Copenhagen (Næss 2006) but not in Frederikshavn (Næss and Jensen 2004). The lack of compensatory travel in Frederikshavn is most likely due to the city's low housing density even in the centre.

The pattern in figure 8.12 is similar to a pattern in the relationship between energy consumption and *city size* found by a number of empirical studies of cities in Norway, Sweden and England (Næss 1997). According to these studies, energy consumption per capita decreases as density increases, up to a certain point, but thereafter energy consumption increases. Thus, the advantages of 'mega-cities' or 'extreme-density areas' seem to be outweighed by the advantages offered by more modest forms of urban compactness. However, the studies in Norway, Sweden and Denmark suggest that residents living in very high-density areas consume less energy for their total transport needs than residents living in very low-density areas (which also can be seen in figure 8.12). Both groups, however, use more energy for transport than residents living in medium-density areas.

Thus, based on the analysis of total energy consumption for transport and the different land-use characteristics, we can divide residential areas into three categories according to their energy consumption:

- *High–energy-consumption residential areas*: These residential areas are dominated by low-density and single-family housing located at the urban fringe. These areas are far from both a local sub-centre and public transport systems. Residents consume a large amount of energy for their daily transportation needs; however, they consume relatively little energy for travel by plane.
- *Medium–energy-consumption residential areas*: These residential areas are dominated by high-density and mainly multifamily housing located relatively close to the city centre. These areas are close to workplaces, public transport systems and private and public services. Residents consume relatively little energy for their daily transportation needs; however, they consume a large amount of energy for travel by plane.
- *Low–energy-consumption residential areas*: These residential areas are dominated by moderate-density housing located close to local sub-centres. These areas are, to a varying extent, close to workplaces, public transport systems and private and public services. Residents consume relatively little energy for their daily transportation needs; and also they consume relatively little energy for travel by plane.

Thesis 14: Decentralized concentration is a more sustainable urban form than the compact city, the dispersed city, and other alternatives.

Based on the material presented so far, three attributes in land-use planning seem to produce the best results in reducing total energy consumption for transport:

- A relatively high degree of housing density in residential areas.
- The shortest possible distance to city centre or local sub-centre.
- Proximity to workplaces, public transport systems and private and public services.

Thus, the research strongly supports the idea of the compact city. However, two important aspects, *degree* of density and urban size, still need to be considered. Also, the importance of access to a private garden or nearby recreational areas must be considered.

In the compact-city concept, two dimensions are often mixed together without further qualification. These are centralization-decentralization and concentration-sprawl. The first pair refers to the population patterns in large national contexts, whereas the second pair refers to the development processes within urban areas. Since the advent of the car era, urban development in most EU-15 countries may be characterized as 'centralized sprawl'. This means that the overall national population pattern is one of centralization, and that sprawl characterizes each of the urban concentrations. In some cases researchers have claimed that the concept of a compact city implies a pattern of further centralization of the population and that large cities are the ideal sustainable urban development pattern (Newman and Kenworthy 1989; CEC 1990). Our research does not support such claims. It suggests, on the contrary, that more favourable ecological footprints result from having several smaller compact towns and cities ('decentralized concentration'), rather than a few large, 'mega' cities. Decentralized concentration is the opposite of the dominant development pattern ('urban sprawl') of the last decades in every respect (see figure 8.13).

It is, however, a fact that an increasingly larger percentage of the world's population live in large cities. Urban planners must face this situation; they cannot, in a modern democracy, simply, in the name of sustainability, transfer people from large, densely populated cities to smaller and less densely populated cities. Urban planners must therefore encourage polycentric cities, that is, densely populated and concentrated centres *within* the large cities. These centres should contain a variety of housing and workplaces, as well as private and public services. It is also vital that

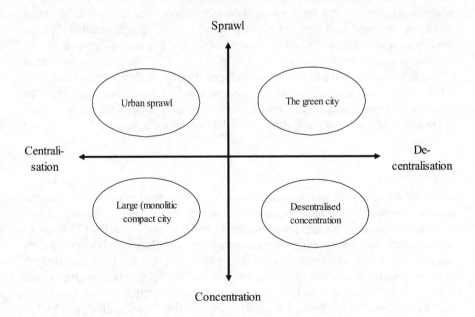

Figure 8.13 Four models of sustainable urban form

polycentric cities be built on an effective and environmentally sound public transport infrastructure that connects the different centres. Decentralised concentration, of single cities or polycentric development within larger cities, offers the best possibility for developing an affordable and well-functioning public transport system which in turn will increase accessibility to transport for low-mobility groups. As the analyses in chapter 7 concluded, decentralised concentration within cities having more than 500,000 inhabitants (that is, creating polycentric cities) could lead to lower energy consumption in households, which is a conclusion that seems to be enjoying widespread support (Breheny 1992a; Banister 1992; Owens 1992; Newman and Kenworthy 2000; Buxton 2000; Masnavi 2000; Høyer and Holden 2001; Holden 2004). Thus, the following two sub-theses can be formulated:

- *Sub-thesis 14.1*: Decentralized concentration reduces people's total energy consumption for passenger transport.
- *Sub-thesis 14.2*: Decentralized concentration increases the possibility for developing an affordable and well-functioning public transport system, which ensures accessibility to transport for low-mobility groups.

According to Breheny (1992a), the concept of decentralised concentration is based on sustainable development and urban form policies, such as slowing down the centralized sprawl process. At the same time, it is based on the realisation that extreme forms of the compact city are unrealistic and moreover, undesirable. Therefore, Breheny makes clear that various forms of decentralised concentration, based around a single city or polycentric cities, might be appropriate. Furthermore, Breheny emphasises that inner cities should be rejuvenated and public transport should be improved both between and within cities. Thus, 'people-intensive' places (dwellings and workplaces) and activities (public and private services) should be developed around public transport nodes, in his opinion. This implies that mixed use must be encouraged and zoning discouraged. Finally, Breheny recommends that urban (or regional) greening be encouraged and efficient remote heating systems be developed in new and existing housing areas. Most of Breheny's recommendations are in line with the empirical findings from the Greater Oslo Region.

Summary

Based on the empirical and theoretical knowledge presented in part II, this chapter presents fourteen theses regarding the roles of technology, public transport, green attitudes and land-use planning in achieving sustainable mobility in the EU. Some of the theses are well known within the sustainable mobility literature but nevertheless can and should be backed by fresh empirical evidence, which this book does. Others are not so well known, and some are even new, bringing new perspectives to the discussion of sustainable mobility, particularly the theses that pertain to leisure-time travel. Some of the theses are supplemented by sub-theses to give them further strength. Taken together, the fourteen theses constitute the basis for a theory of sustainable mobility.

Chapter 9

Sustainable Mobility in the European Union

How can the EU achieve sustainable mobility by 2030? What approach should they apply – the efficiency approach, the alteration approach or the reduction approach – and moreover, what roles will technology, public transport, green attitudes and land-use planning play?

These questions are answered in a four-step process (figure 9.1), and each step is addressed in a separate section below. Step 1 involves constructing seven scenarios each of which reflects different assumptions in terms of the transport situation in 2030. The scenarios use EU-15 data but, in line with chapter 1's fourth rationale, the results apply to the whole EU. Each scenario is based upon different levels of technological improvement in vehicle efficiency, different degrees of change in transport patterns and different growth rates in total passenger transport volumes. In Step 2 the SMART model calculates yearly per capita energy consumption for passenger transport and yearly travel distance by public transport. In Step 3 each scenario's outcome is compared to two 2030 goals of sustainable mobility described in chapter 3:

- The energy consumption for passenger transport in 2030 should not exceed 8 kWh per capita daily (which is half the 1990 per capita energy consumption for passenger transport).
- The available travel distance by public transport in 2030 should not go below 11 km per capita daily.

Thus, the results from the SMART model calculations indicate whether a particular scenario will lead the EU into the SMA. Finally Step 4 involves discussing the roles of technology, public transport, green attitudes and land-use planning in those scenarios that achieve these two sustainable mobility goals. The discussion draws heavily on the fourteen theses presented in chapter 8.

All assumptions in the scenarios are based on 2030. Why? According to the Brundtland Report's low-energy scenario, 1990 levels of per capita energy consumption must be reduced 50 per cent by then. Moreover, because this time frame is reasonably short term, comparisons will not be purely speculative. Finally, by 2030 the full potential of most implemented changes should be relatively clear.

However, in vehicle technology improvement a problem arises: new passenger cars in 2030 will have significantly lower energy consumption than the average of the entire passenger car fleet which will include many old cars. Thus, it might take until 2040 for the fleet's average energy consumption to equal that of the

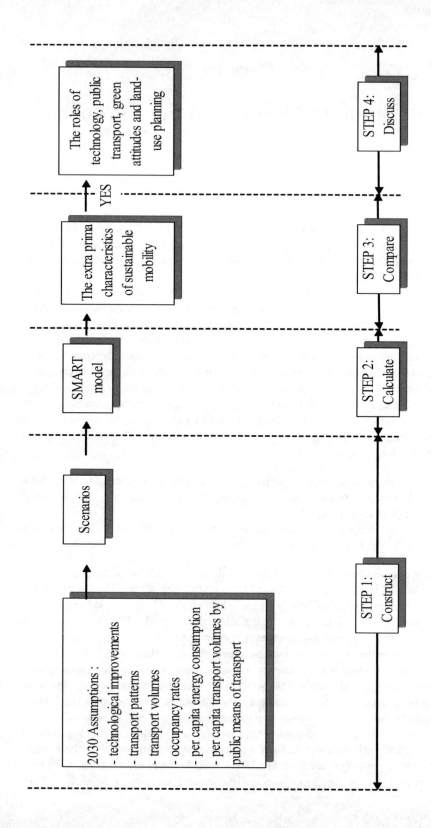

Figure 9.1   A four-step process for assessing the sustainability of EU passenger transport in 2030

Scenario	Short name	Alteration [ii]	Reduction [iii]	Technology [iv]
2030 Business as usual [i]	BAU	BAU	BAU	BAU
2030 Efficiency	EFF	BAU	BAU	+++
2030 Alteration	ALT	+++	BAU	BAU
2030 Reduction	RED	BAU	÷÷÷	BAU
2030 Sustainable 1	SM1	++	÷÷÷	BAU
2030 Sustainable 2	SM2	++	÷÷	++
2030 Sustainable 3	SM3	++	÷	+++

(i) 2030 Business as usual (BAU) = prolonging trends from 1990–2000 to 2030.
(ii) Relative change compared to 2030 BAU: + = increased alteration towards the use of public transport.
(iii) Relative change compared to 2030 BAU: ÷ = reduced transport volume.
(iv) Relative change compared to 2030 BAU: + = increased energy efficiency.

Figure 9.2   The 7 scenarios for the EU-15 in 2030

2030 models. Furthermore, because planes, buses and trains generally have longer lifetimes than passenger cars, even more time will be needed to bring the average energy consumption of those fleets to that of new planes, buses and trains built in 2030. Therefore, in order to accurately estimate the 2030 energy consumption of the entire passenger transport fleet, the calculation must include: the average lifetime of the various vehicles, the distribution of travel distances for new and old vehicles and the energy consumption of vehicles by age. However, although some EU countries have calculated the energy consumption of their *present* passenger transport fleets, no such calculation has been made for 2030. It is probably not worth doing anyway because of the uncertainties involved in estimating vehicle lifetime, travel distances and energy consumption. Therefore, in the scenarios below, I assume that the energy consumption of 2030-model vehicles of each mode of transport equals the respective fleet's average energy consumption. Although this represents a simplification, it gives a powerful indication of what works – and what does not work – in terms of achieving sustainable mobility.

Step 1: Constructing Seven Scenarios for the EU-15

Seven scenarios for 2030 are included in the analysis – shown in figure 9.2. All use 2002 as a base case; thus, assumed *changes* in transport technologies (improved efficiency), transport patterns (increased alteration) and transport volumes (possible reduction) refer to 2002. However, I have used a somewhat different methodology regarding the assumptions made for each scenario, which I will explain after briefly presenting the seven scenarios.

2030 Business as Usual (BAU)

The BAU scenario is included because it shows the effects on yearly per capita energy consumption and yearly travel distance by public transport of simply prolonging until 2030 the 1990–2000 passenger transport pattern in the EU-15. Accordingly, growth in travel distance for all modes follows the same pattern as 1990–2000 (EC 2003). Thus, no additional measures are applied to reduce its growth or to alter present travel patterns. Moreover, the specific energy consumption for all means of transport declines slowly year-by-year in line with the reductions achieved 1990–2000. Thus, no additional measures are applied to further reduce it.

2030 Efficiency (EFF)

The EFF scenario shows the effects on yearly per capita energy consumption and yearly travel distance by public transport when stronger measures than those in the BAU scenario are taken to increase technological efficiency for all means of transport. Accordingly, growth in travel distances for all modes is the same as in the 2030 BAU scenario. Thus, no additional measures are applied to further reduce its growth or to alter present travel patterns. However, strong measures are applied to significantly reduce specific energy consumption compared to the BAU scenario, including implementing ultra-lightweight hybrid cars and high-speed propeller aircraft.

2030 Alteration (ALT)

The ALT scenario shows the effects on yearly per capita energy consumption and yearly travel distance by public transport when very strong measures are applied to alter present transport patterns towards greatly increased use of public transport compared to the BAU scenario. Accordingly, growth in total travel distances and reductions in specific energy consumption for all means of transport follow the BAU scenario. However, very strong measures are applied to alter present transport patterns towards greatly increased use of buses, coaches, trains, trams and inland navigation compared to the BAU scenario. According to the ALT scenario, 2030 average travel distance by public transport in the EU-15 would be three times greater than what Austria has today, which is presently the highest in the EU-15 (EC 2004). Furthermore, occupancy rates for all public transport are assumed to increase by a staggering 32 per cent.

2030 Reduction (RED)

The RED scenario shows the effects on yearly per capita energy consumption and yearly travel distance by public transport when strong measures are applied to halt growth in passenger transport by car and plane. Accordingly, total travel distances by public transport and specific energy consumption for all means of transport follow the BAU scenario. Thus, no additional measures are applied to alter transport patterns or reduce energy consumption; however, strong measures are applied to halt growth in passenger transport by car and plane at the 2002 level.

2030 Sustainable Mobility Scenarios

The three sustainable mobility scenarios show that there are several combinations of approaches that could lead to sustainable mobility. By meeting the minimum requirement for yearly per capita travel distance by public transport and by not exceeding the maximum requirement for yearly per capita energy consumption, the EU-15 can achieve sustainable mobility via several combinations of the EFF and RED approaches. In other words, there is a trade-off between improvement in specific energy consumption and growth in transport volume. On one hand, transport volume, even by car and plane, could grow moderately if specific energy consumption for all means of transport were reduced per the EFF scenario level. On the other hand, transport volume would likely be reduced if specific energy consumption were reduced per the BAU scenario level. The assumptions made in the three sustainable mobility scenarios are described below.

2030 Sustainable mobility scenario 1 (SM1) Specific energy consumption for all means of transport is reduced per the 2030 BAU scenario. Moreover, occupancy rates for all means of transport are assumed to increase by 10 per cent.

2030 Sustainable mobility scenario 2 (SM2) Specific energy consumption for all means of transport is reduced far more than the 2030 BAU scenario but not as much as in the 2030 EFF scenario – a middle point is chosen. Moreover, occupancy rates for all means of transport are assumed to increase by 10 per cent.

2030 Sustainable mobility scenario 3 (SM3) Specific energy consumption for all means of transport is reduced per the 2030 EFF scenario. Moreover, occupancy rates for all means of transport are assumed to increase by 10 per cent.

Methodology

The four first scenarios (BAU, EFF, ALT and RED) employ a 'bottom-up approach'. First, assumptions are put into the SMART model regarding improvements in specific energy consumption, and changes in occupancy rates and annual transport growth rates for each mode. Second, the model calculates 2030 per capita energy consumption and per capita travel distance by public transport. Third, the results are compared to the sustainable mobility goals to determine whether the scenario is sustainable.

Thus, in these four scenarios, the assumptions (independent variables) and results (dependent variables) are:

Assumptions (independent variables):

- The 2002–2030 annual growth rates for each mode of transport.
- The 2030 specific energy consumption.

- The 2030 occupancy rate.
- The 2030 EU-15 population.

Results (dependent variables):

- The 2030 yearly travel distance for all modes of transport.
- The 2030 per capita energy consumption for passenger transport.
- The 2030 per capita travel distance by public transport.

The last three scenarios – the sustainable mobility scenarios SM1, SM2 and SM3 – employ a 'top-down approach'. First, the sustainable mobility goals are set, which means that these scenarios per definition comply with the sustainable mobility requirements. Second, the SMART model finds various *combinations* of the levels of specific energy consumption, occupancy rates and transport growth rates for all means of transport that would fulfil the sustainable mobility goals.

The starting point for all 2030 sustainable mobility scenarios is that energy consumption for passenger transport should not exceed 8 kWh per capita daily and that available travel distance by public transport should not go below 11 km per capita daily. Moreover, the occupancy rate for all means of transport is assumed to increase by 10 per cent compared to the BAU scenario. Thus, all three sustainable mobility scenarios have the following common assumptions (independent variables):

- The 2030 energy consumption for passenger transport should not exceed 8 kWh per capita daily.
- The 2030 available travel distance by public transport should not go below 11 km per capita daily.
- The 2030 occupancy rate for all means of transport increases by 10 per cent compared to BAU scenario.

Moreover, there is a single *unique* assumption which applies to each sustainable mobility scenario above regarding future reductions in specific energy consumption for all means of transport. This assumption, in turn, determines the 2030 allowed yearly total travel distance for each scenario. Thus, the sustainable scenarios have the following unique assumption (independent variable):

- Specific energy consumption in 2030 for each mode of transport.

Finally, the common and unique assumptions above result in two dependent variables:

- Allowed yearly growth rate in travel distance for passenger cars, powered two-wheelers and planes, during the period 2002–2030 and subsequently.
- Allowed yearly total travel distance for passenger transport in 2030 by all means of transport.

Step 2: The SMART Model

The three main approaches towards sustainable mobility can be linked to the three main factors that influence and, in the end, determine total energy consumption for passenger transport: the EFF approach aims at increasing the pace of technological improvements; the ALT approach aims at altering present transport patterns towards increased use of public transport and the RED approach aims at reducing (or slowing) growth in total passenger transport volumes. Thus, the relation between sustainable mobility and the three approaches is:

SM = g (A,R,T)

Where:

SM = sustainable mobility
A = the ALT approach which aims at changing transport patterns towards increased use of public transport
R = the RED approach which aims at reducing – or slowing – growth in total passenger transport volumes
T = the EFF approach which aims at increasing the pace of technological improvements.

This relation can be expressed as a mathematical equation, coined 'the SMART model':

$$E_{PT} = \sum_{i=1}^{n} \frac{d_i}{o_i} * s_i$$

Where:

E_{PT} = yearly per capita energy consumption for passenger transport [kWh/cap/year]
n = number of modes [-]
d_i = yearly per capita travel distance by mode i [pkm/year]
o_i = average occupancy rate for mode i [pkm/vkm]
s_i = average specific energy consumption for mode i [kWh/vkm].

Step 3: Comparing the Scenarios. When is Transport Sustainable?

The results from the scenario analyses are shown in table 9.1 and in figure 9.3. The first column in the table shows the 1990 and 2002 base cases and the seven 2030 scenarios for the EU-15. The second column shows total yearly travel distance – indicating whether a scenario allows for an increase or instead demands a reduction in total yearly

Table 9.1   The 1990 and 2002 base cases and the 2030 scenario analyses for the EU-15 (assumptions in shaded)

Scenario	Yearly total passenger travel distance(i) (1000 mio pkm)	Public transport proportion(ii) (%)	Change in specific energy consumption 2002–2030 (%)			Daily per capita energy consumption (kWh/cap/day)	Daily per capita travel distance by public transport (km/cap/day)
			Car	Public transport (ii)	Plane		
1990 Base case	4,511	15.7	-	-	-	15.9	5.3
2002 Base Case	5,798	13.7	0	0	0	17.0	5.8
2030 BAU	12,494	8.8	- 52	- 10	- 26	24.3	7.6
2030 EFF	12,494	8.8	- 65	- 25	- 56	16.0	7.6
2030 ALT	12,445	32.7	- 52	- 10	- 26	19.9	28.2
2030 RED	6,102	18.0	- 52	- 10	- 26	9.7	7.6
2030 SM1	5,585	28.5	- 52	- 10	- 26	8.0	11.0
2030 SM2	6,592	24.1	- 60	- 18	- 40	8.0	11.0
2030 SM3	7,842	20.3	- 65	- 25	- 56	8.0	11.0

(i) All motorized transport

(ii) Bus and coach, tram and metro, railway, and inland navigation

Notes for the 2002 base case and the 2030 scenarios in table 9.1 (see footnote 7 page 66 for 1990 base case data):

2002 BASE CASE: Data for yearly *total passenger travel distances* by all means of transport from EC (2004), but since this source only includes domestic and intra-EU air travel, I have estimated extra-EU air travel based on EC (2006) = 682,000 mio pkm. *Specific energy consumption* (s) *and occupancy rate* (o): Car, s=0.638 kWh/vkm (CEC 2004), o=1.55 (EEA 2006); Powered two-wheeler, s=0.330 kWh/vkm (SFT 1999), o=1.15 (Holtskog 2001); Bus and coach, s=2.737 kWh/vkm (SFT 1999), o=30% (EEA 2006); Tram and metro, s=17.534 kWh/vkm (20% improvement of 1990 data, CEC 1992), o=30% (EEA 2006) of 300 (CEC 1992); Railway, s=35.755 kWh/vkm (20% improvement of 1990 data, CEC 1992), o=30% (EEA 2006) of 536 (CEC 1992); Inland navigation, 0.780 kWhpkm (Holtskog 2001); Plane, domestic and intra-EU travel, s=33.015 kWh/km (Fitzgerald et al. 1999), o=60% (EEA 2006) of 85 (Cox et al. 1999); Plane, extra-EU travel, s=57.175 kWh/km (Fitzgerald et al. 1999), o=60% (EEA 2006) of 184 (Cox et al. 1999). *Population:* 379 mio (EC 2003).

2030 BAU: Data for *annual % change in passenger travel distances* for all means of transport 2002–2030 (EC 2003): Car and powered two-wheeler = 1.7; Bus and coach = 1.1; Ttram and metro = 1.2; Railway = 1.2; Inland navigation = 1.5; Plane (domestic, intra-EU and extra-EU) = 6.0. *Total per cent reduction in specific energy consumption 2002–2030*: Car and powered two-wheeler = -52%; Bus and coach, tram and metro, railway and inland navigation = -10%; Plane (domestic, intra-EU and extra EU) = -26%. *Occupancy rate*: unchanged 2002–2030. *Population*: 396 mio (EC 2003).

2030 EFF: Data for *annual % change in passenger travel distances* for all means of transport 2002–2030: 2030 BAU. *Total per cent reduction in specific energy consumption 2002–2030*: Car and powered two-wheeler = -65%; Bus and coach, tram and metro, railway and inland navigation = -25%; Plane (domestic, intra-EU and extra EU) = -56%. *Occupancy rate*: Unchanged 2002–2030. *Population*: 396 mio (EC 2003).

2030 ALT: Data for *annual % change in passenger travel distances* for all means of transport 2002–2030: Car and powered two-wheeler = 1.1; Bus and coach, tram and metro, railway and inland navigation = 6.0; Plane (domestic, intra-EU and extra-EU) = 4.0. *Total per cent reduction in specific energy consumption 2002–2030*: 2030 BAU. *Occupancy rate*: Car, powered two-wheeler and plane = unchanged 2002–2030; Bus and coach, tram and metro, railway and inland navigation = increased from 30% (2002) to 40% (2030). *Population*: 396 mio (EC 2003).

2030 RED: Data for *annual % change in passenger travel distances* for all means of transport 2002–2030: Car, powered two-wheeler and plane = 0.0 (i.e., equals 2002); Bus and coach, tram and metro, railway and inland navigation = 2030 BAU. *Total per cent reduction in specific energy consumption 2002–2030* = 2030 BAU. *Occupancy rate*: Unchanged 2002–2030. *Population*: 396 mio (EC 2003).

2030 SM1: Data for *necessary annual % change in passenger travel distances* for all means of transport 2002–2030: Car, powered two-wheeler and plane (domestic, intra-EU and extra EU) = -0.8; Bus and coach, tram and metro, railway and inland navigation = 2.5. *Total per cent reduction in specific energy consumption 2002–2030*: 2030 BAU. *Occupancy rate*: 10% increase for all modes 2002–2030. *Population*: 396 mio (EC 2003).

2030 SM2: Data for *necessary annual % change in passenger travel distances* for all means of transport 2002–2030: Car, powered two-wheeler and plane (domestic, intra-EU and extra EU) = 0.0; Bus and coach, tram and metro, railway and inland navigation = 2.5. *Total per cent reduction in specific energy consumption 2002–2030*: Car and powered two-wheeler = -60%; Bus and coach, tram and metro, railway and inland navigation = -18%; Plane (domestic, intra-EU and extra EU) = -40%. *Occupancy rate*: 10% increase for all modes 2002–2030. *Population*: 396 mio (EC 2003).

2030 SM3: Data for *necessary annual % change in passenger travel distances* for all means of transport 2002–2030: Car, powered two-wheeler and plane (domestic, intra-EU and extra-EU) = 0.8; Bus and coach, tram and metro, railway and inland navigation = 2.5. *Total per cent reduction in specific energy consumption 2002–2030*: 2030 EFF. *Occupancy rate*: 10% increase for all modes 2002–2030. *Population*: 396 mio (EC 2003)

travel distance compared to 2002. The third column shows the proportion of the total travel distance that is performed by public transport – indicating the importance of public transport for each scenario. The fourth column shows total percent change in 2002–2030 specific energy consumption for cars and powered two-wheelers, public transport, and planes, respectively – indicating the level of technological improvement for each scenario. The fifth and sixth columns show per capita daily energy consumption and per capita daily travel distance by public transport for each scenario – indicating whether the sustainable mobility goals are met. Moreover, the table indicates which factors are assumptions (shaded) and which are results. Figure 9.3 shows where the scenarios are located in the SMA diagram.

The scenario analyses show that BAU will not bring the EU-15 closer to the SMA. On the contrary, BAU moves the EU-15 further from it because rather than leading to a 50 per cent reduction in per capita energy consumption for passenger transport, BAU leads to a 53 per cent *increase*. Moreover, although BAU slightly increases per capita travel distance by public transport – from 5.8 to 7.6 km/day – it does not achieve the goal of 11 km/day.

Two aspects are worth elaborating on regarding the assumptions about growth in transport volume and improved specific energy consumption in the BAU scenario. First, the assumed reductions in specific energy consumption for cars and planes in the BAU scenario *are* very significant – more than 50 per cent for cars and nearly 30 per cent for planes. Nevertheless, the BAU scenario fails to reach sustainable mobility's energy goal; this powerfully indicates how difficult it is to achieve sustainable mobility at the present level of annual growth in transport volumes. Second, at present transport volume growth rates it would take about an 85 per cent reduction in the specific energy consumption of cars and planes (corresponding to 1 litre/100vkm for cars and 1 litre/100pkm for planes) for the BAU scenario to be compatible with sustainable mobility's energy goal. However, the technological revolution necessary to achieve such reductions is not yet in sight. Moreover, even if such a technological revolution were to happen, the large transport volume would likely make it impossible to comply with the *prima* characteristics of sustainable mobility such as reduced local pollution in towns and cities.

The scenario analyses also show that none of the three main approaches *alone* will get the EU-15 into the SMA. The EFF scenario – based on the use of ultra-lightweight hybrid cars and high-speed propeller aircrafts – will not meet sustainable mobility's energy goal. Rather than achieving a 50 per cent reduction, the EFF scenario merely stabilizes per capita energy consumption at 2002 levels. Moreover, it does not do much to meet sustainable mobility's public transport goal. On the other hand, the ALT scenario – based on a massive change of present transport patterns towards the increased use of public transport – ensures that the public transport goal is met. However, under this scenario per capita energy consumption will increase about 25 per cent. The RED scenario – based on keeping travel distances by car and plan at 2002 levels and on keeping travel by public transport at BAU levels – will reduce per capita energy consumption by 39 per cent. However, this reduction is still not enough to comply with sustainable mobility's energy goal. Moreover, under this scenario the public transport goal is not met.

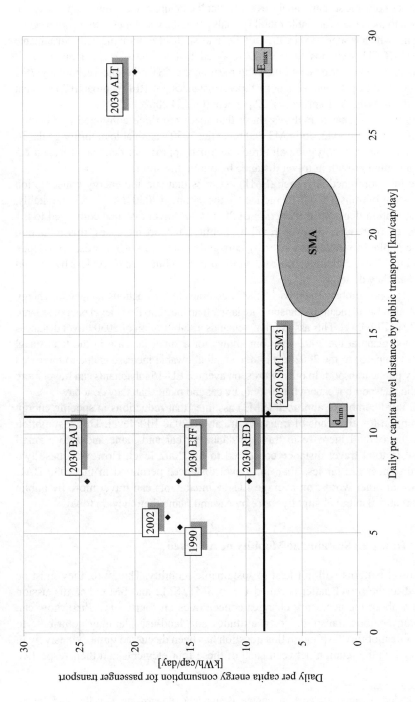

Figure 9.3   The 1990 and 2002 base cases and the 2030 scenarios for the EU-15

Furthermore, the scenario analyses show that the failure of these three approaches on their own to meet the sustainable mobility goals paves the way for *combined approaches* – a finding which is supported by the OECD. In its study of Environmentally Sustainable Transport (EST) scenarios the OECD reported that the three main approaches, if combined, would contribute as follows to meeting the EST criterion: Technology[1] (the EFF approach) 52 per cent, reduction of travel distances (the RED approach) 26 per cent and mode shift (the ALT approach)[2] 22 per cent (OECD 2002c).

Finally, the scenario analyses show that there are three combined approaches illustrated by SM1, SM2, and SM3 that meet the 2030 sustainable mobility goals. To meet the public transport goal, all three combined approaches demand at least a 2.5 per cent annual growth in travel distance by public transport.

The first combined approach (SM1) assumes that specific energy consumption for all means of transport will be reduced to the assumed 2030 BAU level. Inevitably, this assumption demands a *reduction* of 2030 *total* travel distance compared to the 2002 level; moreover, because travel by public transport increases, this reduction must be applied to travel distances by cars and planes. In other words, on average EU-15 inhabitants can travel more by public transport but must travel less by car and plane than they do today.

The second combined approach (SM2) assumes that reductions in specific energy consumption for all means of transport are larger than the 2030 BAU level but not as large as the 2030 EFF level. This assumption demands a stabilization of 2030 travel distances by car and plane at the 2002 level but allows for a small increase in the total travel distance compared to the 2002 level – the small allowable increase is due to increased travel by public transport. In other words, on average EU-15 inhabitants can travel more by public transport but cannot travel more by car and plane than they do today.

The third combined approach (SM3) assumes that reductions in specific energy consumption for all means of transport are at the 2030 EFF level. This assumption allows for a small increase in travel distance by car and plane and also a small increase in total travel distance compared to the 2002 level. However, these two travel distances are far less than the travel distances permitted in the 2030 BAU scenario. In other words, on average EU-15 inhabitants can travel more by public transport and also travel slightly more by car and plane than they do today.

Step 4: How Can Sustainable Mobility be Achieved?

BAU travel patterns will not lead to sustainable mobility. Therefore, they must be changed to the travel patterns called for in SM1, SM2 and SM3. The discussion in step 4 about the necessary changes concentrates on four issues: First, how can technology, public transport, green attitudes and land-use planning contribute to sustainable mobility? Although this question has been discussed quite extensively in chapters 4–8, the relation between each of these four elements and their respective

---

1 Including improvements in engine design and downsizing (smaller and lighter vehicles).

2 Including increased occupancy rates.

influence on sustainable mobility will be elaborated on here. Second, and not much discussed so far in this book, there is a mutual relation between these four elements; that is, they influence each other. Thus, it is important to clarify these relations and moreover discuss how they can contribute to sustainable mobility. Third, due to the present strong increase in leisure-time mobility, special attention should be given to how technology, public transport, green attitudes and land-use planning can contribute to sustainable leisure-time mobility. Fourth, and finally, I present some thoughts regarding what I consider to be the most important issue in achieving sustainable mobility.

Step 4 presents a synthesis of the empirical evidence and the theoretical knowledge presented throughout the book. However, it also points at knowledge gaps and raises a number of issues for further research.

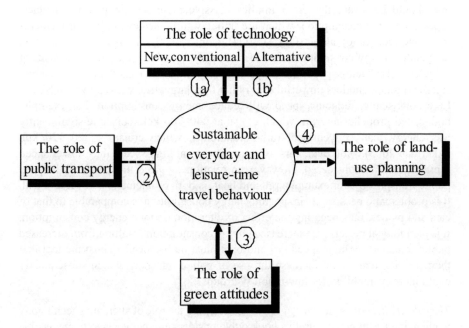

Figure 9.4   How to achieve sustainable mobility – I

The Roles of Technology, Public Transport, Green Attitudes and Land-use Planning

The relation between each of these four elements and changes towards sustainable everyday and leisure-time travel behaviour is shown in figure 9.4.

As indicated by the solid arrows in figure 9.4, the main relation is assumed to be one where each element changes travel behaviour. However, as indicated by the dotted arrows, changes in travel behaviour could also influence the elements themselves. For example, changes in travel behaviour trends – due to, say, increased environmental concern – could increase the demand for public transport and subsequently enhance the role of public transport. Thus, there is a reciprocal relation between each element and its influence on travel behaviour, which will be discussed in the next section.

The role of new, conventional technology (1a)   The role of new, conventional technology in achieving sustainable travel behaviour was presented in the scenario analyses: On one hand, to reduce specific energy consumption for all means of transport at the BAU level demands that 2030 average yearly travel distances by car and plane be less than today (SM1). On the other hand, reductions in specific energy consumption for all means of transport at the EFF level allow for a small increase in 2030 yearly travel distances by car and plane compared to the 2002 level (SM3).

The scenario that allows for an increase in yearly travel distance up to 2030 (SM3) is probably more attractive than the one that demands its reduction (SM1). However, one should be aware that SM3 implies massive reductions in present vehicles' specific energy consumption, which are unlikely to be achieved by improvements in engine technology alone (OECD 2004). Consequently, the necessary reduction in specific energy consumption in SM3 can only be achieved by *also* downsizing vehicles and reducing speed. Cars in particular must be downsized; people must buy smaller, lighter, and less powerful cars rather than large, heavy and powerful SUVs. Like downsizing, reducing speed will reduce energy consumption. For example, high-speed propeller aircraft, which cruise at 640–700 kph, consume significantly less energy than conventional turbofan aircraft, which cruise at 820–920 kph (Åkerman 2005). Moreover, cars use more energy at high speed; thus, lower speed limits should be considered. However, in relation to speed, improved high-speed public transport by, for example, rail and boat, is both problematic and paradoxical. It is problematic because their specific energy consumption is comparable to that of cars and planes, thus negating the effect of alteration on total energy consumption. It is paradoxical because the increased energy consumption resulting from increased public transport by high-speed rail and boat must be balanced against the fact that their development could increase the use of public transport, which subsequently could increase mobility for low-mobility groups.

The role of alternative technology (1b)   Concerning the role of alternative technology in changing travel behaviour, this book only considers alternative energy chains, that is alternative energy sources, alternative fuels and alternative drive trains for vehicles. Unfortunately, implementing alternative energy chains will not reduce overall energy consumption because so much energy is required to produce and distribute alternative fuels, which counteracts the benefits derived from their use. Thus, because alternative energy chains, as we know them today, do not reduce total energy consumption, their use is not a central part of a sustainable mobility strategy.

If, however, alternative energy chains that do reduce total energy consumption were to be developed, their use would indeed be a central part of a sustainable mobility strategy. Moreover, there are other legitimate reasons for increasing the use of alternative fuels: the use of domestically sourced natural gas or biomass fuels could increase national energy security; their use could solve environmental problems like local air pollution in towns and cities, and could moreover support sectors having a declining labour market like agriculture.

The role of public transport (2) Public transport's role in changing travel behaviour has three parts. First, improved public transport ensures the basic mobility needs of low-mobility groups. Perhaps extensive urban rail systems are the solution. As demonstrated by Kenworthy and Laube (2002b), passenger transport by rail is a major component of public transport in cities with high levels of public transport use. Second, improved public transport encourages mode switching away from travel by car and plane. Although this mode switching does not contribute much to reducing total energy consumption (unless the total transport volume is reduced), it has other benefits, for example less local pollution and congestion. Third, improved public transport would make it easier for both present high- and low-mobility groups to meet their basic mobility needs if restrictions were to be put on travel by car on plane due to, for example, fuel scarcity or very high fuel prices.

The role of green attitudes (3) Apparently, green attitudes play a limited role in changing travel behaviour. People who express concern about green issues, or those who are members of green NGOs, simply do not translate their concern into sustainable travel behaviour. However, their green attitudes play a very important *indirect* role in changing travel behaviour because green people are more likely to accept or even demand changes in technology, land-use planning and public transport (more about this in the final section).

The role of land-use planning (4) Land-use planning's role in changing travel behaviour is complex. Indeed, some scholars dismiss the very idea that land-use planning might influence travel behaviour. They argue that other factors are far more important and that land-use planning's role in changing travel behaviour is at best negligible. Moreover, even those who support the idea that land-use planning can promote sustainable travel behaviour admit that it reduces energy consumption relatively little. For example, over a thirty-year period, the energy saving potential through land-use planning in Norway is a modest 7 per cent of total energy consumption (Næss 1997).

However, I will argue that the main case for employing land-use planning to change travel behaviour is that it contains significant *potential* to change travel behaviour. Indeed, certain urban forms resulting from land-use planning do, to a much larger extent than other forms, *make possible* sustainable travel behaviour. A large and growing literature suggests that decentralized concentration of cities and towns and polycentric development within large cities are the urban forms that best exploit land-use planning's potential to change travel behaviour. Furthermore, like improved public transport, certain urban forms would make it easier for both present high- and low-mobility groups to meet their basic mobility needs in the future if restrictions were to be put on travel by car on plane.

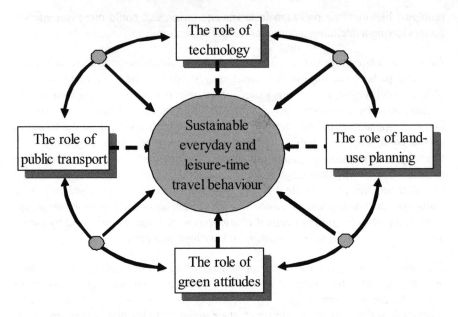

Figure 9.5   How to achieve sustainable mobility – II

The Relation between Technology, Public Transport, Green Attitudes and Land-use Planning

More important than studying the respective elements one-by-one would be to study how the *relation* between them could contribute to sustainable mobility (figure 9.5).

Thus, rather than assuming that the effect of applying the respective elements would be additive:

- SM = f {TE (effects of technology) + PT (effects of public transport) + GA (effects of green attitudes) + LU (effects of land-use planning)},

    the following is more relevant:

- SM = f {[TE+PT+GA+LU] + [(TE*PT)+(TE*GA)+(TE*LU)]+ … + [TE*PT*GA*LU]}.

The latter 'formula' is not an equation in any quantitative sense. Rather, it merely illustrates the issues that occur due to the complex relation between the elements in terms of making sustainable mobility achievable. I will discuss seven issues here:

First, how can the apparent lack of consistency between green attitudes and leisure-time travel behaviour be understood? I have argued in this book that because of the desire to indulge themselves, people with green attitudes seem to cast aside those attitudes when travelling for leisure. But, are there alternative explanations for this inconsistency? For example, do green people merely lack information about the environmental problems caused by their leisure-time travel? Thus, would they behave consistently if they were to have such information?

Second, how can the apparent inconsistency between sustainable urban form and people's energy consumption for everyday and leisure-time travel be understood? For example, the empirical evidence presented in this book suggests that people living in high-density residential areas consume less energy for everyday travel than people living in low-density residential areas, but that they consume more energy for leisure-time travel by plane than the latter. Does this inconsistency result from so-called 'compensatory travel behaviour,' or rather because people living in high-density areas have different lifestyle preferences than people living in low-density residential areas?

Third, how can public transport become attractive for leisure-time travel? Today, car and plane are preferred for such travel. Can new technology in terms of more attractive and efficient pubic transport – for example automatically guided vehicles or magnetically levitated trains – change such preferences? Would such improved public transport attract commuters and, moreover, affect these commuters' leisure-time travel behaviour? The relation between public transport and leisure-time travel raises another interesting issue. Some researchers suggest that attractive and efficient public transport to, say, a tourist destination could show people that this indeed is an appealing mode of transport. Thus, would it be possible to increase people's use of public transport in their everyday travel by educating them about its use for leisure travel?

Fourth, how important is the *indirect* effect of green attitudes on sustainable travel behaviour? To what extent do green people indirectly reduce their energy consumption for transport by, for example, choosing housing close to public transport infrastructures, shops and workplaces? Moreover, to what extent do green people indirectly reduce their energy consumption for transport by downsizing their cars and by accepting slower means of transport?

Fifth, are there other and more effective ways to promote green attitudes than through public information and awareness campaigns? Would it for example be possible to increase peoples' green attitudes by developing, say, green neighbourhoods? Thus, should the authorities promote green attitudes through urban planning rather than through information and awareness campaigns?

Sixth, does information and communication technology (ICT) influence everyday and leisure-time travel differently? For example, is the relation between ICT and travel behaviour such that ICT reduces the need for everyday travel (for example, by allowing some people to work from home) but at the same time generates the desire for leisure-time travel (for example, by conveying more effectively tourism promotional messages)?

Seventh, what is the role of economics in promoting sustainable mobility? How can economics be incorporated in figure 9.5 and what are the relations between it and the other elements illustrated in the figure? I argue in chapter 2 that economic growth is not one of sustainable development's goals, but rather a *potential means* to facilitate the fulfilment of sustainable development's three extra prima characteristics. A similar relation exists between economic growth and sustainable mobility:

economic growth is not one of sustainable mobility's goals. However, this does not mean that economic *measures* are unimportant to achieving sustainable mobility. On the contrary, economic measures like differentiated taxation (to promote unleaded gasoline), carbon tax (to combat global warming), subsidies (to encourage public transport modes) and marketable permits (to reduce a particular polluting substance) are probably necessary to lead developed countries into the SMA. However, such economic measures might affect everyday travel and leisure-time travel differently; for example, household travel surveys in three Norwegian cities showed that whereas people with low incomes consume less energy for leisure-time travel than people with high incomes, they do not consume significantly less energy for everyday travel (Holden 2001, 2004; Holden and Norland 2005).

Elements	Reduces energy consumption for everyday travel?	Reduces energy consumption for leisure-time travel?
Technology (for example the use of electric cars)	Yes	No
Public transport (for example 'mode switch effects')	Yes	No
Green attitudes (for example membership in NGOs)	Yes	No
Land-use planning (for example compact cities)	Yes	No
ICT (for example increased use of the Internet)	Yes	No
Economy (for example increased taxes on travel)	No	Yes

Figure 9.6   Various elements affect energy consumption for everyday travel and leisure-time travel differently

The Troublesome Leisure-time Mobility

Many of the issues raised in the previous section concern how the four elements – technology, public transport, green attitudes and land-use planning – seem to influence energy consumption for everyday and leisure-time travel differently as shown in figure 9.6. The figure summarizes the relations between the four elements and travel behaviour presented in chapters 4–8 and moreover illustrates some hypothetical relations between ICT, economy and travel behaviour.

The ambiguity regarding the role of technology can be illustrated by the effect of using electric cars and promoting downsizing. Electric cars, which consume considerably less energy than conventional petrol and diesel cars but which have a significantly shorter driving range, are fine for everyday travel but probably hard to sell as a means of transport for leisure-time travel. Moreover, downsized, less powerful cars with less storage space are fine for everyday travel, but few people find them attractive for leisure-time travel.

The ambiguity regarding the role of public transport is that whereas an improved public transport system would increase the use of public transport for everyday travel, it would not to any great extent increase the use of public transport for leisure-time travel.

The ambiguity regarding the role of green attitudes has powerfully been demonstrated concerning members of environmental organisations. These members comply with their green attitudes and use public transport in their everyday lives, whereas they cast aside those attitudes when travelling for leisure.

The ambiguity of the role of land-use planning can be illustrated by the development of large, high-density compact cities. Residents in such cities consume less energy for everyday travel than do residents of other urban forms, but consume much more energy for long-distance leisure-time travel than do residents of other urban forms.

The respective ambiguities of the role of ICT and the role of the economy have already been touched upon in the sixth and seventh issues above: they seem to influence everyday and leisure-time travel differently. Indeed, more knowledge of the six elements and their ambiguous effects on everyday and leisure-time travel is important for achieving sustainable mobility. This knowledge must lead to an answer to the following question: What measures will have the maximum effect on reducing *total* energy consumption for *all* travel?

The Tipping Point

Implementing new technology, improving public transport, increasing individuals' green attitudes and promoting sustainable land-use planning are all important elements in achieving sustainable mobility, as are ICT and economic measures. However, I believe that there is a hierarchy between these elements, and that individuals' attitudes are most important. Thus, changes towards sustainable mobility must start with the transformation of the attitudes and values of a *large* majority of people. Indeed, I believe that changes cannot and should not take place unless and until they are accepted by or demanded by a *large* majority of people. Therefore, the transformation of attitudes and values must precede regulation. Some scholars, however, argue that changing attitudes and values takes too long and that regulations therefore must come first. Moreover, they would argue that regulation could transform attitudes and values and thus could be used as a means to promote sustainable mobility without much prior popular support. I am sceptical about this argument for three reasons:

First, forcing people to do something they strongly oppose, for example to use their cars less or to buy small, efficient cars, will likely cause *negative* attitudes amongst them towards sustainable mobility. Thus, regulation without prior popular support might be counterproductive long term.

Second, in a democracy the majority must approve regulation towards sustainable mobility. True, the government can put forward measures which favour the common good, for example to prevent climate change, or measures that are based on moral grounds, for example to ensure accessibility for low-mobility groups. However, for such measures to be effective, there must be acceptance by a large majority that this common good is worth favouring and moreover that the measures are justified on moral grounds.

Third, even after extensive regulation by government, there is almost always some freedom of choice left for the individual. Thus, the final outcome depends on individual choice. The importance of attitudes and values should therefore not be underestimated. In fact, some of history's most sensational events and changes are the result of gradually changed attitudes (Petty and Krosnick 1995). Notable transformations in history include the shift from the overt racist attitudes of the 1950s in the US, and more recently, access for women to significant leadership roles in society. Collective attitude change in these instances was a prerequisite for the transformations. To change our presently unsustainable mobility pattern requires a similar collective attitude change.

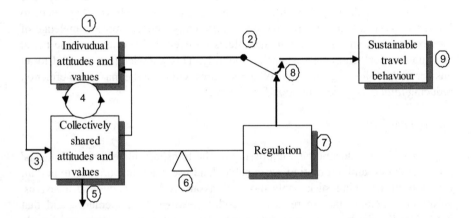

Figure 9.7   How to achieve sustainable mobility – III (see text for explanations of numbers)

The relation between individual attitudes, collectively shared attitudes, regulation and sustainable travel behaviour is illustrated in figure 9.7. The switch (2) that connects individual attitudes (1) and sustainable travel behaviour (9) is currently 'off,' indicating that most developed countries currently have an unsustainable transport system. This in turn explains the attitude-behaviour inconsistency of most green people; that is, sustainable travel behaviour is almost impossible in an unsustainable transport system.

Turning the switch 'on' (8) requires four steps: First, individual attitudes must change (1). This requires that people be more knowledgeable about transport's negative consequences; moreover, they must know how their *personal* travel behaviour contributes to those negative consequences. Second, a large majority of people must change their attitudes (3). Being green must become the *social norm*; as such, being green will perhaps become more attractive, thereby facilitating the greening of ever more individuals. This mutual relation between individual attitudes (personal norms) and collective attitudes (social norms) would continue (4), until the number of green people were to reach a critical value (5). Third, there must be a majority of greens before we reach the tipping point (6). Then regulation towards sustainable mobility can begin (7). Such regulation would likely include the introduction of fuel efficiency standards for vehicles, the initiation of massive investments in an improved public transport system and the development of decentralised concentration and polycentric urban form. Fourth, there must be extensive regulation of this sort to finally turn the switch 'on' (8).

Figure 9.7 illustrates a critical issue – that the transition from a few dedicated greens to a large majority with collectively shared green values would ultimately reach the tipping point. Alas, we are currently far from such a point. Moreover, it will probably take quite some time to reach it, although 2030 *could* be a realistic target. The good news, however, is that once we reach it we should know fairly well how to turn the switch 'on.'

Bibliography

Aall, C. et al. (1997), *Scenarier for transportutvikling i Norge (Scenarios for transport development in Norway)*, Note 29 (Sogndal: Western Norway Research Institute).

Aall, C. et al. (2003), *Bustad, forbruk og økologiske fotavtrykk (Housing, consumption and ecological footprints)*, Report 16 (Sogndal: Western Norway Research Institute).

Aall, C. and Norland, I.T. (2002), *Det økologiske fotavtrykket for Oslo kommune (The ecological footprint of Oslo municipality)*, Report 1 (Oslo: ProSus/University of Oslo).

Adams, J. (1992), 'Towards a Sustainable Transport Policy', in Roberts et al. (eds), *Travel Sickness: The Need for a Sustainable Transport Policy for Britain* (London: Lawrence & Wishart).

Ajzen, I. (1996), 'The directive influence of attitudes on behaviour', in Bargh, J.A. and Golwitzer, P. (eds), *Psychology of action*, pp. 385–403 (New York: Guilford).

Ajzen, I. and Fishbein, M. (1977), 'Attitude–behaviour relations: A theoretical analysis and review of empirical research', *Psychological Bulletin* 84, 888–918.

Alexander, E. (1981), 'If planning isn't everything, maybe it's something', *Town Planning Review* 52:4, 131–142.

Allport, G.W. (1935), 'Attitudes', in Murchinson, C. (ed.), *Handbook of Social Psychology*, pp. 798–844 (Worcester, MA: Clark University Press).

Anable, J. (2002), 'Picnics, Pets, and Pleasant Places: The Distinguishing Characteristics of Leisure Travel Demand', in Black and Nijkamp (eds), pp. 181–190.

Anda, O. and Larssen, S. (1982), *Luftforurensninger fra vegtrafikk: Slitasje av vegdekke, bildekk og bremsebånd (Air pollution from road traffic. Wear of roads, car tyres and brakes)*. Report 31 (Kjeller: Norwegian Institute for Air Research).

Andersen, O. et al. (2004), 'Transport Scenarios in a Company Strategy', *Business Strategy and the Environment* 13, 43–61.

Bagozzi, R.P. (1982), 'A field investigation of causal relations among cognitions, affect, intentions, and behaviour', *Journal of Marketing Research* 19, 562–584.

Bang, J.R. and Holden, E. (1991), *Elektriske biler – en utslippsanalyse (Electric vehicles – an impact assessment)* (Oslo: Norwegian Institute of Technology).

Banister, D. (1992), 'Energy Use, Transport and Settlement Patterns', in Breheny (ed.), pp. 160–181 (London: Pion Limited).

Banister, D. (2002), *Transport Planning,* 2nd Edition (London and New York: Spon Press).

Banister, D. (2005), *Unsustainable Transport* (London: Routledge).

Banister, D. and Button, K. (eds) (1993), *Transport, the Environment and Sustainable Development* (London: E & FN Spon).

Banister, D. et al. (2000), *European Transport Policy and Sustainable Mobility* (London/New York: Spon Press).

Bauman, Z. (2000), *Globalisation* (Columbia University Press).

Beckerman, W. (1994), 'Sustainable development: is it a useful concept?', *Environmental Values* 3, 191–209.

Beckmann, J. (2002), 'Keeping the Holy Grail: The "Mobility View" of the Danish Automobile Club FDM', in Black and Nijkamp (eds), pp. 101–106.

Black, W.R. (2003), *Transportation. A Geographical Analysis* (New York/London: The Guilford Press).

Black, W.R. and Nijkamp, P. (eds) (2002), *Social Change and Sustainable Transport* (Bloomington: Indiana University Press).

Black, W.R. and Nijkamp, P. (2002a), 'Introduction: Pathways to Sustainable Transport and Basic Themes', in Black and Nijkamp (eds), pp. xi–xiii.

Boarnet, M.G. and Crane, R. (2001), *Travel by design. The influence of urban form on travel* (Oxford: Oxford University Press).

Breheny, M.J. (ed.) (1992), *Sustainable Development and Urban Form* (London: Pion Limited).

Breheny, M.J. (1992a), 'The Contradictions of the Compact City: A Review', in Breheny (ed.), pp. 138–159.

Breheny, M.J. (1996), 'Centrists, Decentrists and Compromisers: Views on the Future of Urban Form', in Jenks et al. (eds), pp. 13–35.

Buxton, M. (2000), 'Energy, Transport and Urban Form in Australia', in Williams, K. et al. (eds), pp. 54–63.

Callon, M. (1999), 'Society in the Making: The Study of Technology as a Tool for Sociological Analysis', in Bijker, W.E., Hughes, T.P. and Pinch, T. (eds), *The Social Construction of Technological Systems*, 7th Edition, pp. 83–103 (Massachusetts: MIT Press).

Campbell, C. (1987), *The Romantic Ethic and the Spirit of Modern Consumption* (Oxford: Macmillan).

CARB (1979), *Fine particle emissions from stationary and miscellaneous sources in the south coast air basin*, Final Report KVB5806–783 (Sacramento, California: California Air Resources Board).

CARB (1998), *Emissions factors scenario. Predicted California vehicle emissions*, Ozone planning inventory, Scenario MVE17G (Sacramento, California: California Air Resources Board).

Carson, R. (1962), *Silent Spring*. (Greenwich, Connecticut: Fawcett Publications).

CEC (1990), *Green Paper on the Urban Environment* (Brussels: Commission of the European Communities).

CEC (1992), *Green Paper on the Impact of Transport on the Environment. A Community strategy for 'sustainable mobility'*, COM (92) 46 Final (Brussels: Commission of the European Communities).

CEC (1993), *The Future Development of the Common Transport Policy – A global approach to the construction of a community framework for sustainable mobility*,

Bulletin of the European Communities, Supplement 3/93 (Brussels: Commission of the European Communities).

CEC (1998), *The Common Transport Policy – Sustainable Mobility: Perspectives for the Future*. COM (98) 716 Final (Brussels: Commission of the European Communities).

CEC (2000), *Monitoring of ACEA's Commitment on CO_2 Emission Reduction from Passenger Cars (1995–1999)'*, Final version. Joint Report of the European Automobile Manufacturers Association and the Commission Services (Brussels: Commission of the European Communities).

CEC (2001), *White paper. European transport policy for 2010: Time to decide*, COM (2001) 370 Final (Brussels: Commission of the European Communities).

CEC (2004), *Implementing the Community Strategy to Reduce CO_2 Emissions from Cars: Fourth annual report on the effectiveness of the strategy (Reporting year 2002)*. COM (2004) 78 Final (Brussels: Commission of the European Communities).

Chambers, N. et al. (2000), *Sharing Nature's Interest. Ecological Footprints as an Indicator of Sustainability* (London: Earthscan).

Cole, M. et al. (1997), 'The Environmental Kuznets curve: an empirical analysis', *Environment and Development Economics* 2, 401–416.

Cox, J.A. et al. (1999), 'Part F. Applications of the Meet Methodology', in Hickman, A.J (ed.). *Methodology for calculation transport emissions and energy consumption*. Project report SE/491/98. Berkshire: Transport Research Laboratory.

Daly, H.E. (2005), 'Economies in a full world', *Scientific American*, September, 100–107.

Djupskås, O.T. and Nesbakken, R. (1995), *Energibruk i husholdningene 1993 (Energy Use in Households 1993)*, Report 10 (Oslo: Statistics Norway).

EC (2003), *European Energy and Transport Trends to 2030* (Brussels: European Commission).

EC (2004), *EU Energy and Transport in Figures. Statistical pocketbook 2004* (Brussels: European Commission).

EC (2006), 'Air Transport in Europe in 2004', *Statistics in Focus – Transport* 2 (Brussels: European Commission).

ECIP (2003), *European Common Indicators: Towards a Local Sustainability Profile* (Milano: Ambiente Italia).

Ecotraffic (2001), *Well-to-wheel Efficiency for Alternative Fuels from Natural Gas or Biomass* (Stockholm: Ecotraffic ERD3 AB).

Edinger, R. and Kaul, S. (2003), *Sustainable Mobility: Renewable Energies for Powering Fuel Cell Vehicle* (London: Praeger).

EEA (2002), *Energy and environment in the European Union*, Environmental issue report 31 (Copenhagen: European Environment Agency).

EEA (2005), *Household Consumption and the Environment*, EEA Report 11 (Copenhagen: European Environment Agency).

EEA (2006), *Transport and Environment: Facing a Dilemma*, EEA Report 3 (Copenhagen: European Environment Agency).

Eir, B. (1997), *Cykelregnskab og Grønne Cykelruter (Cycle Account and Green Cycle Routes)*, Paper presented at the Conference 'Trafikdage på Aalborg Universitet 1997'.

Elkin, T. et al. (1991), *Reviving the City: Towards Sustainable Urban Development* (London: Friends of the Earth).

Elkington, J. (1997), *Cannibals with Forks: The Triple Bottom Line for 21st Century Business* (Oxford: Capstone).

Elkington, J. (2004), 'Enter the Triple Bottom Line', in Henriques, A. and Richardson, J. (eds), *The Triple Bottom Line. Does it all add up?*, pp. 1–16 (London: Earthscan).

Elster, J. (1989), *Nuts and Bolts for the Social Sciences* (Cambridge: Cambridge University Press).

Enwicht, D. (1992), *Towards an Eco-City: Calming the Traffic* (Sydney: Envirobook).

Fazio, R.H.and Zanna, M.P. (1981), 'Direct experience and attitude-behaviour consistency', in Berkowitz, L. (ed.), *Advances in Experimental Social Psychology* vol. 14, pp. 161–202 (New York: Academic Press).

Feitelson, E. (2002), 'Introducing Environmental Equity Concerns into the Discourse on Sustainable Transport: A Research Agenda', in Black and Nijkamp (eds), pp. 141–148.

Fishbein, M. and Ajzen, I. (1972), 'Attitudes and opinions', *Annual Review of Psychology* 23, 487–544.

Fishbein, M.and Ajzen, I. (1975), *Belief, Attitude, Intention, and Behaviour* (Reading, MA: Addison-Wesley).

Fitzgerald, P. et al. (1999), 'Part D. Air Transport', in Hickman, A J (ed.), *Methodology for calculation transport emissions and energy consumption*, Project report SE/491/98 (Berkshire: Transport Research Laboratory).

Frey, H. (1999), *Designing the City. Towards a More Sustainable Urban Form* (London: Spon Press).

Frey, B.S. and Foppa, K. (1986), 'Human behavior: Possibilities explain action', *Journal of Economic Psychology* 7, 137–160.

Gabriel, Y. and Lang, T. (1995), *The Unmanageable Consumer* (London: SAGE Publications).

Gatersleben, B. and Uzzell, D. (2002), 'Sustainable Transport and Quality of Life: A Psychological Analysis', in: Black and Nijkamp (eds), pp. 135–140.

Geenhuizen, M. von et al. (2002), 'Social Change and Sustainable Transport: A Manifesto on Transatlantic Research Opportunities', in Black and Nijkamp (eds), pp. 3–16.

General Motors (2001a), *Well-to-wheel Energy Use and Greenhouse Gas Emissions of Advanced Fuel/Vehicle Systems – North American Analysis*, vol. 2 (Detroit: General Motors Corporation).

General Motors (2001b), *Well-to-tank Energy Use and Greenhouse Gas Emissions of Transportation Fuels – North American Analysis*, vol. 3 (Detroit: General Motors Corporation).

General Motors (2002), *Well-to-wheel Energy Use and Greenhouse Gas Emissions of Advanced Fuel/Vehicle Systems – A European Study* (Detroit: General Motors Corporation).

Giddens, A. (1991), *Modernity and Self-Identity* (Oxford: Polity Press).

Giddens, A. (2001), *Sociology*, 4th Edition (Oxford: Blackwell Publishers Ltd).

Giddings B. et al. (2002), 'Environment, economy and society: fitting them together into sustainable development', *Sustainable Development* 10:4, 187–196.

Gilbert, R. (2002), 'Social Implications of Sustainable Transport', in Black and Nijkamp (eds), pp. 63–70.

Gillespie, A. (1992), 'Communications Technologies and the Future of the City', in Breheny (ed.), pp. 67–78.

Giuliano, G. and Gillespie, A. (2002), 'Research Issues Regarding Societal Change and Transport: An Update', in Black and Nijkamp (eds), pp. 27–34.

Glaser, B. and Strauss, A. (1967), *Discovery of Grounded Theory* (Aldine: Chicago).

Goodwin, P. et al. (1992), *Modifying our volume of traffic: the primary route to sustainable transport* (Oxford: University of Oxford, Transport Studies Unit).

Gordon, P. and Richardson, H.W. (1989), 'Gasoline consumption and cities – a reply', *Journal of the American Planning Association* 55:3, 342–345.

Gorham, R. (2002), 'Car Dependence as a Social Problem: A Critical Essay on the Existing Literature and Future Needs', in Black and Nijkamp (eds), pp. 107–116.

Gullestad, M. (1989), *Kultur og hverdagsliv (Culture and Everyday life)* (Oslo: Scandinavian University Press).

Hasic, T. (2000), 'A Sustainable Urban Matrix: Achieving Sustainable Urban Form in Residential Buildings', in Williams et al. (eds), pp. 329–336.

Halkier, B. (1999), *Miljø – til daglig bruk?(Environmental issues – for everyday life?)* (Forlaget Sociologi, Frederiksberg).

Hanley, N. et al. (2001), *Introduction to Environmental Economics* (Oxford: Oxford University Press).

Haq, G. (1997), *Towards Sustainable Transport Planning: A Comparison between Britain and the Netherlands* (Aldershot: Avebury).

Hellevik, O. (1991), *Forskningsmetode i sosiologi og statsvitenskap (Reserch Method in Sosiology and Political Science)* (Oslo: Scandinavian University Press).

Hellman, K.H. and Heavenrich, R.M. (2001), *Light Duty Automotive Technology and Fuel Economy Trends, 1975–2001*, Report no. EPA420-R-01-008 (US Environmental Protection Agency).

Hille, J. (1995), *Sustainable Norway* (Oslo: The Project for an Alternative Future).

Hine, J. and Mitchell, F. (2001), *The Role of Transport in Social Exclusion in Urban Scotland* (Edinburgh: Scottish Executive Central Research Unit).

Hochleitner, R.D. (1998), 'Foreword', in Weizäcker et al., pp. xiii–xiv.

Holden, E. (2001), *Boligen som grunnlag for bærekraftig forbruk (Housing as basis for a sustainable consumption)*, PhD-thesis 2001:115 (Trondheim: Department of Town and Regional Planning, Norwegian University of Science and Technology).

Holden, E. (2003), *Energi og miljødata for alternative og konvensjonelle drivstoffer – år 2010* (Energy use and emissions for conventional and alternative fuels – year 2010), Report no. 2 (Sogndal: Western Norway Research Institute).

Holden, E. (2004), 'Ecological Footprints and Sustainable Urban Form', *Journal of Housing and the Built Environment* 19:1, 91–109.

Holden, E. (2005), 'En rett og to vrange … Tre teser om miljøholdninger og husholdningenes forbruk' (One plain and two purl… Three theses about the relationship between environmental attitudes and household consumption), *Sosiologisk tidskrift* (Norwegian Journal of Sociology) 13, 261–286.

Holden (forthcoming), '"Green" attitudes and sustainable household consumption of energy and transport – Six conditions that improve attitude-behaviour consistency', in: Bergman, S., Sager, T. and Hoff, T (eds), *Spaces of Mobility* (London: Equinox).

Holden, E. and Høyer, K.G. (2005), 'The Ecological Footprints of Fuels', *Transportation Research Part D: Transport and Environment* 10:5, 395–403.

Holden, E. and Norland, I.T. (2004), *SusHomes – En undersøkelse av husholdningers forbruk av energi til bolig og transport i Stor-Oslo* (SusHomes – A survey of household consumption of energy and transport in Greater-Oslo), ProSus Report 3/4 (Oslo: ProSus, University of Oslo).

Holden. E. and Norland, I.T. (2005), 'Three Challenges for the Compact City as a Sustainable Urban Form: Household Consumption of Energy and Transport in Eight Residential Areas in the Greater Oslo Region', *Urban Studies* 42:12, 2145–2166.

Holden, E and Linnerud, K. (2006), 'The sustainable development area: Satisfying basic needs and safeguarding ecological sustainability', *Sustainable Development* (Published Online: 10 October 2006).

Holter, Ø. et al. (1979), *Alternative Energi Ressurser* (Alternative Energy Resources) (Oslo: Scandinavian University Press).

Holtskog, S. (2001), *Direkte energibruk og utslipp til luft fra transport i Norge. 1994 og 1998* (Energy use and emissions to air from transport in Norway. 1994 and 1998), Report 16 (Oslo: Statistics Norway).

Holtskog, S. and Rypdal, K. (1997), *Energibruk og utslipp til luft fra transport i Norge* (Energy use and emissions to air from transport in Norway), Report 7 (Oslo: Statistics Norway).

Holtz-Eakin, D. and Selden, T.M. (1995), 'Stoking the fires? CO_2 emissions and economic growth', *Journal of Public Economics* 57, 85–101.

Hopwood, B. et al. (2005), 'Sustainable Development: mapping different approaches', *Sustainable Development* 13:1, 38–52.

Horvath R.J. (1997), *Energy consumption and the environmental Kuznets curve debate* (Department of Geography, University of Sydney).

Høyer, K.G. (2000), *Sustainable Mobility – the Concept and its Implications*, PhD-thesis, Report 1 (Sogndal: Western Norway Research Institute).

Høyer, K.G. (2003), *Husholdninger, forbruk og miljø. Et historisk perspektiv* (Households, consumption and environment. A historical perspective) (Sogndal: Western Norway Research Institute).

Høyer, K.G. and Heiberg, E. (1993), *Persontransport – konsekvenser for energi og miljø* (Passenger transport – an assessment of energy and environmental impacts), Report 1 (Sogndal: Western Norway Research Institute).

Høyer, K.G. and Holden, E. (2001), 'Housing as Basis for Sustainable Consumption', *International Journal on Sustainable Development* 1:4, 48–58.

Høyer, K.G. and Holden, E. (2003), 'Household consumption and ecological footprints in Norway – Does Urban Form matter?', *Journal of Consumer Policy* 26, 327–349.

Høyer K.G and Holden, E. (forthcoming), 'Alternative Fuels and Sustainable Mobility – Is the Future Road paved by Biofuels, Electricity or Hydrogen?', *International Journal of Alternative Propulsion*.

IEA (2002a), *Bus Systems for the Future* (Paris: The International Energy Agency).

IEA (2002b), *Transportation and Energy* (Paris: The International Energy Agency).

IEA (2004), *World Energy Outlook 2004* (Paris: The International Energy Agency).

IEA (2005), *Key World Energy Statistics 2005* (Paris: The International Energy Agency).

Illich, I.D. (1974), *Energy and Equity*, Open Forum Series (London: Calder & Boyars).

International Union for Conservation of Nature and Natural Resources (1980), *World Conservation Strategy: Living Resources Conservation for Sustainable development* (Gland, Switzerland: IUCN).

IPCC (2001), *Climate Change 2001. The Scientific Basis*, Contribution of Working Group I to the Third Assessment Report of the Intergovernmental Panel on Climate Change, Published for the Intergovernmental Panel on Climate Change (Cambridge University Press).

Jacobs, J. (1961), *The Death and Life of Great American Cities. The Failure of Town Planning* (New York: Random House).

Jahn Hansen, C. et al. (2000), *Nordisk transport i fremtiden. Krav til bærekraft og effektivitet*, Report 8/2000 (Sogndal: Western Norway Research Institute).

Janelle, D.G. and Beuthe, M. (2002), 'Globalization and Transportation: Contradictions and Challenges', in Black and Nijkamp (eds), pp. 49–54.

Jenks, M. et al. (eds) (1996), *The Compact City: A Sustainable Urban Form?* (London: E & FN Spon).

Jensen, C. (1998), *Jeg har sett verden begynne* (I have seen the beginning of the world) (Oslo: Forlaget Geelmuyden Kiese).

Jones, P.M. (1987), 'Mobility and the Individual in Western Industrial Society', in Nijkamp P. and Reichman S. (eds), *Transportation Planning in a Changing World*, pp. 29–47 (Aldershot: Gower).

Jørgensen, A.E. et al. (2002), *Assessing the ecological footprint. A look at the WWFs living planet report 2002* (København: Environmental Assessment Institute).

Kaiser, F. (1993), *Mobilität als Wohnproblem – Ortsbindung im Licht der emotionalen Regulation* (Bern: Peter Lang Publishing Group).

Kennedy, M. (1995), 'Ekologisk stadsplanering i Europa' (Ecological Urban Planning in Europe), in *Den miljövänliga staden – en Utopi?* (The Ecological City – an Utopia?) (Gøteborg: Miljöprosjekt Sankt Jörgen).

Kenworthy, J. and Laube, F. (2002a), 'Urban transport patterns in a global sample of cities & their linkages to transport infrastructure, land use, economics & environment', *World Transport Policy and Practice* 8:3, 5–19.

Kenworthy, J. and Laube, F. (2002b), 'Travel demand management: The potential for enhancing urban rail opportunities & reducing automobile dependence in cities', *World Transport Policy and Practice* 8:3, 20–36.

Kirchler, E. (1988), 'Household economic decision-making', in Raaij, W.F.v. et al. (eds), *Handbook of economic psychology*, pp. 144–204 (Dordrecht: Kluwer Academic Publishers).

Koski, H.A. (2002), 'Information and Communication Technologies and Transport', in: Black and Nijkamp (eds), pp. 43–48.

Lafferty, W.M. (ed.) (2004), *Governance for Sustainable Development. The Challenge of Adapting Form to Function.* (Cheltenham: Edward Elgar).

Lafferty, W.M. and Langhelle, O. (1999), 'Sustainable Development as Concept and Norm', in Lafferty, W. M. and Langhelle, O. (eds), *Towards Sustainable Development. On the Goals of Development – and the Conditions of Sustainability* (London: Macmillan Press LTD).

LaPiere, R.T. (1934), 'Attitudes vs. actions', *Social Forces* 13, 230–237.

Larssen, S. (1987), *Støv fra asfaltveier. Karakterisering av luftbåret veistøv. Fase 1: Målinger i Oslo, våren 1985* (Dust from asphalt roads. Characterisation of air-borne road dust. Phase 1: Measurements in Oslo, spring 1985), OR 53/87 (Kjeller: Norwegian Institute for Air Research).

Larssen, S. (1997), *Har piggdekk virkelig skylden for all luftforurensing i de store byene?* (Can studded tyres really be blamed for all air pollution in the large cities?), Paper presented at the STOR-seminar 1997 – the Scandinavian Tire and Rim organization, Høvik, 11 December 1997, F 26/97 (Kjeller: Norwegian Institute for Air Research).

Litman, T. (2003), *Social Inclusion as a Transport Planning Issue in Canada* (Victoria: Victoria Transport Policy Institute).

Lorek, S. and Spangenberg, J.H. (2001), 'Indicators for environmentally sustainable household consumption', *Int. J. Sustainable Development* 1:4, 101–120.

Lovins, A.B. (1977), *Soft Energy Paths. Toward a Durable Peace* (Cambridge, Mass.: Ballinger Publishing Co).

Luke T.W. (2005), 'Neither sustainable nor development: reconsidering sustainability in development', *Sustainable Development* 13:4, 228–238.

Lyons, G. and Kenyon, S. (2003), 'Social participation, personal travel and internet use', Proceedings from *the 10th International Conference on Travel Behaviour Research*, Lucerne, August 2003.

Martinez Alier, J. (2006), Socio-Metabolic Profiles and Ecological Conflicts. *What Future for Environmentalism? Conference*, 10 May, Oxford Brookes University, Oxford.

Martinussen, W. (1999), *Sosiologiske forklaringer* (Sociological explanations) (Bergen: Fagbokforlaget).

Masnavi, M-R. (2000), 'The New Millennium and New Urban Paradigm: The Compact City in Practice', in Williams (eds), pp. 64–73.

Masser, I. et al. (1992), 'From Growth to Equity and Sustainability: Paradigm Shift in Transport Planning?', in *Transportation Planning and Technology* 17:4, 232–247.

McGuire, W.J. (1985), 'Attitudes and attitude change', in Lindzey, G. and Aronson, E. (eds), *Handbook of Social Psychology*, vol. 2, pp. 233–346 (New York: Random House).

McGuire, W.J. (1986), 'The vicissitudes of attitudes and similar representational constructs in twentieth century psychology', *European Journal of Social Psychology* 16, 89–130.

McLaren, D. (1992), 'Compact or dispersed? Dilution is no solution', *Built Environment* 18:4, 268–84.

Meadows, D.H. et al. (1972), *The Limits to Growth* (New York: Potomac Associates Book).

Meadows, D.H. et al. (1993), *Beyond the Limits: Confronting Global Collapse, Envisioning a Sustainable Future* (Post Mills, Vermont: Chelsea Green Publishing Company).

MoE (2002), *Bedre miljø i byer og tettsteder* (A better environment in cities and towns), Parliamentary White Paper no. 23 (2001–2002) (Oslo: Ministry of Environment).

Moisander, J. and Uusitalo, L. (1994), 'Attitude-behaviour inconsistency: Limitations of the reasoned action approach in predicting behavior from pro-environmental attitudes', in Antonides, G. and Raaij, W. F. v. (eds), *IAREP/SABE Conference*, pp. 560–579. Rotterdam, July 10–13.

Nachmias, D. and Nachmias, C. (1992), *Research methods in the social sciences* (New York: St. Martin's Press).

Newman, P.W.G. and Kenworthy, J.R. (1989), 'Gasoline consumption and cities – a comparison of US cities with a global survey'. *Journal of the American Planning Association* 55:1, 24–37.

Newman, P.W.G. and Kenworthy, J.R. (1999), *Sustainability and Cities. Overcoming Automobile Dependence* (Washington DC: Island Press).

Newman, P.W.G. and Kenworthy, J.R. (2000), 'Sustainable Urban Form: The Big Picture', in Williams et al. (eds), pp. 109–120.

Newton, P. (2000), 'Urban Form and Environmental Performance', in Williams, K. et al. (eds), pp. 46–53.

Nielsen, T.S. (2002), *Boliglokalisering og transport i Aalborg* (Residential location and transport in Aalborg), PhD thesis (Aalborg: Aalborg University).

Næss, A. (1991), 'Den dypøkologiske bevegelse: aktivisme ut fra et helhetssyn' (Deep Ecology), in Gjerdåker, S., Gule, L. and Hagtvedt, B. (eds), *Den uoverstigelige grense. Tanke og handling i miljøkampen* (The insurmountable limit. Thoughts and action in the environmental battle), pp. 21–43 (Oslo: J. W. Cappelens Forlag).

Næss, P. (1996), *Urban Form and Energy Use for Transport. A Nordic Experience*, PhD thesis 1996:20 (Trondheim: The Norwegian Institute of Technology).

Næss, P. (1997), *Fysisk planlegging og energibruk* (Spatial Planning and Energy Use) (Oslo: Tano Aschehoug).

Næss, P. (2000), 'Urban Land Use Changes and Mobility', Paper for the NTF Workshop, *Driving forces of mobility*, Stockholm, November 16–17.

Næss, P. (2006), *Urban Structure Matters* (Routledge).

Næss, P. and Jensen, O.B. (2004), 'Urban Structure Matters, Even in a Small Town', *Journal of Environmental Planning and Management* 47, 35–56.

OECD (2000), 'Environmentally Sustainable Transport, futures, strategies and best practices', Synthesis Report of the OECD project on Environmentally Sustainable Transport EST, presented on occasion of the *International est! Conference* 4th to 6th October in Vienna, Austria (Organisation for Economic Co-operation and Development).

OECD (2002a), *Towards Sustainable Household Consumption? Trends and Policies in OECD Countries* (Paris: Organisation for Economic Co-operation and Development).

OECD (2002b), *Report on the OECD Conference 'Environmentally Sustainable Transport (EST): Futures, Strategies and Best Practice'*. Palais Auersperg, Vienna, Austria 4–6 October 2000. ENV/EPOC/WPNEP/T(2001)8/FINAL (Organisation for Economic Co-operation and Development).

OECD (2002c), *Policy Instruments for Achieving Environmentally Sustainable Transport* (Paris: Organisation for Economic Co-operation and Development).

OECD (2004), *Can Cars Come Clean? Strategies for low-emission vehicles* (Paris: Organisation for Economic Co-operation and Development).

OECD (2005), *Making Cars More Fuel Efficient. Technology for Real Improvements on the Road* (Paris: Organisation for Economic Co-operation and Development).

Ölander, F. and Thøgersen, J. (1995), 'Understanding of consumer behaviour as a prerequisite for environmental protection', *Journal of Consumer Policy* 18, 317–357.

O'Riordan, T. (1993), 'The Politics of Sustainability', in Turner, R.K. (ed.), *Sustainable environmental economics and management,* pp. 37–69 (Chichester: John Wiley & Sons).

Orrskog, L. and Snickars, F. (1992), 'On the Sustainability of Urban and Regional Structures', in Breheny, M. J. (ed.), pp. 106–121.

Ostrom, T.M. (1969), 'The relationship between the affective, behavioural and cognitive components of attitude', *Journal of Experimental Social Psychology* 5, 12–30.

Owens, S. (1992), 'Energy, Environmental Sustainability and Land Use Planning', in Breheny (ed.), pp. 79–105.

Peden, M. et al. (eds) (2004), *World report on road traffic injury prevention* (Geneva: World Health Organisation).

Petty, R.E. and Krosnick, J. A. (eds) (1995), *Attitude strength: Antecedents and consequences* (Mahwah, New Jersey: Lawrence Erlbaum Associates).

Pieters, R. (1988). 'Attitude-behavior relationships', in Raaij, W.F. v. et al. (eds), *Handbook of economic psychology*, pp. 144–204 (Dordrecht: Kluwer Academic Publishers).

Posch, M. et al. (eds) (2001), *Modelling and Mapping of Critical Thresholds in Europe: Status Report 2001*, RIVM Report No. 259101010 (Bilthoven: Coordination Center for Effects, National Institute for Public Health and the Environment).

Rietveld, P. and Stough, R.R. (2005), *Barriers to Sustainable Transport. Institutions, Regulations and Sustainability* (London and New York: Spon Press).

Roberts, J. et al. (1992), *Travel Sickness: The Need for a Sustainable Transport Policy for Britain* (London: Lawrence & Wishart).

Ronis, D.L. et al. (1989), 'Attitudes, decisions, and habits as determinants of repeated behavior', in: Pratkanis, A.R. et al. (eds), *Attitude structure and function*, pp. 213–239 (Hillsdale, N.J.: Lawrence Erlbaum).

Root, A. et al. (2002), 'Women and Travel: The Sustainability Implications of Changing Roles', in Black and Nijkamp (eds), pp. 149–156.

Rudinger, G. (2002), 'Mobility Behaviour of the Elderly: Its Impacts on the Future Road Traffic System', in Black and Nijkamp (eds), pp. 157–164.

Rådberg, J. (1995), 'Termitstack eller ekobyar? En diskussion om täthet och bärekraftig stadsutvecling' (A Discussion of Density and Sustainable Urban Development), in Lehtonen, H. and Johansson, M. (eds), *Att omringa ekologi* (Encircling Ecology), C 36, pp. 115–123 (Esbo: VTT Byggnadsteknik).

Sager, T. (2005), 'Footloose and forecast-free: Hypermobility and the planning of society', *European Journal of Spatial Development*, September, article no.17.

Salomon, I. and Mokhtarian, P.L. (2002), 'Driven to Travel: The Identification of Mobility-Inclined Market Segments', in Black and Nijkamp (eds), pp. 173–180.

Sandqvist, K. (2002), 'Growing Up With and Without a Family car', in Black and Nijkamp (eds), pp. 117–124.

Sayer, A. (1992), *Method in Social Science. A Realist Approach*, 2nd edition (London and New York: Routledge).

Schafer, A. (1998), 'The Global Demand for Motorized Mobility', *Transportation Research A* 32:6, 455–477.

Scherlock, H. (1991), *Cities are Good for Us* (London: Paladin).

Schlich, R. and Axhausen, K.W. (2002), *Wohnumfeld und Freizeitverkehr – eine Untersuchung zur Fluchttheorie*, Arbeitsberichte Verkehr- und Raumplanung 155 (Zürich : ETH/IVT)

Schmidt, P. (2006), *Schmidt's Auto Publications*. AID 0604, <www.eagleaid>.

Schmidt-Bleek, F. (1994), *MIPS – Das Mass für Ökologisches Wirtschaften* (Basel: Birkhäuser).

SFT (1993), *Utslipp fra veitrafikken i Norge* (Emissions from road traffic in Norway), Report 93:02 (Oslo: Norwegian Pollution Control Authority).

SFT (1999), *Emissions from road traffic in Norway* Report 99:04 (Oslo: The Norwegian Pollution Control Authority).

Simmonds, D. and Coombe, D. (2000), 'The Transport Implications of Alternative Urban Forms', in Williams, K. et al. (eds), pp. 121–130.

SINTEF (1994), *Vegstøvdepot i Trondheim – partikkelstørrelsesfordeling, kjemisk og mineralogisk sammensetning* (Road dust depot in Trondheim – particle size distribution, chemical and mineralogical composition), STF36 A94037 (Trondheim: SINTEF).

Skjeggedal, T. et al. (2003), *Fortettingsrealisme* (TheRealism of Densification), *Plan* 6, 56–63.

Smyth, H. (1996), 'Running the Gauntlet: A Compact City within a Doughnut of Decay', in Jenks, M. et al. (eds), pp. 101–113.

SPSS (1998). *SPSS Base 8.0 Application Guide* (Chicago: SPSS Inc.).

Stead, D. et al. (2000), 'Land Use, Transport and People: Identifying the Connections', in Williams, K. et al. (eds), pp. 174–186.

Stern, P.C. and Oskamp, S. (1987), 'Managing scarce environmental resources', in Stokols, D. and Altman, I. (eds), *Handbook of environmental psychology*, pp. 1043–1088 (New York: Wiley).

Stoel, T.B. jr. (1999), 'Reining in Urban Sprawl', *Environment* 41:4, 6–11.

Tengström, E. (1999), *Towards Environmental Sustainability? A comparative study of Danish, Dutch and Swedish transport policies in a European context* (Aldershot: Ashgate).

Thompson-Fawcett, M. (2000), 'The Contribution of Urban Villages to Sustainable Development', in Williams, K. et al. (eds), pp. 275–287.

Thøgersen, J. (1999), *Making ends meet. A synthesis of results and implications of a research programme,* Working Paper No. 99–1 (Aarhus: Marketing and Environment, Department of Marketing, The Aarhus School of Business).

Tillberg, K. (1998), 'The impact on travel patterns due to residential location', *European Network for Housing Research Conference Housing Futures: Renewal, Sustainability and Innovation*, Cardiff, 7–11 September 1998.

Tillberg, K. (2001), *Barnfamiljers dagliga fritidsresor i bilsamhället – ett tidspussel med geografiska och könsmässiga variationer* (The daily leisure trips of families with children in the automobile society: a time puzzle with geographical and gender variations) Geografiska regionstudier nr. 43 (Uppsala: Uppsala University)

Tillberg, K. (2002), 'Residential Location and Daily Mobility Patterns: A Swedish Case Study of Households with Children', in Black and Nijkamp (eds), pp. 165–172.

Titheridge, H. et al. (2000), 'Assessing the Sustainability of Urban Development Policies', in Williams, K. (eds), pp. 149–159.

Triandis, H.C. (1977), *Interpersonal behavior* (Monterey: Books/Cole).

Troy, P.N. (1996), 'Environmental Stress and Urban Policy', in Jenks, M. et al (eds), pp. 200–212.

Turner, R.K. (1993), 'Sustainability: Principles and Practice', in Turner, R.K. (ed.), *Sustainable Environmental Economics and Management*, pp. 3–36 (Chichester: John Wiley & Sons).

UNDP (1990), *Human Development Report 1990*, United Nation Development Programme (Oxford: Oxford University Press).

UNDP (2005), *Human Development Report 2005*, United Nation Development Programme (Oxford: Oxford University Press).

Uteng, T.P. (2006), 'Mobility: Discourses from the non-western immigrant groups in Norway', *Mobilities* 1:3, 435–462.

Vallacher, R.R. and Wegner, D.M. (1987), 'What do people think they're doing? Action identification and human behavior', *Psychological Review* 94, 3–15.

van Dieren, W. (ed.) (1995), *Taking Nature Into Account: A Report to the Club of Rome* (New York: Springer Verlag).

Vegdirektoratet (1997), *Veg-grepsprosjektet. Delprosjekt 5.4: Vegstøv – helseskader og kostnader. Økonomiske konsekvenser av endret piggdekkbruk, helse og trivsel* (The Road-grip Project. Subproject 5.4: Road dust – health damages and costs. Economical consequences of changed use of studded tyres, health and comfort), Internal Report no. 1980 (Oslo: The Norwegian Public Roads Administration).

Victor, P.A. (1991), 'Indications of sustainable development: Some lessons from capital theory', *Ecological Economics* 4, 191–213.

Vilhelmson, B. (1990), *Vår dagliga rørlighet. Om resandes utveckling, førdelning och gränser* (Our daily mobility. On the development, distribution and limits of travelling), TFB Report 16 (Stockholm: The Swedish Transport Board).

Vilhelmson, B. (1992), 'Daglig resande: utveckling, gränser, påverkbarhet' (Everyday travel: development, limits and influence), in Lundgren, L. J. (ed.), *Livsstil och miljö – på väg mot ett milövänligt beteende? (Lifestyle and the environment)* (Lund: Universitetet i Lund).

Wachs, M. (2002), 'Social Trends and Research Needs in Transport and Environmental Planning', in Black and Nijkamp (eds), pp. 17–26.

Wackernagel, M. and Rees, W. (1996), *Our Ecological Footprint. Reducing Human Impact on the Earth* (Gabriola Island: New Society Publisher.

WBCSD (2001), *Mobility 2001* (World Business Council for Sustainable Development).

WBCSD (2004), *Mobility 2030: Meeting the Challenges to Sustainability*, The Sustainable Mobility Project, Full Report 2004 (World Business Council for Sustainable Development).

WCED (1987), *Our common future*, The World Commission on Environment and Development (Oxford: Oxford University Press).

Wegener, M. and Greene, D.L (2002), 'Sustainable Transport', in Black and Nijkamp (eds), pp. 35–42.

Weiss, M.A. et al (2000), *On the Road in 2020. A life-cycle analysis of new automobile technologies*, Energy Laboratory Report (MIT EL 00-003) (Cambridge, Massachusetts: Energy Laboratory, Massachusetts Institute of Technology).

Weizsäcker, E.v. et al. (1998), *Factor Four* (London: Earthscan).

Western Norway Research Institute and National Institute of Technology (2002), *Beregningsmodell for alternative drivstoffer i transportsektoren – dokumentasjonsrapport* (Computer model for comparing the environmental impacts of alternative fuels in the transport sector) (Sogndal and Oslo: Western Norway Research Institute and National Institute of Technology).

Weterings, R.A.P.M. and Opschoor, J.B. (1992), *The Ecocapacity as a Challenge to Technological Development*, Publication 74a (Rijswijk: Netherlands Advisory Council for Research on Nature and Environment).

Wetlesen J. (1999), 'A Global Ethic of Sustainability?', in Lafferty and Langhelle (eds), pp. 30–47.

Whitelegg, J. (1993), *Transport for a Sustainable Future. The Case for Europe* (London/Chichester: Wiley).

Whitelegg, J. (1997), *Critical Mass* (London/Chicago: Pluto Press).

Wicker, A.W. (1969), 'Attitudes versus actions', *Journal of Social Issues* 25, 41–78.

Wildavsky, A. (1973), 'If planning is everything, maybe it's nothing', *Policy Sciences* 4:2, 127–153.

Williams, K. et al. (eds) (2000), *Achieving Sustainable Urban Form* (London: E & FN Spon).

Williams, K. et al. (2000a), 'Achieving Sustainable Urban Form: An Introduction', in Williams et al. (eds).

Williamson, O.E. (1994), *Institutions and Economic Organizations – The Governance Perspective* (Washington, DC: World Bank).

Wonnacott, T.H. and Wonnacott, R.J. (1990), *Introductory Statistics*, 5th edition (John Wiley & Sons).

World Bank (1996), *Sustainable Transport: Priorities for Policy Reform* (Washington, DC: World Bank).

WWF (2004), *The Living Planet Report 2004* (Gland, Switzerland: World Wide Fund for Nature).

WWF (2006), *The Living Planet Report 2006* (Gland, Switzerland: World Wide Fund for Nature).

Yin, R.K. (1994), *Case Study Research. Design and Methods*, 2nd Edition (Sage Publications).

Østerberg, D. (1990), 'Det sosio-materielle handlingsfelt' (The Socio-material Field of Action), in Deichman Sørensen, T. and Frønes, I. (eds), *Kulturanalyse* (Culture analysis), pp. 65–79 (Oslo: Gyldendal).

Åkerman, J. (2005), 'Sustainable air transport – on track in 2050', *Transportation Research Part D* 10, 111–126.

Index